MW00632415

SINS OF THE SHOVEL

SINS OF
THE SHOVEL

*Looting, Murder, and the Evolution of
American Archaeology*

Rachel Morgan

The University of Chicago Press CHICAGO

The University of Chicago Press, Chicago 60637
Published 2023
Printed in the United States of America

32 31 30 29 28 27 26 25 24 23   1 2 3 4 5

ISBN-13: 978-0-226-82238-9 (cloth)
ISBN-13: 978-0-226-82239-6 (e-book)
DOI: https://doi.org/10.7208/chicago/9780226822396.001.0001

Library of Congress Cataloging-in-Publication Data

Names: Morgan, Rachel (Archaeologist), author.
Title: Sins of the shovel : looting, murder, and the evolution of American
archaeology / Rachel Morgan.
Description: Chicago : The University of Chicago Press, 2023. | Includes
bibliographical references and index.
Identifiers: LCCN 2023002877 | ISBN 9780226822389 (cloth) |
ISBN 9780226822396 (e-book)
Subjects: LCSH: Excavations (Archaeology)—United States. | Indians of
North America—Antiquities. | United States—Antiquities.
Classification: LCC CC101.U6 M67 2023 | DDC 970.004/97—dc23/
eng/20230123
LC record available at https://lccn.loc.gov/2023002877

♾ This paper meets the requirements of ANSI/NISO Z39.48-1992
(Permanence of Paper).

Contents

Prologue

"Ohmygod."

All one word, no spaces, that was how the archaeologists summarized the artifacts in the sand. The expression lacked scientific precision or descriptive clarity, but it fit archaeology's history of awestruck exclamations—like Howard Carter's 1922 description of the contents of Tutankhamen's burial chamber: "wonderful things." But the Ohmygod Site was not that.

It was now 1981. American archaeology had become a different sort of enterprise—fewer entranced journeys into the past; more regulated endeavors governed by the Antiquities Act (1906), the National Historic Preservation Act (1966), the Archaeological Resources Protection Act (1979), state regulations, and executive orders. Some of these contemporary archaeologists were surveying Chaco Canyon in northwestern New Mexico, near one of the basin's many great houses, Pueblo Bonito. The site consisted of a scattering of wood, daub, and debris, and it was in the path of a planned roadway. They named it the Ohmygod Site not for its troves of gold or insights into the past, but out of surprise at finding anything at all. And then they moved on.[1]

Three years later, another archaeologist dug deeper. An old photograph revealed two nineteenth-century buildings standing near Pueblo Bonito. These were the apparent source of Ohmygod's wood, daub, and debris. The photo was captioned: "Wetherill House and Store, Looking West."[2]

The Wetherill family had begun moving into Chaco Canyon in the

1890s to excavate Pueblo Bonito. Their largely unregulated excavations evolved into a trading post and then a ranch. Each endeavor turned a profit, but there was always more to be had. The Wetherills built a home and business in Chaco Canyon, where ancient artifacts, Indigenous art, and disinterred humans lined the walls and the owners' pockets. When archaeology, business, and power come together, there's almost always tension, occasionally erupting in violence. Some of those tensions led to the collapse of the Wetherill regime.

By the time archaeologists were recording the remnants of the Wetherill buildings as the Ohmygod Site, much had changed. But American archaeology was continuing to dance awkwardly with the intersecting interests of the past, present, and future. Even in our highly regulated present, the wild roots of the past continue to intrude. The historic excavations and their aftermath explored in these pages highlight American archaeology's efforts to reconcile with a complicated past. It's a story full of big personalities, noble intentions, questionable behavior, enchanting ancient monuments, and occasional bursts of idealism and valor. But it's not a story that has an ending.

ONE

A Palace in the Sky

On December 18, 1888, Richard Wetherill rode deep into the canyons of Mesa Verde, Colorado. At thirty years old, Richard stood about five foot nine. His eyes were black and startling. A local paper remembered: "His deep set eyes had an assurance, a steadiness, a penetration that made weaker men uneasy."[1] His hair and mustache were black too, yet streaks of grey crept in at the temple, hinting at the pressures Richard faced in keeping the family ranch afloat.[2] His four younger brothers, little sister, and parents were all waiting at the family home, Alamo Ranch. It was a large family to support and only growing larger as evidenced by the man riding beside him.

Three years before, Charlie Mason had married Richard's sister Anna. He was taller and thicker than Richard and sported a beard.[3] There was a more obvious warmth to Charlie than to his brother-in-law, who could come across as "frigid" even when trying to show affection.[4]

They followed tracks in the snow, scanning the land for any trace of the family's livestock. A wild herd had swept through Alamo Ranch and the Wetherill cattle followed the feral ones to freedom without any sense of loyalty to the people who had branded them.[5]

It was cold and the cattle were nowhere to be seen. As the branches and brambles cut into the legs of both the men and the horses, they had to ask themselves: where are we?

Terra incognita would be the optimistic, adventurous response. But others had been there before. Richard's little brother Al traversed the area a year or so earlier, and he was not the first.[6]

Beginning in 1882, Virginia Donaghe, a New York journalist,[7] explored the region. A wealthy woman in her early twenties, she had accepted a job with the *New York Daily Graphic* to report on "buried cities." Her hair often fell in a fashionable pile of tight curls, her sharp features reflecting a seriousness and drive that few underestimated. She discovered no buried cities on her first venture, but she did spot the cliff dwellings of the Mesa Verde region.[8]

During a later visit, she had to hide in the canyons of Colorado for days. She was hungry, thirsty, and weary. A fall from a cliff had nearly ended her life, but Virginia was not deterred.[9] She stood in view of the cliff dwellings. The red towers and rooms that rose out of the past mesmerized her and fortified her against the elements and her enemies.

Pictures of the cliff dwellings had circulated since William Henry Jackson photographed the ruins in the 1870s, but with the railroad in its infancy and no roads nearby, few got to enter the monuments as Virginia did.

Few who looked like Virginia, that is. The "hostile" Indigenous peoples she hid from and their ancestors had known of Mesa Verde for centuries, but they were no longer welcome in Colorado. In 1876, Colorado's first governor rode to electoral victory on the slogan: "Get the Utes out of Colorado."[10] Three years later, a sheriff's posse killed a young Ute named Tabernash. In return, some Ute inflicted a series of bloody reprisals on White settlers and agents.[11] The entire Ute Tribe did not commit the crimes, but the entire tribe paid. They were driven out of Colorado to new reservations, leaving their much-coveted lands to settlers, railroads, and miners.

In their absence, the local papers declared that "the Utes are gone, and the white man is here. . . . The wigwam of the savage has passed away, and the cabin of the pale face marks the beginning of a new era and a new history."[12]

Virginia admired the antiquity and beauty of the cliff houses, but she also saw their vulnerability. She wrote of Colorado, "To mighty multitudes her wealth she yields, As shifting seasons pass and years increase."[13] Trains and legislation favorable to homesteading threw Colorado wide open. It was only a matter of time before the new arrivals laid siege to the ancient cliff dwellings. Virginia felt the artifacts and architecture of Mesa Verde were one type of resource that should never be tapped. The cliff dwellings of Mesa Verde needed to be preserved and protected. Come hell or high water, Virginia Donaghe was going to see that they were.

While not on new earth, Wetherill and Mason could still call themselves lost. The tracks had led them to a part of the canyons they had never seen before. This was not unusual. The family had been living in Colorado for less than a decade. They were busy and the land was vast. There was plenty of unknown territory to explore.

Yet Richard was never really lost. The Wetherills were Quakers guided by the principle of the Inward Light. Founder of Pennsylvania and leading Quaker theorist William Penn described Inward Light: "The light of Christ within, who is the world, leads all that take heed unto it, out of the darkness into God's marvellous [sic] light."[14] So while momentarily uncertain of their location, Richard had other guidance.

Ordained by a higher power or not, the search had been a long, hard ride in bleak weather. The horses would have been tired. The men may have rested their steeds.[15] They could probably have done with a bit of rest themselves. In warmer weather, a glance across the canyon offered a sea of reddish-brown rock adorned with cedar and piñon trees, but winter offered a gray and tan landscape dotted with snow. It was hardly inviting. One wrong step and the careless visitor would careen into the canyon straight to their death. It was a dangerous environment, but the land captivated the eye and the mind.

And then it happened. In an instant, Richard and Charlie caught a glimpse of something. Below an overhang of red and tan rocks, a series of red walls and towers peeked out above the trees. It was a cliff dwelling. Red sandstone homes cut into cliffs dotted Colorado and interested many, but there was something different here. The men suspended the search for the cattle; they had to get across the canyon into the red fortress.*

* A later retelling of the discovery of Cliff Palace credits a Ute man named Acowitz with either showing Richard and Charlie the cattle footprints in the snow or pointing to the

Figure 1. The brothers Wetherill, from left to right, Win, Al, John, Clayt, and Richard (BLM Canyons of the Ancients Visitor Center and Museum, Wetherill Archives, 2000.19.P.559.O).

This break from the herd was no quick pit stop. A canyon separated Richard and Charlie from the cliff dwelling. Twenty-seven-year-old Al Wetherill had spotted this very cliff dwelling but had been too tired to trek across the void.[16] Richard and Charlie would not be so easily deterred. They found some downed trees, chopped them up, and used their lassos to bind the logs together. They threw their rickety excuse for a ladder over the edge of the cliff and descended.[17]

Southwesterly winds blew across Mesa Verde for approximately one million years, bringing with them deposits of fine silt from drier regions. The silt settled and formed a moist, productive soil. People arrived in Mesa Verde in approximately 550 CE and soon began farming. The mesas were quickly depleted by tree harvesting and began to erode.[18]

Vicissitudes in the soil or the climate or both led the people down from the mesas into the alcoves below around 1200 CE. They pulled

---

cliff dwelling or both. However, Charlie makes no mention of Acowitz in his retelling of the discovery of Cliff Palace, and there is some uncertainty regarding his participation.

stones from riverbeds in the canyon and crafted sandstone blocks. They stacked the blocks on top of each other, adding a layer of mortar made of mud and water. By laying the stones in regular courses and adding tiny bits of stone into the mortar,* the makers of the cliff dwellings built strong walls. Some buildings rose as high as four stories. The builders cut T-shaped and rectangular doors into the rooms and added timber support beams. They installed courtyards and underground chambers between the buildings, crafting domestic and ceremonial spaces where people acted out the full spectrum of life from the mundane to the extraordinary.[19]

But as with all construction endeavors, it was the location that mattered most. The Western Interior Seaway had fluctuated for millions of years, depositing sand and shale across the region. In time, erosion carved out alcoves that would become prime real estate.[20] This was a strategic, defendable location, home to around a hundred people, most of whom did not make it to age forty.

Spanish explorers were the first European eyes to see the area. They named the land Mesa Verde, which was incorrect. *Mesa* translates to table in English, implying a flat land, whereas this "mesa" dips to the south and is therefore a *cuesta*. The cuesta does contain many mesas within the canyon, so the Spanish were not all wrong. And there is no dispute on *verde*. For much of the year, the land remains awash in green that gives way to the orange, red, and gray of the cliffs and the dwellings.

There would be no stopping to consider geographic semantics or Indigenous beliefs for Richard and Charlie. For many Indigenous peoples the past is alive, thus the cliff dwellings were not abandoned relics but special places, home to the spirits of the ancestors. Hopi archaeologist Stewart B. Koyiyumptewa writes of the past as footprints: "Our footprints are living pieces of history on the landscape. They are not abandoned. We believe that our ancient ancestors who have passed on return to these dwellings in the afterworld."[21]

Did the spirits of the ancestors hear the cowboys as they scaled the ancient stone steps that led into the cliff dwelling?

Did they know that after six centuries, they were under siege, that

---

* This technique is called chinking.

they would never be at peace again, that every superficial and intimate scrap of their lives would be torn out and paraded around the world?

As far as anyone knows, Richard and Charlie were the first White men to enter the cliff dwelling. Years later Charlie would describe their first venture:

> We spent several hours going room to room, and picked up several articles of interest: among them a stone ax with the handle still on it. There were also parts of several human skeletons scattered about. . . . Another strange circumstance is that so many of their valuable possessions were left in the room, and covered with the clay of which the roofs and upper floors were made. . . . It would seem that their intention was to conceal their valuables so that their enemies might not secure them.[22]

For their part, Richard and Charlie pocketed only a handful of artifacts that day. There was no need to rush. They knew they would be

Figure 2. Nineteenth-century photo of Cliff Palace, Mesa Verde, Colorado (Library of Congress, 2008678195).

back. They could collect more then, and they would. Al described the experience of excavating as one of optimism: "Day after day we have dug in the dust of untold ages with the hope that something new would show up—the excitement of the work was the same as a prospector has when working on a Claim."[23]

As Richard and Charlie headed home, they ran into "some old friends, Charles McLoyd, Howard Graham, and L.C. Patrick." They told them about their discovery and presumably showed them the items they had taken from the alcove. Another of Richard's brothers, twenty-two-year-old John, joined McLoyd, Graham, and Patrick to make their own claims. Charlie remembered, "They only had provisions for three or four days, but before this was gone they had found as much stuff as they could carry."[24] A few more visits to the alcove later, McLoyd took a collection of artifacts called the "Ancient Aztec Relics" to the Colorado Historical Society and left with $3,000.[25]

As America became aware of its antiquities and people like Virginia Donaghe began to press for their protection, the past became profit. In 1888, there was nothing to stop the commercialization of the past. Archaeology was not a discipline. There were no university archaeology departments. At most, there were societies, where those educated in other sciences coalesced to share their interests in the past and sponsored explorations of ruins. They had no authority, and neither did anyone else. There were no laws safeguarding archaeological sites or agencies monitoring ruins. The past was consigned to the personalities who found it; some inclined to protection, some to profit, some indifferent. In this void, the tangible remnants of the past became vulnerable.

There was only one word for the fortress Richard and Charlie stood in that December day: palatial. And so, Richard named it Cliff Palace. Al later explained how momentous such a discovery felt:

To know that you are the first to set foot in homes that had been deserted for centuries is a strange feeling. It is as though unseen eyes watched, wondering what aliens were invading their sanctuaries and why. To complete the absolute isolation of the dwelling, there was a buzzard's nest on the small ledge in the cliff back of the buildings. According to ancient mythology, anyone finding a buzzard's nest is in luck forever after. But, to our deep disappointment, they quit the nest and were not seen again.[26]

Much would never be the same after that day. Richard fell under Mesa Verde's spell just like Virginia. They would both remain enchanted and struggle to maintain control of the past. They would both accomplish much and sacrifice more. The coming years would bring arrests, vilification by professionals, investigations by federal authorities, damaged reputations, and untold losses. A federal injunction and an act of Congress would come and go. And yet they would carry on until they could no longer.

For one of them, it would take a bullet to the chest and then another to the face to break the spell of antiquity.

Or perhaps it was a curse.

The Robber Baron

Gustaf Erick Adolf Nordenskiöld stepped off the train with more names than experience. The summer air of July 1891 welcomed the twenty-three-year-old Swede to Colorado. He dressed the part of the scholarly aristocrat and kept his hair cut neatly, wore thin framed glasses over his blue eyes, and sported a long English-style mustache. Less flattering angles revealed that he was in recovery from tuberculosis. His thin body showed the stress of the injections.[1]

His weak constitution contrasted strongly with his father's reputation as an accomplished Arctic explorer. The elder Nordenskiöld, Baron Adolf, headed the Vega Expedition and the first successful crossing of the Northeast Passage. Colorado was an opportunity to make a discovery worthy of his father's praise.

Gustaf had been around the world. Earlier he enjoyed the stunning Alps,[2] the Roman ruins of Verona, and boring Antwerp, before crossing the Atlantic.[3] He landed in New York, "a terribly unpleasant and dirty city." He tarried just long enough to enjoy the Museum of Natural History, which he pronounced "beautiful and well organized, although not especially large."[4]

At the beginning of June, he jumped on a steamer bound for South Carolina. Accustomed to the rigors of travel, Gustaf decided to experiment, buying a second-class ticket rather than a first, quite a risk for a Swedish aristocrat. He later wrote to his mother to assure her he would not repeat the experiment.[5]

Figure 3. Gustaf Nordenskiöld, the aristocratic visitor to Mesa Verde who led the first formal archaeological investigation of the cliff dwellings (BLM Canyons of the Ancients Visitor Center and Museum, Wetherill Archives, 2000.14.P.1.O1200).

As with thousands of others, rumors of Colorado's riches pulled Gustaf west. Durango was a mining town of around three thousand people who spent their days trying to extract gold from the desert. Others came for silver, minerals, or oil. Gustaf came for "some good mineral samples," but soon heard about other subterranean treasures.[6] According to reports, a family of Quaker ranchers lived near Durango and had discovered and harvested incredible archaeological wonders. Gustaf carried a letter of introduction to the head of this family, Mr. Benjamin K. Wetherill. If he could find the Wetherills, he might have something bigger to send home.

The road from Durango to the Wetherills' home in Mancos was a well-worn if remote path. Gustaf was a little frustrated to find that there was no train connection.[7] He had to rent a buggy and mules and drive himself down the rocky road that followed the Rio Mancos. Cliffs framed either side of the river across the land that the Ute once occupied. But Gustaf saw no sign of Indigenous people as he drove deeper into the valley. Even as an outsider, he understood why: "Like most of the North American tribes the Ute Indians are rapidly dying out, and form but the last remnant of a once great and powerful nation."[8]

Eurocentric histories typically begin with a setting and treat geographic movement, migrations, or diasporas as telltale signs of meaningful change. There is nothing wrong with that approach; it simply works poorly when applied to people who used land seasonally or tracked herds of seasonal mammals. The Ute, like many Indigenous groups in America, lived such a life. The Ute fall under the umbrella of the Shoshonean-speaking people. They moved into the Great Basin prior to European contact. They hunted the big game of the valleys and mountains, and their riches grew.[9]

Speaking of the Ute as a homogenous, unified group gives a historically inaccurate impression. People identified as Ute belonged to family-oriented bands. Identity revolved around links to family-oriented hunting, fishing, and foraging locations, rather than present-day conceptions of national unity.[10] However they defined themselves, they had to adapt to numerous invasions beginning in the sixteenth century.

First came the Spanish.

It was not all death and disease when the first Europeans found the Ute. Following Vasquez de Coronado's 1540–1542 expedition, guns and horses entered the Ute world. The technology was transformative. The Ute could hunt faster and kill more bison and other large mammals, but so could others. Thus, the Ute saw reduced access to hunting and raiding lands.[11]

Then came the trappers and traders.

By 1821, the Ute would have noticed a greater stream of eastern visitors. Many came for furs. While the pressures that fur trapping and trading brought to the Southwest were real, these easterners were temporary visitors, who got their goods and returned home. The Utes' seasonal mobility and migration was minimally threatened by them.[12]

Then came the farmers and the miners.

Americans heard about gold in the Rocky Mountains around 1858–1859. Utes began to see a shift in the newcomers. These easterners were settling down. With increased threats of violence, the Ute turned to diplomacy and built alliances with the ranchers and miners, protecting themselves from the massacres that other Indigenous peoples faced during this time.[13] But the Ute were also feared by the settlers of Colorado as adroit warriors and prolific raiders.

In 1867, Congress unveiled the Doolittle Report, which concluded that the Indigenous peoples of the West had to give up their traditional ways of life, concede to acculturation, settle down on lands determined by the US government, and pick up a plow. Founding American anthropologist Lewis Henry Morgan agreed. He had formulated a view of cultural evolution that said humans began as savages, transitioned to barbarians, and then to civilization. No exceptions. Everyone was the same. Indigenous people would be able to proceed toward his view of civilization more easily if they were on reservations being trained as peaceful farmers.[14]

Despite the Utes' traditional band organization, the US government treated them as a unified group. A handful of leaders signed a treaty subjecting all Utes to life on the reservation, though they retained the right to roam for hunting for some time.[15]

Congress passed a new Indian Homestead Act in 1884; others had been previously passed in 1862 and 1875 offering Indigenous people land claims for the low, low price of their tribal affiliation.

Then in 1887, Congress ratified the General Allotment Act.

Redistribution of Indigenous lands destroyed territorial and political alliances and hastened the erosion of traditional ceremonies and customs. Indigenous communities resisted these intrusions both through direct combat and legal recourse. Resistance resulted in arrest, imprisonment, and/or death.[16] Helen Hunt Jackson published *A Century of Dishonor* outlining injustices against Indigenous peoples, but it failed to improve matters, as new settlers poured into the land buoyed by hope and a dash of manifest destiny.

Amid these tensions, Benjamin Wetherill moved his family to Mancos, Colorado. His five strapping sons, Richard, John, Al, Clayt, and Win, built the ranch. They chopped log after log to build the family home on an old riverbed. They felled more trees to build the white fences that sheltered the cattle and the land. They cut a long irrigation ditch diagonally across the front yard and lined it with rows of cottonwood trees. The family called their home Alamo Ranch, after this green alley.[17] As one visitor put it: "Everything about Alamo Ranch gives evidence of thrift and comfort. . . . The whole neighboring scene is pastoral; a picturesque home has been established in the wilderness of sage-brush and piñon pine."[18]

Gustaf pulled up to Alamo Ranch on July 2, 1891.[19] Flowers brightened the lawn and hammocks swung from the cottonwood trees. The man Gustaf was searching for was a small, bald gentleman growing weak from lead poisoning.[20] Benjamin and his wife Marion welcomed Gustaf to their home with kindness and generosity. This was their way with everyone.

President Grant had appointed Benjamin a trail agent back in 1867, and he enjoyed regaling guests with tales from the trail. His daughter-in-law remembered them as full of "clear thinking and quiet humor."[21]

Marion and her only surviving daughter, Anna, kept the boys and the guests well fed and comfortable. Though so modest, Marion shed her traditional gray Quaker garb to avoid attention, and she had modern interests. "Many of the leaders of the woman's movement were her friends. She knew Harriet Beecher Stowe. She heard Frances Willard lecture in Leavenworth. . . . Mrs. Wetherill was interested in the new point of view."[22] The smell of roast chicken, homemade bread, and fresh pies filled the home, and up to twenty-five people could eat in the dining room each night.[23] Though their guests included wealthy European and American tourists and prominent scholars, they all retired either to cornshuck mattresses or to simple floor pallets.[24]

As bullets flew and bodies fell over the years, the Wetherills carved out a different sort of existence in Mancos. Their neighbors were the Ute and ranchers. The Ute continued to hunt on horseback throughout the Four Corners region. But legally they were confined to two small reservations and barred from the great expanses they had roamed for centuries.

Many have posited that due to his Quaker faith, Benjamin Wetherill chose to treat peacefully with his Ute neighbors. When his White neighbors lobbied him to join defensive efforts against the Ute, Benjamin rejected their call to arms, reportedly saying, "They are our friends. We don't fortify against friends!" When the locals pushed back, Benjamin remained defiant. "You don't fight them, you feed them!"[25] His sons followed his example, and the Ute allowed the family to graze their cattle on their few precious pieces of land.

Al casually swept away the typical sources of discord over Colorado's limited resources, writing: "To be sure, we had cattle killed and horses stolen, but who did not? We had cattle: the Utes had cattle; we both ran them in the canons and on top of the Mesa Verde. Perhaps we ate Indian beef and we knew they ate ours." Summarizing the family's relations with the Ute, he continued: "Staying on the good side of the Utes did not require much effort, since we had lots of wheat for flour, plenty of beef, and pasture. Indians were expensive friends, but it was good policy. . . . We maintained a friendly attitude and accepted friendship in return."[26]

It sounds nice.

In 1863, Special Agent John Nicolay recommended that officials "buy [the Utes'] good will. . . . The expense of such a system will in a given number of years be found to be less by far than the expense of active military campaigns against them."[27] Seen in a broader context, the Wetherills' treatment of their Ute neighbors may also be interpreted as the wisdom of soft conquest.

Still, many in Mancos saw the Wetherill family as different. They

dressed like cowboys and worked like cowboys, but there was something unusual about them:

> In that frontier town of hard-riding, hard-drinking, hard-swearing
> pioneers, the gentle mistress of the Alamo Ranch put no restraint on
> her sons, but the Wetherill boys soon became known as boys who
> were held quietly in the Quaker way of austerity by their mother and
> their father, taking no part in the gambling or the drinking of that
> wide-open frontier town.[28]

Unbeknownst to the Wetherills or the Ute, acts of neighborly kindness between peoples of uncommon faiths would make the Wetherill
name notorious.

The Wetherills showed Gustaf their collection of artifacts from the cliff
dwellings. The pottery and stone tools were as impressive as he had
hoped. He asked for a tour of the canyon. Richard Wetherill obliged. By
this time, the Wetherill brothers had cliff dwelling tours down to an art.

Cliff Palace remained the showstopper. The road to Cliff Palace was
"long and tiring." They traveled through miles of piñon forest until
they reached a precipice. Then, just as Richard and Charlie had years
before, visitors looked across the canyon and caught their first glimpse
of the fortress in the "wild and gloomy" gorge. Though he had surely
been exposed to Europe's grand castles, Cliff Palace was worthy of the
title in Gustaf's estimate: "This ruin well deserves its name, for with its
round towers and high walls rising out of the heaps of stones deep in
the mysterious twilight of the cavern and defying in their sheltered site,
the ravages of time, it resembles at a distance an enchanted castle."[29]

Gustaf quickly fell under Cliff Palace's spell. He had planned to make
only a short sightseeing tour in Mancos, collect some more minerals,
and be on his way. But he was suddenly aware of the possibilities of
Mesa Verde. No archaeologist had conducted in-depth excavations in
the cliff dwellings. The Wetherills had collected ravenously from the
sites, to be sure, but there was still plenty a scientific mind could extract.
Gustaf could lead the first extensive archaeological exploration of Mesa

Verde. He could dig his heels in, excavate widely, obtain a hoard of artifacts, and take them back to Sweden to introduce the world to the works of mysterious ancient peoples. Upon his return from the cliff dwellings, he wrote urgently, "It would be good if Father could send answer by telegram yes or no as to whether I should stay on longer here."[30]

The Wetherill brothers agreed to escort Gustaf, for a price of course, three dollars a day. Gustaf thought the price high, but the Wetherills had the market cornered.[31] So, Gustaf dipped into the family fortune and the brothers saddled up the horses.

Gustaf assembled a field crew before they set out. He hired two Mexican men as excavation assistants and later brought on one additional assistant.[32] Only one of his assistants' names survived, Joe.[33] Europeans and Americans rarely saw fit to credit their workers, assistants, or informants, even though they likely could not have completed their studies without them. This has led to the false narrative that archaeology was the field of rich White men. In fact, the real work in the trenches was completed by people of all colors and all walks of life for much of history. Only credit was marginalized.

For their part, the Wetherills were happy to help with Gustaf's larger social mobility effort. The way they saw it, "he had a desire to succeed to a title by some worthwhile scientific work."[34]

Though eager to begin, Gustaf, on Richard's advice, started off not with the massive Cliff Palace but with a smaller site at Cliff Cañon.[35] There were several rooms and underground chambers, called kivas. Richard and Al headed up the first round of excavations. Now thirty years old, Al sported a lighter mustache than his brother and flashed kinder eyes that revealed his friendly, good-humored nature.[36] They covered their faces with bandanas to keep the dust out of their lungs.[37] Then they entered the kivas.

They had dug around in the first kiva before. Previously, they recovered "half a bow, three or four arrows, a stone axe with handle, and bone knife."[38] Gustaf's workers began removing the rubble that had fallen into the kivas over the centuries. This sent clouds of dust into the dry air, a considerable nuisance for a man recovering from tuberculosis. Removal of the rubble exposed wooden and bone tools, fragments of hide (possibly deer or sheep), pieces of cloth, yucca fiber, sandals, pottery, maize, stone axes, and projectile points.[39] It was not a bad start, considering archaeologists can dig for days and days without finding anything.

They moved on to the second kiva and then to the rooms, but they struggled to find anything else promising. Was the first kiva beginner's luck? Gustaf was ready to move on. So were Richard and Al. They were needed back at Alamo Ranch. They packed up their gear and headed home. Their younger brother John stepped in to lead the rest of the excavation.

The small crew trekked across Montezuma Valley, climbed a slope of 600 meters, and crossed several canyons. Out of gratitude for the family's help, Gustaf named the mesa they arrived at Wetherill Mesa.[40] Thin and mustached like his brothers, John Wetherill was a quiet, calm, and witty middle child with plenty of experience and passion for the cliff dwellings. At twenty-five, he was only two years older than Nordenskiöld.[41] His brothers trusted him and often gave him the most difficult task of all—transportation. "The beautiful, fragile pieces had to be carefully wrapped and carried down to the main canons where our horses were. We always trusted brother John to this special class of work because he seemed to have a knack of packing and of dodging trees and rocks in the trails."[42] The new crew made their camp close to the only spring near Wetherill Mesa.

Their days fell into a familiar pattern. At 6 a.m., the camp came to life. John rose and whipped up a breakfast of bread, fried pork, tomatoes, oatmeal, and coffee. Joe got the horses ready. Gustaf had "the privilege of stretching out a bit longer."[43] Al had noticed Gustaf "was helpless as a babe when it was camp work or horse hunting."[44] Then John shouted, "Breakfast ready!" They ate, washed up, saddled the horses, and headed up the trail to the ruin of the day. They dug and dug until noon. Then they stopped, devoured a can of corned beef and a piece of bread, and dug some more.[45]

Eat, dig, eat, dig, eat, sleep, repeat.

Of the cliff dwellings at Wetherill Mesa, Long House looked most promising. It contained approximately 150 rooms and 21 kivas. For about a month, they heaved up shovels full of dirt. The cliffs provided some cover from the summer sun, but the dust from the digging proved a constant challenge. After a month "without any particularly good results,"[46] Gustaf was ready to roll again.

From August to September, the team moved from dwelling to dwelling like Goldilocks struggling to find the right fit. As they dug, the rest of the team could hear Gustaf mumbling about money, complaining "he was paying John as much per day as a professor earned in Sweden."[47] They spent long enough at one dwelling to name it after "the well-known instantaneous camera 'Kodak.'" They did a brief stint at Mug House, where ceramic mugs had once been found. They excavated some perforated shells that Gustaf believed to be a necklace, but otherwise the larger dwelling failed to produce anything exciting.[48] If they had looked closely at the ceiling of the alcove, they would have noticed two handprints in white. Gustaf left his own permanent mark on Mug House and several other cliff dwellings. He carved "No. 19" into a rock as part of his site tracking system, permanently disfiguring a site that stood unscathed for hundreds of years but keeping his records nice and tidy.

They pressed on to Step House. It was a smaller dwelling of twenty rooms and three kivas. But here, Gustaf and his team unearthed several burials and some impressive pottery. Gustaf still wanted more and preferably somewhere previously untouched. The Wetherills' methods were rough. They had already drained many of the dwellings they took Gustaf to. He wanted his own cliff dwelling free of their fingerprints.

Gustaf's wish came true at Spruce Tree House. At around 130 rooms and eight kivas, it was on the larger side. Inside, Gustaf counted the rings on a spruce tree poking out of a wall. He determined that the dwelling was at least a couple hundred years old, likely older. With just a little digging, artifacts in the form of "some handsome baskets and pieces of pottery" emerged.[49] He planned to get all he could from Spruce Tree House.

First, though, he needed to take the artifacts they had collected already back to town. He made trips to Mancos and Durango often and put barrels and crates on trains bound for Stockholm via New York. He sent instructions home: "Please be sure that the skeletons from the different sacks are not mixed together."[50]

The first sign of trouble appeared on one of these trips to town. On the wall of the Mancos post office hung a notice: "Nobody is allowed in this reservation for the purpose of procuring Indian (!) relics from Aztec (?) ruins. . . . No foreigner is allowed on the Indian land without permission . . . fine 1000 dollars."[51] No additional information was provided about the Indigenous residents' objections to excavations on reservation lands or Mesa Verde specifically. Ramon Riley, former Tribal Historic Preservation Officer of the White Mountain Apache Tribe, shared in an interview that growing up he learned, "Don't take anything that's not yours, especially things left behind by those who are no longer living . . . misdeeds always catch up with you."[52] Perhaps similar sentiments were on the minds of those who heard about Gustaf's collections.

Worried, Gustaf rode to a military station. An officer gave him a pass to travel back to the Ute Reservation, but with "the inconvenient addendum that 'this pass not include any right of making excavations in the ruins.'"[53] An acquaintance assured Gustaf that he could carry on digging without fear of reprisal.

But Durango buzzed with discontent over the excavations that summer and into the cooler days of September. What right did a foreign aristocrat's son have to sail away with ancient artifacts from the lands selected by the US government for the imprisonment of Indigenous Americans? The cliff dwellings of Mesa Verde sat on Ute land and the citizens of Colorado were entitled to dictate what happened to the resources on that land, right?

The Wetherills received praise and money for their collections from the cliff dwellings, but locals labeled Gustaf a greedy vandal. One Colorado newspaper editor had a solution: Gustaf, he concluded, "ought to be lynched."[54]

Gustaf felt the tension. He wrote his father on September 17, "It is getting time to leave Mancos. An ignorant newspaper article containing expressions such as 'vandalism' 'robbery' and 'must be stopped at once' appeared soon after I had made my first shipment, which is why I prefer to get the rest of my collection to safety as soon as possible."[55]

He quickly loaded eight crates of artifacts onto a train bound for New York. He then checked into Room 323 at the Strater Hotel. After weeks of strenuous excavations and travels, he probably looked forward to a meal not made over a campfire and a good night's sleep in a nice bed.

Gustaf's sleep came to an end at midnight. US Deputy Marshal Sargent and Indian Agent Bartholomew entered the room and arrested Gustaf for plundering pottery, skeletons, and other relics from the Colorado cliff dwellings. The Ute and Indian Agent Bartholomew contended he had violated the terms of his visit. He could visit the cliff dwellings on the Ute Reservation, but "not injure anything."[56]

Gustaf tried to remain calm. He telegraphed his father, "Much trouble some expense no danger."[57] Easy to say, but southwestern hanging judges needed very little cause to sentence a man to death. People died by the noose for crimes as serious as rape and murder, but as minor as theft.

The press turned the spotlight on Colorado. Iowa's *Muscatine News-Tribune* reported Gustaf's arrest under the geographically inaccurate headline, "An Antiquarian in Trouble. A Swedish Nobleman Despoils the Arizona Cliff Dwellings."[58] Across the country the Associated Press ran the headline, "A Noted Baron Arrested." Just in case a scandal involving a European aristocrat failed to entice readers, the subtitle specified, "He Wanted to Leave the Cliff Dwellings Barren of Interest."[59]

At his initial hearing, Judge Cyrus Newcomb released Gustaf on a bond of $1,000 with instructions to return to court on October 2.[60] The bigger issue for the sheriff of Durango and the court soon became apparent. They had arrested a man for violating a law that did not exist. In 1891, there was no law preventing someone from looting an archaeological site or for transporting artifacts across the country or the world.

Gustaf and the Wetherills passed the weeks ahead of the court appearance in Mesa Verde. They photographed ruin after ruin. Sometimes they posed for a picture in a cliff dwelling, other times they focused on capturing the magnificence of the ancient architecture. They did not collect any artifacts, though. Gustaf resigned himself to the fact that "Americans would rather that cowboys, miners, etc., dig their antiquities, than foreigners."[61]

Across the United States, citizens and professionals alike decried the vulnerable state of ancient sites. In 1880, Adolph Bandelier, a Swiss-American archaeologist and one of the first to study the Indigenous communities of the Southwest, reported widespread destruction:

"Treasure hunters, inconsiderate amateurs, have recklessly and ruth-lessly disturbed the abodes of the dead." At another site he complained: "These premises have been thoroughly ransacked by visitors, and every striking object has already been carried off."[62] The barrels of artifacts bound for Stockholm were the symptom of a much larger problem.

When Gustaf returned to court, Judge Newcomb dismissed the charges. Vindicated or not, his arrest marked the end of his explorations of the cliff dwellings. In total, Gustaf collected over 1,400 pounds of artifacts and individuals from Mesa Verde.[63] Eventually the collection ended up in the Finnish National Museum.

Though he, too, was arrested and released for looting Mesa Verde just weeks after Gustaf,[64] Richard Wetherill returned to the ruins again and again. The excavations and arrests of 1891 marked the beginning of the legal battle in the fight to control the past. But with no legal restrictions to protect archaeological sites, America's antiquity remained up for grabs.

THREE

All the World's a Fair

Richard Wetherill tried to put on a professional front when he arrived at the Chicago World's Fair in the fall of 1893. Just 400 years after Christopher Columbus got lost and landed in the Americas (perhaps a circumstance Richard understood all too well), a 260-foot-tall Ferris wheel welcomed the world to Chicago. With 250,000 displays from 46 nations, the United States was out to show just how far the young republic had come.

For Richard, the past held more allure than the present. Visitors could find American antiquities at two main locations: the Government Building and the Anthropology Building. The two structures embodied competing visions of archaeology, one grounded in anthropology, the other in ethnology.

Balding, with a large mustache, William Henry Holmes worked in the Government Building. His colleagues regarded him as "an eminent man of science in whom the various phases of art and science were fused to a degree seldom given in one man."[1] Holmes began investigating a hillside in Piney Branch, Washington, DC, in 1889, the same year he began working for the Smithsonian Institution's Bureau of American Ethnology (BAE).*

Congress established the BAE in 1879. By that time the Smithsonian had published its first archaeology monograph, *Ancient Monuments of*

---

* The BAE was originally called the Bureau of Ethnology and later renamed.

the Mississippi Valley, and Samuel Haven's *Archaeology of the United States.*[2] From Congress's point of view, the mission of the BAE was collection. They wanted specialists to descend across the country and acquire Indigenous objects for display in a national museum. But renowned explorer John Wesley Powell had other—he would probably insist better—ideas. Powell subscribed to Lewis Henry Morgan's evolutionary trajectory. He believed Indigenous communities were headed toward civilization and that their languages, traditions, and culture were doomed. He felt it imperative to record their languages and ways of life. Congress and Powell never really resolved this issue in the many years Powell led the BAE.[3]

Holmes's hill in Piney Branch was covered in cobbles and stone tools. Analyzing the stone fragments, Holmes theorized that ancient toolmakers selected a stone, crafted a tool, used it, and discarded it. Mistakes happened, and the toolmaker tossed out defunct arrowheads or spearpoints. Holmes called those tossed-out points "rejects." These rejects resembled Paleolithic tools found in much deeper European soils, *but* they did not appear in glacial geological deposits in the United States. Thus, Holmes deduced that they were more recent rejects and that Paleolithic people never made it to America.[4] Holmes's interpretation touched off a "controversy, characterized by no little acrimony . . . between what might be termed the old school and the new school on this subject."[5]

With the BAE, Holmes set up shop in the prominently located Government Building.[6] Archaeological wunderkind Frank Hamilton Cushing helped Holmes create an engaging exhibit of the Piney Branch discoveries. Cushing "was an anthropologist 'born and made,' if there ever was one" and started working for the Smithsonian while in his teens. He gained prominence after living with the Zuni for six years, becoming one with the tribe, in his mind.[7] Then in 1887, he headed to the Southwest to lead the Hemenway Southwestern Archaeological Expedition. The expedition discovered abandoned cities composed of two-story adobe structures, mounds, irrigation systems, and hundreds of ancient individuals.[8]

Cushing's expedition took its name from its benefactor, as was customary. Some said Mary Hemenway was the wealthiest woman in Boston. She was certainly a very generous woman, who often gave money to historical and archaeological projects. In 1889, she and thirteen other prominent Bostonians signed a petition to Congress requesting federal protection of Casa Grande, the ancient structure in Arizona built around the fourteenth century CE. They first called for federal protection of archaeological sites on all public lands, but when Congress rejected that idea, they settled for protection of Casa Grande. They explained that the site "is at present entirely unprotected from the depredations of visitors and that it has suffered more in eleven years from this source than in the three hundred and fifty years preceding." Congress agreed and President Benjamin Harrison signed an executive order that made the Casa Grande Ruins the first national archaeological reserve.[9]

The expedition was on its last legs that summer, but Cushing had been pushed out years before. Suffering from chronic illness, Cushing simultaneously faced accusations of fraud and financial mismanagement from his own brother-in-law. The allegations added to his reputation as an "inveterate complainer," and he lost his job. Powell, who valued Cushing, lamented his "unfortunate temperament," noting "he fancies he has enemies where none exist."[10]

One or two might have existed.

BAE ethnologist Matilda Coxe Stevenson also worked with the Zuni and Cushing. Like most ethnologists of the day, she frequently purchased cultural items including sacred religious objects from the people she studied. Some, like Adolph Bandelier, complained about the amounts she and others spent. When cash failed to persuade people to part with items, Matilda resorted to intimidation and manipulation, as did Cushing and their colleagues. Despite their similarities, there was great animosity between Cushing and Matilda. She wrote on the back of a picture of Cushing dressed in Zuni attire, "This man was the biggest fool and charlatan I ever knew." Matilda was also at the World's Fair to help set up the displays in the Government Building and to judge the displays in the Department of American Ethnology.[11]

Cushing struggled with the Piney Branch display. He slept poorly and complained, "It is dreadful to be so poor and in ill health too with so much to lose forever thereby!"[12] Still, he crafted and named Indigenous mannequins weaving, making beads and baskets, and performing traditional ceremonies. As the display slowly came together, Cushing began to hope for redemption among the rejects.

The BAE's displays were just a fraction of the archaeology in Chicago. The fair appointed Frederic Ward Putnam, Harvard professor of anthropology and curator of the Peabody Museum, to organize ethnology, archaeology, anthropology, history, and natural history exhibits. Aged fifty-four, Putnam was well placed to bring together a wide range of specimens from around the globe.

Putnam's views could be described as old school when compared with the BAE's. He relied on a string of amateurs to collect evidence of the Paleolithic. A New Jersey surgeon with a poor bedside manner, Charles Conrad Abbott, was one of Putnam's collectors. Abbott turned to writing to support his family, along with other odd jobs.[13] For almost two decades he worked as a field assistant for the Peabody Museum of Archaeology, collecting more than 20,000 stone fragments from the Delaware River Valley.[14] Abbott argued that these stones proved the existence of Paleolithic people in America because they resembled Paleolithic tools found in European glacial deposits.

He was not alone. Teacher Frances Babbitt found 1,200 quartz blades in a Minnesota washout. After conferring with prominent members of the field, she concluded that the tools "were distinctly paleolithic in general tone."[15] Trusting in this evidence, Putnam chided Holmes for dismissing the Paleolithic camp.[16]

Putnam may have been defending a long-term investment from criticism, but perhaps something more personal lurked behind the conflict. Years before, Abbott complained to Putnam: "I believe myself a fool to try, being poor, to take a prominent part in the scientific world. Money makes science, as well as the man, go."[17]

Putnam could sympathize with feelings of inadequacy. He attended a lot of school, but never obtained a degree.[18] That failure haunted Putnam but did not make him jealous. He welcomed students into his home, helped them secure jobs, and loaned them funds when he could. He viewed his students as "human beings in need of encouragement and assistance, not mere thought machines to be perfected and turned adrift."[19] His mentorship was such that they were proud to call themselves Putnam's "boys" and revere him as "'the Professor,' as if there were really only one."[20]

Although anthropology and archaeology were male dominated, a few women were joining the ranks. Putnam welcomed female students. Of his first three students, one was a woman named Cordelia Studley. He would also later mentor one of the first Indigenous archaeologists— Arthur Parker.[21]

He beamed with pride at his students as they accomplished what he had not: "keenly alive to the value of degrees and distinctions: they were the reward of valor and an earnest of future work. . . . And he never forgot to address a new PhD as 'Doctor' on his emergence from a successful examination."[22]

Degree or no degree, on July 4, 1893, Putnam had more important things to worry about than rejects of the human or object variety. Time was up.

Forget mummies and burial grounds. The curse no archaeologist can escape is the stubborn finiteness of time. No matter the era, there is always too much land to excavate and too many artifacts to curate. Most excavations bring more questions than answers. And the only thing that slips away faster than the minutes is the money. Putnam was cursed; he was an archaeologist.

Independence Day marked the opening of Putnam's Anthropology Building, over two months behind schedule. Plans began years before, but the building took far longer to complete than expected.[23] Putnam was aided by his student Franz Boas. Boas's background was in physics, but after 1883, he pursued a career in anthropology.[24] That pursuit left him working a series of temporary, insecure positions. As he did for his other students, Putnam tried to look out for Boas, employing him as his chief assistant and head of physical anthropology at the fair.[25]

Putnam saw Indigenous peoples as essential to communicating the importance of anthropology to the public. He argued:

These peoples, as great nations, have about vanished into history, and now is the last opportunity for the world to see them and to realize what their condition, their life, their customs, their arts were four centuries ago. . . . Without them the Exposition will have no base. It will show the material prosperity and the development of our race in the arts and in culture, but it will have no beginning; it will be a monument standing upon nothing.[26]

It would be absurd for Indigenous people of great nations to stand beside Putnam's own White race. Someone had to be on top. It was perhaps one thing Putnam and Powell agreed on.

Ida B. Wells helped produce 20,000 copies of the pamphlet *The Reason Why the Colored American Is Not in the World's Columbian Exposition*. The pamphlet underlined the irony of the fair's exclusion of Black Americans: "The exhibit of progress made by a race in 25 years of freedom as against 250 years of slavery, would have been the greatest tribute to the greatness and progressiveness of American institutions which could have been shown in the world."[27] But the fair organizers chose to represent the progress of only one group of Americans.

Putnam envisioned Indigenous representatives encamped in a wooded isle going about their traditional lives as visitors ambled through the human zoo. Getting those representatives to Chicago proved more difficult than he had hoped.[28] Putnam turned to a Tuscarora man named Cornelius C. Cusick and then a man named Antonio Apache to lure participants to his village, but neither succeeded. The tick of the clock grew louder.

Putnam got the people before the building. He was disappointed to learn that some Indigenous people claimed not to practice the traditional crafts of four hundred years ago, as if they had changed over time. But slowly groups of Navajo, Inuit, and Iroquois, among other nations, made their way to Chicago.

The Inuit set up a replica village along a pond. For twenty-five cents, visitors could see reindeer and dogs in harnesses and a skin tent that housed Inuit people wearing traditional clothing.[29] During the fair, some Indigenous people earned financial compensation for their participation; others earned nothing; and wage disputes remained a source of conflict.[30] The births of four Inuit—Columbia Susan Manak, Kotuktooka, Christopher Columbus Palliser, and Nancy Helene Columbia Parker—warmed hearts. But after living in unheated buildings and plagued by measles in the harsh Chicago winter, Manak and a baby born before arrival in Chicago died. Palliser would die of malnutrition after the close of the fair, aged seventeen months.[31]

Putnam maintained all Indigenous peoples were treated well and given the opportunity to civilize.[32] If they could just keep breathing, the Indigenous people on display in Chicago could learn to be as civilized, intelligent, and empathetic as those who brought unvaccinated people to live outside by a pond in the Chicago winter.

Putnam acknowledged that few Americans even knew what anthropology was in 1893.[33] Anthropology is the study of humans in the past and the present, unlike archaeology, which is the study of the material remains of past human activity, not present. With the help of others, Putnam introduced the world to the Americas' archaeological treasures. Boas felt four archaeological subjects were well documented there: (1) human antiquity in North America; (2) the mystery of the mound builders; (3) the archaeology of Central America; (4) the archaeology of Peru.[34]

Some of the most visible antiquities across America were burial mounds. Their size, scale, contents, and origins intrigued the public and professionals alike. Ohio was the location of the Smithsonian's inaugural archaeology survey, and its earthen mounds were a staple of research. The Anthropology Building displayed pictures, maps, and artifacts of Ohio's mounds.

Many burial mounds appeared as rounded piles of earth, while others were shaped like animals and called effigy mounds. Putnam had worked at many mounds across the nation, including the Serpent Mound of Ohio. The over 1,300-foot earthen viper slithers through the state with an open mouth holding an oval object. The first time Putnam saw the Serpent Mound, he exclaimed: "The most singular sensation of awe and admiration overwhelmed me at this sudden realization of my long cherished desire, for here before me was the mysterious work of an unknown people, whose seemingly most sacred place we invaded."[35] Putnam quickly found that others had made it to the Serpent Mound before him, digging holes into the monument, taking artifacts, and plowing portions of the site. Putnam turned to Alice Cunningham

Fletcher, an ethnologist and anthropologist. With the help of "a few ladies in Boston," they raised enough money to buy the Serpent Mound and donate it to the Peabody Museum. Putnam hoped "the example thus set must bear good fruit, and we can now feel sure that greater interest than ever before will be taken in the preservation of the ancient monuments of America."[36]

Inside and outside the Anthropology Building, visitors also explored the architecture of ancient Mexico. Large models of temples from Uxmal and Labná, Yucatan, offered guests a realistic glimpse of the ancient cities. One of Putnam's students, George Dorsey, returned from South America with 4,000 "earthenware vessels, wood carvings, gold and silver pieces, weapons, textiles, tools, and human remains." His display included Peruvian mummies with their knees tucked under their chin and "wands, silver bracelets, feather cloth, ivory ornaments."[37]

Elsewhere in the building were displays that fell outside the four themes. Gustaf Nordenskiöld organized an exhibit of the Mesa Verde collection. It consisted of photos and maps of the cliff dwellings. No artifacts. He had a new book coming out, *The Cliff Dwellers of Mesa Verde*, which provided descriptions of the cliff dwellings and kivas. He offered detailed directions on how to reach each cliff dwelling, making it possible for others to assess his claims. He also incorporated pictures of artifacts and individuals.[38] The book was and remains a high-quality, invaluable source of information.

The Indigenous village remained open. Whatever the Indigenous people at the fair hoped for, to the anthropologists they were living evidence. Few placed more value on the Indigenous people as specimens than Boas. His previous work in British Columbia included collecting Indigenous skulls and complete skeletons. He complained, "It is most unpleasant work to steal bones from a grave, but what is the use, someone has to do it."[39] Apparently, someone also had to sell said bones because Boas exchanged crania for cash with museums.

In Chicago he focused on the living. He measured the skulls of approximately 50,000 schoolchildren and used the Indigenous village as a laboratory. One newspaper explained, "Whenever Professor Putnam's associates get hold of an aboriginal person they measure him. A series of results obtained by measuring skulls and skeletons have been collected and placed on charts.... Seventy-five men worked two years measuring nearly twenty thousand Indians. They thus found one use to which an Indian could be put."[40] Boas spent his days stockpiling an enormous dataset on the physical attributes of the people of America. He would use it later.

Richard tried to fit in. Appearances mattered. He wrote, "Clothes do not make the man But a man without clothes had better stay at home."[41] He was parroting Marcia Lorraine Billings, a Denver native with strawberry blonde hair and blue eyes. Like so many others, she had come to Alamo Ranch to see the cliff dwellings. He fell for her, but if Marcia ever felt the same, she cooled quickly, sending him a "kind, but cold hearted letter" in response to his affectionate messages. His letters to Marcia reveal a man sensitive to his place in life and his financial instability. But he was no grand romantic.

By the summer of 1893, Marcia was gone. Richard had spent part of the summer expanding the tourist trade, partnering with Pennsylvania photographer Charles Lang. They advertised themselves as specialists in cliff dwelling images. And Richard recovered from Marcia with the arrival of family friend Julia Cowing, who frequently made Alamo Ranch her summer retreat.[42]

Chicago had beckoned for some time. Charlie Mason noted that by 1889 the tone of the Wetherill family's explorations of the cliff dwellings had shifted: "We went at it in a more businesslike manner, as our previous work had been carried out to satisfy our own curiosity than for any other purpose." The State of Colorado paid the family to raid the cliffs specifically for the World's Fair.[43] Richard's biographer wrote that Colorado used a legislative appropriation of $100,000 to buy this collection from the family.[44] But the *Grand Junction News* reported that in 1891 the legislature was considering a bill to purchase a collection from the Wetherills for $10,000.[45] One zero makes quite a difference. The prices paid for similar collections make it tempting to believe the *Grand Junction News*. The Wetherills' colleagues in the cliffs, Charles McLoyd and J. H. Graham, sold a collection to C. D. Hazzard, who then sold part of the collection to Phoebe Hearst for $14,500.[46] McLoyd and C. C. Graham also sold a collection to Reverend C. H. Green for $3,000.[47] It seems most likely that Colorado stuck to this general pay range. According to one Alamo Ranch visitor, the state paid the Wetherills a regular exploration fee: "These sons are now in the pay of the State of Colorado at $50.00 per month each for three of them, the elder receiving $100.00 per month, to work up the subject of the cliff dwellings."[48] Business was good.

Charlie Mason, Richard, Al, John, and Clayt Wetherill sold a collection to the H. Jay Smith Exploring Company and C. D. Hazzard in 1892.[49] The H. Jay Smith Exploring Company stole the show at the fair. They crafted a replica of Battle Rock Mountain, a cliff dwelling in southwestern Colorado. They used timber and iron to create the basic shape of the mountain, then painted the cliff a shade of reddish brown and covered the exterior in grasses. For twenty-five cents, visitors could step inside the exhibit, where some two thousand artifacts from cliff dwellings lay on display.[50] Tourists found "large coarse jars . . . hundreds of stone hatchets, knives, arrow heads, hammers and mortars, bows, paddles, hoes, lances, etc." Mummified individuals found in the cliff dwellings were also on display.[51]

Richard would have felt at home among the ruins that fascinated him. Cushing paid a visit one day and commented, "They are remarkably realistic, but not so impressive as might have been made."[52] In Boas's estimate, "The ancient culture of the cliffdwellers is one of the best represented subjects at the exposition."[53] Criticisms aside, the Battle Rock Mountain experience made the H. Jay Smith Exploring Company $87,366.28 during the fair.[54] For those paying attention, it paid to own the past.

The popularity of Battle Rock Mountain must have made Richard proud of his work. But the fair also offered a chance to put faces to names. The Wetherills had been trying to get the professional archaeological community interested in Mesa Verde for years.

Richard's father had written to the Smithsonian expressing his hope that Mesa Verde would be preserved as a national park; if not, he warned of the cliff dwellings' imminent destruction by curious visitors.[55] He neglected to mention that his sons would be leading them down the path of destruction. Holmes responded. He had traveled through the region, seen cliff dwellings, and seemed unimpressed by the Wetherills' work but did not offer tips for improvement. He admonished them for failing to record the place and circumstances of each discovery and suggested the Wetherills required "scientific supervision." He was not interested in their collections. Instead, he asked: "Is it not possible for you to map the ruins visited and to preserve for this Bureau a series of descriptive notes of work done."[56]

It may not have been the message the Wetherills were hoping for, but it was good archaeology. Context is crucial. At its most basic it is the location of discovery. But archaeologists scour that location for clues about antiquity, recording the layer and type of soil, the relationship between artifacts and surrounding cultural or environmental features. The act of excavation is destructive. As the dirt and artifacts start moving, the integrity of the evidence starts to diminish. If the scene is not analyzed and recorded, the artifacts and site lose their value.

Holmes informed the secretary of the Smithsonian, Samuel Langley, that there was no need for continued communication with the Wetherill family. Langley told the Wetherills that the Smithsonian could not accept any of the Mesa Verde collection. Benjamin's daughter-in-law adds that the family offered the collection for "the cost of excavating" and that the Smithsonian replied "that they had no money to buy the collection and could only accept it as a donation."[57]

So, Richard wrote to Putnam in 1890. He parroted Holmes's message: "We recognize the fact, the principal scientific value of collections existed in the circumstances of their original position, or reference to the implements or objects with which they were associated, and we worked accordingly."[58] He invited the professor to visit Mesa Verde, but Putnam did not. The fair offered an opportunity for Richard to connect in person.

Perhaps the men could have bonded over their personal miseries. Putnam had plenty of personal problems. He had founded a press decades earlier that printed academic reports and was now failing, costing Putnam thousands of dollars.[59] As the crowds passed through the Anthropology Building, Putnam found himself in debt, defending theories under siege, dramatically behind schedule, and delivering far less than he had promised.

To some extent his financial struggles were a sign of the times. A series of banking disturbances in 1873, 1884, and 1890 had already shaken the American economy. But on May 3, 1893, the stock market collapsed.[60]

Well before then, Richard had left Alamo Ranch on the hustle. In December 1892, he jumped into the San Juan gold fields looking for a quick fix. *The Idaho Springs News* soon reported Richard's disappointment: "At no place is there enough for any man to make more than $1.50 a day in the process of panning."[61] In April, a grand jury indicted Richard for grand larceny. This time, the charges involved cattle, rather than artifacts. A jury found him not guilty, but lawyer fees still needed to be paid.[62] He returned to Mancos in June with "a large assortment" of Navajo blankets to sell.[63] Meanwhile the brothers invested in a sluice and began harvesting the ranch in hopes of mineral wealth. The local paper was supportive of their endeavor, declaring, "We believe the boys will be astounded with their success as soon as they get in more boxes and learn how to manipulate them. Boys, you are on the true road to wealth and eventually will become the possessors of loving wives and children."[64] Whatever else they were, the Wetherills proved that they were resourceful and adaptable capitalists.

As an undervalued, underfunded profession, archaeology is an unenviable occupation when stocks start crashing. These men must have felt financially vulnerable and uncertain. Two of Putnam's first three students, including Cordelia Studley, had to withdraw because of financial difficulties.[65] With the demand for the past clearly established and no legal restrictions on the antiquities trade, it must have seemed irrational to some not to leverage the past for all it was worth.

Serious professionals gathered en masse at the fair in August at the International Congress of Anthropology. Putnam discussed the exhibits in the Anthropology Building and the surveys behind them. Zelia Nuttall, a specialist on ancient Mexico, spoke on "The Mexican Calendar System." Boas read a paper on seven Indigenous languages of the Northwest Coast.[66]

Cushing discussed the origins of the cliff dwellers. He linked them to the southwestern Indigenous peoples such as the Zuni. Reflecting on Cushing's paper, Holmes observed that the for-profit cliff dwelling exhibit was spouting contradictory information: "These conclusions were antagonized by the extraordinary and utterly unreliable teachings of the principal exhibitor of cliff dwellers' remains on the exposition grounds, through whose agency many erroneous notions respecting these remains have been disseminated."[67]

That was exactly what concerned Mrs. McClurg, who lectured in the Women's Building at the fair. Virginia Donaghe had married journalist Gilbert McClurg in 1889 and gained another name. She was now living in Colorado, where she worked for the *Daily Republic* and kept a close watch over Mesa Verde. Yet in addition to lecturing at the fair, she also sponsored a cliff dwelling exhibit.[68]

One contrary opinion later appeared in print. Anthony James wrote of the cliff dwellers at the fair that they had Caucasian skulls that demonstrated intelligence. He repeated an Aztec tale of Quetzalcoatl, the god of the air, who had "white skin, long, dark hair, and a flowing beard," and posited that the story held some factual foundation. He interpreted the cliff dwellers as a vanished race of White ancestral Americans. He pointed to a mummy of a child collected by Wetherill that displayed "a goodly quantity of a fine silky hair of lightish [*sic*] shade, such as belongs to no other people on earth save the Caucasian."[69] This superficial and flimsy analysis aligned with interpretive standards of the day wherein descriptive evidence was used to make sweeping speculations.

James was wrong but in Holmes's criticism lay signs of a communication issue that still plagues American archaeology. As professional archaeologists created boundaries to site access, artifact accumulation, and interpretation of the past, a gulf between the professionals and the public opened. Archaeologists found that entertainers, profiteers, and charlatans proved frustratingly good at sliding into the gap and manipulating the past for profit.

The congress continued with papers on a variety of topics. Egyptologist Sarah Stevenson spoke on the ceremonial rights of the dead in ancient Egypt. Matilda Coxe Stevenson's paper was on Zuni mythology. Cushing criticized it as "a poor effort, rambling, superficial, and in its differences from my well-known statements, really silly and somewhat venomous."[70] Holmes discussed the stone tools from Piney Branch and the absence of evidence of Paleolithic people in America.

This was American archaeology in 1893. There, but not there. Pinballing between ethnography and anthropology and commodity, but unable to stand on its own with any authority. It was a hodgepodge of ambitious, competitive, passionate individuals who went where they wanted, dug where they wanted, took what they wanted, and believed what they wanted. They were all flawed with blind spots of varying magnitudes, and with their imperfections and love of the past, they paved the way.

Although much of the archaeological, anthropological, and ethnographic work presented at the fair revolved around Indigenous communities, Indigenous Americans were not offered seats at the professional table. At best, professionals used Indigenous Americans as informants. Others objectified living and deceased Indigenous peoples as specimens. But the people who made much of the work on display at the fair possible were not treated as collaborators or colleagues.

The objectification and dehumanization of Indigenous peoples left many ostracized from a field obsessed by them. Choctaw archaeologist Joe Watkins explores various interpretations of the rareness of published Indigenous perspectives on archaeology:

> Does the paucity of published comment mean Indigenous groups have no issues with the way archaeology is practiced or the way archaeology impacts them, or does that quietude mean only that no one has asked their opinion? Perhaps the air is silent only because Indigenous people are unable to get their opinions published, or maybe the Indigenous group is afraid to draw attention to their situation for one reason or another.[71]

American archaeology in 1893 was not a field focused on inclusion, much less the accumulation and interpretation of data. Archaeologists collected things. Lots of things. Then they speculated based on the appearance of things and little more. With such a low bar, the archaeological community found interesting ways to settle their differences.

Abbott chose poetry to commit himself to the existence of Paleolithic people in America:

> The stones are inspected,
> And Holmes cries 'rejected,
> They're nothing but Indian chips'
> He glanced at the ground,
> Truth, fancied he found,
> And homeward to Washington skips.
> They got there by chance
> He saw at a glance
> And turned up his nose at the series;
> 'They've no other history,
> I've solved the whole mystery,
> And to argue the point only wearies'
> But the gravel is old,
> At least, so I'm told;
> 'Halt, halt! cries out W.J.,
> It may be very recent,
> And it isn't quite decent,
> For me not to have my own way.'
> So dear W.J.
> There is no more to say,
> Because you will never agree
> That anything's truth
> But what issues, forsooth,
> From Holmes or the brain of McGee.[72]

Poetic rivalries aside, Holmes had criticisms of the congress: it was organized too quickly, the papers could have been better, but he acknowledged, "The great richness of the American field of investigation was made apparent to all. The importance of the outcome of the whole group of anthropologic features connected with the fair depends largely on the action of Chicago with respect to the opportunity of the century in museum-making."[73] At last Putnam could agree with Holmes. He too hoped that a new museum was on Chicago's horizon.[74] As well as a prestigious new job for someone . . .

Twenty-year-old Talbot Hyde and his eighteen-year-old brother Fred wanted for little in life. Their grandfather Benjamin Talbot Babbitt was a successful inventor and chemist, who developed a cheap form of saleratus, a key ingredient in baking powder. He opened a business selling his low-cost yeast, baking powder, and soap.[75] Babbitt led the way in the commercialization of soap, cutting soap into tiny bars wrapped in alluring paper. Marketing was a key strength of the Babbitt enterprise. Some said Babbitt was one of the founders of the loyalty scheme.[76] In 1889, Benjamin T. Babbitt died, leaving a substantial inheritance, possibly bolstered by tax evasion.[77] His daughter Ida married Frederick Erastus Hyde and together they had six children, including Talbot and Fred.

Talbot and Fred found plenty of time for travel. In 1892, they embarked on a world tour, beginning in Colorado. Like Nordenskiöld, they stayed at the Strater Hotel before making their way to Alamo Ranch. Clayt Wetherill, the second youngest of the brothers, was their guide. Talbot and Fred's father wrote, "The trip was a very hard one taking several hours to go to the camp at the cliffs a distance of about twenty-seven miles." Clayt prepared a meal of "fried bacon, fried potatoes, griddle bread, canned apricots." After dinner, the senior Hyde wrote: "A large canvas was laid upon the sand upon this was put our shawls and such bedding quilts as they had, we then lay down with all our clothes on except our shoes and a long flap of canvas was folded from our feet over us to our necks. Thus we were put to bed. As I could not sleep at once I amused myself watching the stars."[78] The next day they carried on to the cliff dwellings. And it would seem the ruins worked their usual magic.

From Colorado, the Hydes explored Japan, China, Singapore, Ceylon, Egypt, and Palestine. Back in Chicago, they explored all that the fair had to offer. Suddenly, they found themselves face to face with Richard Wetherill once more. Perhaps inspired by the antiquities surrounding them, the Hydes offered to sponsor an archaeological expedition with Richard as the leader.

How could Richard resist? With a sizable investment, he could finally launch an in-depth exploration of the Southwest. Think of the artifacts he could collect if he could extend his time in the ruins. Think of the money. He accepted the Hydes' offer, and the Hyde Exploring Expedition was born.

This spur-of-the-moment proposition resulted in an archaeological endeavor that would parallel methodological and legal shifts in American archaeology. As they mulled over the details, Richard, Talbot, and Fred had no way of knowing their deal would eventually pull in Putnam, play a role in the evolution of American archaeology, and leave a century-size mess for future archaeologists to clean up.

FOUR

Toward the Grand Gulch

There was much to do and little time before Richard launched the Hyde Exploring Expedition, so he headed east. He took in Niagara Falls and indulged in the horse racing in Saratoga Springs.[1] By mid-October 1893, his eastward voyage ended in Brooklyn, New York. Julia Cowing welcomed him, and they got down to business.

Julia appears to have been a moderately well-off woman in New York society. She made the local paper from time to time for her involvement in various clubs and social causes. She shared with Richard a love for the cliff dwellings. She shared that passion with New York audiences, giving at least one lecture entitled "Cliff Dwellers of the Mancos Canon" in 1895.[2] Richard's biographer cast a critical eye on Julia, describing her as "a tall, slender woman in her early thirties, her medium blonde hair worn in the short, curly bangs then fashionable. . . . cheerful, curiously different. . . . She wasn't really pretty, but engaging." He went on to describe her as naively taking on the painful horse ride to Mesa Verde, suffering from her foolishness, and requiring days of recovery.[3] Fred and Talbot Hyde's father contradicted the damsel-in-distress caricature, writing that she went into Mesa Verde in "a man's saddle and riding astride."[4] Perhaps she had wised up to the hindrance that was the female horse riding style; perhaps she was wise all along.

Richard had half of what he wanted. The Hyde money meant that he could launch an expedition of considerable size for an extended period. Maybe it was Holmes's criticism of the contextless collection from Mesa Verde; maybe it was the general lack of interest from the professional archaeological community; maybe it was Nordenskiöld's well-received book; but it was no longer enough just to explore and collect. Richard wanted to do *good* archaeology, a very subjective concept.

He wrote to the Hyde brothers, who lived in New York, letting them know that he was in town to get organized. He reckoned there were tools and supplies there that he would not be able to get in Colorado. Then there was the matter of the excavation itself.[5] Despite what he told Putnam, he knew that the Wetherill way of digging and grabbing was subpar. He wrote to Gustaf a year before, "As it stands you have the only collection that has been taken out properly."[6] So with Julia, he devised a new strategy for the Hyde Exploring Expedition.

If they knew where to look, there were a few opinions on archaeological excavation floating around. However, as British archaeologist Sir Mortimer Wheeler later warned, "There is no right way of digging, but there are many wrong ways."[7] The history of archaeology up to 1893 attested to that.

The earliest archaeological endeavors amounted to forceful mad grabs on behalf of regal pack rats. An account from Babylon credits King Nabonidus (555–539 BCE) with excavating temples in his kingdom and placing the finds on display in a quasi-museum.[8] Kings carried on with this tradition for centuries, with Henry III and Henry VIII presiding over the raiding of barrows in England.[9] There is no indication of a scientific framework in these forays.

In 1748, King Charles II of Naples paid engineers to blast through the ruins of Herculaneum.[10] The violent assaults on the world's nonrenewable antiquities were only getting started in the eighteenth century. Richard may have been aware of Richard Vyse's work in Egypt, where in 1837, the colonel blasted through Giza with gunpowder.[11] Or he could have followed the exploits of Heinrich Schliemann in the 1870s as he cut massive trenches across Hissarlik and threw "battering rams, iron levers, and more English spades and pickaxes" in pursuit of Homer's Troy.[12] Perched in the twenty-first century, it is easy to see the destructiveness of these techniques. But as newspapers filled with images of the treasures of these legendary landscapes, Richard and any other lover of the past with a shovel and some time could have easily gotten the wrong idea.

Some in America were aware that archaeology had an issue or two. In the mid-1880s, Putnam gave a legendary* lecture, "On the Methods of Archaeological Research in America." He emphasized the need to expose, identify, and record the association of objects. Chief among the methods of opening the earth were trenching and slicing. In what he would later refine and title the wedding cake method, he encouraged the slow, cautious exploration of mounds. He explained the data that could be accrued by this method: "Each slice thus made is a section, and whenever the slightest change in the structure is noticed or any object found, that section should be drawn or photographed, and measured as at first, and the exact position noted of any object . . . or change in the character of the structure of the mound."[13]

If Richard had access to these guidelines, they would have offered some resolution to his previous struggles with archaeological context; however, the archaeology of the East differs dramatically from that of the West, so Putnam's guidance would have helped only so much. And overall, the discipline remained an unstandardized jumble of personal preference. A summary of the field in 1890 concluded, "The average archaeologist of the United States has been in times past but little more than a collector of Indian relics. He sought to gather or obtain rare or handsome objects, and these qualities measured their value in his eyes. Such collections viewed from the standpoint of the real archaeologists, are but little if any value."[14] They knew the modern maxim "It's not what you find, but what you find out" to be true. Despite Putnam and his colleagues' best efforts, change in their methods of finding out remained sluggish.

Regardless of the lack of formalized excavation methods and his previously destructive pothunting, Richard was determined to do better. He wrote to Talbot Hyde explaining how. Before jumping into any ruin, they would photograph it. Each ruin would be assigned a number. Once inside, they would also assign numbers to any artifacts and record the

---

* Legendary in the sense that no original copies of the lecture are currently known to exist. We rely on an audience member's recollection of Putnam's lecture at Johns Hopkins University Graduate School.

number of floors and rooms in each cliff house. Each ruin would be sketched, and every artifact numbered with "Indian ink and fine pen or with tube paints white, red or black." He concluded on a prescient note, "This whole subject . . . is in its infancy and the work we do must stand the most rigid inspection, and we do not want to do it in such a manner that anyone in the future can pick flaws in it."[15]

If only.

Richard wanted the survey to be more along the lines of Gustaf's work in Mesa Verde than his own. His intended techniques point toward improved record keeping, rather than excavation methods. It is possible that he remained unaware of the data loss inherent in destructive, intensive excavation techniques. And it is apparent that his mind remained on the artifacts and thereby the money. Still, this time his proposal demonstrates an effort at improvement. An epigram in the Wetherill Family Archives reads, "Judge a man not so much by what he does, but by what he would like to do."[16] As he finalized his plans, Richard could only hope for such mercy.

He said goodbye to Julia after little more than a week. Somewhere along the way, he determined that the expedition would not concentrate on Mesa Verde. For some time, Richard had been aware of another archaeological haven: southeastern Utah's Grand Gulch. Charles McLoyd, whom Richard had stumbled into after first seeing Cliff Palace, had been doing work in the gulch for some time. Much like Richard, McLoyd was a hustler working variously as a miner and rancher and leveraging any resources he could find to get by. In 1891, McLoyd explored the Grand Gulch region with another miner and rancher, Charles Cary Graham.[17]

The US Geological and Geographical Survey of the Territories brought the Grand Gulch out of obscurity when it published the results of the 1878 Hayden Survey.[18] The terrain proved more arduous than that of Mesa Verde, but beginning on New Year's Day 1891, McLoyd and Graham barreled into the gulch, leaving their marks as they went. Coming upon a kiva in Bullet Canyon, Graham graffitied the ancient site, writing "C.C. Graham—Jan. 11, 91'" on the canyon wall.[19] By April, they had amassed a collection of large corrugated jars, baskets, sandals, stone and bone tools, cradle boards, hammers, awls, feather blankets, and individuals. Putnam allowed the collection to go on display in the Anthropology Building in Chicago.[20]

John Wetherill joined McLoyd and Graham on their second expedition in the Grand Gulch in 1892, giving Richard a direct line to the conditions in Utah. That year, McLoyd left his mark on a site known as Turkey Pen Ruin, tattooing the wall with "C. McLoyd 1892."[21] McLoyd and Graham had aptly demonstrated that the region contained a high quantity of ruins and artifacts that had not yet been ransacked by tourists. They had also shown that there was demand for the gulch's artifacts. Whether for the quantity, quality, or fiscal value of its antiquities, Grand Gulch was now the Hyde Exploring Expedition's destination.

Home by early November, Richard did not tarry long. He assembled supplies and his team. He brought along two of his brothers, Al and John, leaving Clayt and Win behind to manage the ranch. Charles Lang, with whom Richard had gone into the photography business, tagged along. Two other men, Richard's friend Harry French and blond-haired, blue-eyed Jim Ethridge, an Alamo Ranch laborer, filled out the crew. On November 29, 1893, the team left Alamo Ranch, destination Utah.[22]

Utah's European-American footprint was still young. The earlier peopling of the Southwest is a phenomenon that archaeologists are still working to understand. The answer to this riddle will likely only continue to evolve, rather than ever be solved. The discovery in 2021 of ca. 21,000–23,000-year-old human footprints in White Sands National Park, New Mexico, is the latest break in this search.[23] Certainly by at least 16,000 years ago, people were trickling into the region, but they were not the people Richard and his team encountered as they arrived in San Juan County.

Groups of Mormons immigrated to Bluff, Utah, in the 1880s. These members of the Church of the Latter-Day Saints lived in houses made of rough cottonwood logs and made their living much as the Wetherills did. In 1892, the region witnessed its first gold rush and as "the last civilized outpost, before the canyons and sand dunes went on for miles," the citizens of Bluff benefited from their ability to supply weary miners and travelers.[24] Bluff thus became the Hyde Exploring Expedition's first headquarters.

From Bluff, they continued north toward the Grand Gulch.[25] In the distance, red and brown cliffs lined the horizon with two particularly eye-catching triangular buttes reaching roughly 2,000 feet into the sky. They appeared to many to resemble bears' ears and one day would be the namesake of a controversial national monument. The expedition's route followed Cottonwood Canyon, which also presented a tan and red wonderland interspersed with green for part of the year, balding for the rest. Thirty miles in, the expedition came upon an alcove facing west by northwest. It was small, only 105 feet wide by 10 feet high.[26] That people had been there before Richard and his team was clear. Sandstone rubble and yellow mortar lay strewn across the floor. They recorded a two-room structure on the alcove floor and two more rooms along a ledge approximately ten feet above the alcove opening.[27] As dictated by Richard's new approach, they took pictures of the alcove, which they named Cave 7.* They wandered around the rooms of the ancient edifice, but there was nothing there. The rubble outside proved more fruitful, and they collected a few items. But on the surface, Cave 7 was far less impressive than Mesa Verde and the adobe rooms "inferior to those found in Mancos Canon."[28]

They dug in anyway. Al poetically advised, "You must always take a second look at everything you find; For there's lots of gold you'd not expect in places never mined."[29] Richard established a grid within Cave 7 dividing the alcove into twelve-foot numbered sections.[30] Theoretically, this allowed the team to record the locations of each find in tighter contexts. As their shovels moved below the foundation of the rooms, they came upon the familiar artifacts of the cliff dwellers of Mesa Verde: pottery, sandals, and three individuals.[31]

Three feet down, "a clean, yellow sand" emerged. They noticed dampness in the soil. But they carried on, uncovering dark stains among the yellow sand that gave way to more ancient individuals. As they dug "four and a half to seven feet" below the alcove surface, they continued to disinter more and more individuals.[32] Though absent from this discovery, a writer presumed to be Clayt Wetherill felt such moments called for respect: "There will always be something that appeals to the

---

* Technically, caves are below ground, while alcoves are above ground.

innermost soul compelling one to respect the tombs of the ancient dead of whom we know so little."[33]

Looking back, Al remembered the feeling of encountering the past and its people as a powerful experience:

> It was so much like treading "holy ground" to go into those peaceful-looking homes of a vanished people. . . . It recurred again and again as we found new houses, untouched through all those long years. We knew that if we did not break into that charmed world someone else would, sometime—someone who might not love and respect those emblems of antiquity as we did. It was a strange feeling: perhaps all this had been given into our keeping until someone else might do it more capably than we.[34]

The Hyde Exploring Expedition felt entitled to these ancient places and all that they contained. They maintained intellectual and commercial interests in the ruins, but many saw these sites differently. Hopi archaeologist Lyle Balenquah explains: "The sites, the ancestral sites, the rock art, the pictographs, the artifacts, even the burials that are left in place in some of these places . . . they're all metaphorical footprints within our culture."[35] Thus, describing Cave 7 as a "holy ground" would be apt. Many members of Indigenous communities view the final resting places of the dead as sacred places, not to be disturbed. The interred individuals are viewed as ancestors in need of tranquility, rather than "emblems of antiquity" or specimens brimming with untapped research potential. But neither of these mindsets floated around Cave 7 in 1893. The Hyde Exploring Expedition treated the individuals they discovered as characters in a story of the past that they got to narrate.

Eventually, they uncovered around ninety-two individuals. They removed the bodies from the earth. How is worth asking. Dr. J. L. Wortman had worked on the Hemenway Southwestern Archaeological Expedition with Cushing and had cautioned the archaeological community on the appropriate treatment of human remains. Assessing the field, he wrote: "Some of the methods are so crude, and the skill of collectors so primitive, that the material when collected is almost worthless." He told his readers to drop the picks and shovels and approach the dead with only a hand trowel moving carefully around the "anterior superior curve of the spine, possibly the ribs . . . the frontal eminence of the skull, etc." Wortman gave special instructions for human remains found in caves, which may have been relevant in the alcove: "It is best to take the specimen out in a block of the matrix if possible."[36]

Did Richard instruct the team to move with such care and precision? Possibly, but probably not. Soon they could see the spines of the individuals, which suggests they did not remove the bodies with blocks of earth. There, they saw, in two cases, "the ends of spear points firmly imbedded." They noted fractures in the skulls, ribs, arm, and leg bones. Surrounding these individuals, they found "baskets, spear points, bone awls and ornaments." Richard was more intrigued by what wasn't there. Pottery. While they had recovered pottery above the yellow sand, they found no sherds or complete vessels among these individuals. Then Richard noticed their skulls. They were different from the flattened craniums he had seen so often in Mesa Verde. Instead, the skulls appeared "longheaded or dolicocephalous."[37] In short order, the Expedition formulated a story about them.

Today, archaeologists abide by the maxim "Absence of evidence is not evidence of absence." But Richard was sure that the individuals they unearthed in Cave 7 evinced something big, something new. He dashed off a letter to Talbot Hyde in December 1893, declaring, "Our success has surpassed all expectations." In the alcove, he announced, they had discovered "a different race from any thing [sic] to have ever seen" and especially from the cliff dwellers of Mesa Verde.[38] And they were people with a dramatic past.

The expedition explained: "The number of skeletons found at one level and in one place, would suggest a sudden and violent destruction of a community by battle or massacre." They described one individual as "a mother with an infant on each arm, and another lying on her breast with its head under her chin." They viewed the male individuals through an equally dramatic lens, summarizing: "There are warriors, 'mighty men of valor,' with ten or twelve spear points lying near; younger men with bone tools near them, and the unwarlike counsellors or priests."[39] Richard valued these disinterred individuals above all their other findings. He wrote, "What I consider the most valuable finds in the History of Americas is the finding in one . . . of the back bone of skeleton 103 — a spear point of stone sticking into the bone at least an inch."[40]

Untrained in skeletal analysis, how did they know the ages of these people? Did they really know their sex? Their occupations? How did they know those individuals were the heroes of this tale?

Remembering the Mesa Verde days, Al admitted: "As the work went along we could let our imaginations run riot, thinking of the people who had been there and were now gone. With the proper spirit of romance, you can gradually . . . let the silence speak and the mind's eye bring back to life and being the people whose book of life is forever closed."[41] Letting the imagination drift into the past is natural, but it becomes an issue when imagination takes fact's place and spurious explanations are used to subjugate descendant communities.

The expedition photographed Cave 7 and the individuals they had disinterred. They developed the negatives there, among the sand and the rubble, "so that there should be a certainty of success." Barely a month in, Richard felt confident that the Hyde Exploring Expedition was already a success. With Cave 7, they could "prove the existence of an earlier tribe of Indians than those formerly occupying the cliff houses."[42] Richard concluded, "The whole thing is truly wonderful."[43] They had not even made it into the Grand Gulch proper yet.

It was all a bit too swell for many archaeologists who heard the news of Cave 7. The discovery of a new race of ancient peoples after less than thirty days of exploration seemed far too fortunate. Sitting in class at Harvard, Alfred Kidder heard his professors condemn the finds as a lucrative hoax. As he recalled, the general attitude was, "Richard Wetherill had increased the sales value of his collection if not its credibility."[44]

The team's graffiti indicates that Richard ordered them back to work as soon as Christmas ended. Wirt Billings, hired after they left Alamo Ranch, inscribed "W. Billings Dec-31–1893" in Butler Wash, just outside the Grand Gulch.[45] As they continued exploring the alcoves of the Grand Gulch, Richard grew more confident that Cave 7 was groundbreaking. By February, he wrote Talbot, "I named the cliff dwellers, and you should have the honor at least of naming these, since it is your expedition." Richard's preference seemed to be for the term "Cave dwellers."[46]

At twenty-two, Talbot was only just out of school. He had tried and failed to get into MIT, but with the family name at his disposal, he planned to begin working at his grandfather's company shortly. He, too, was mustached, though his hair was thinning early.[47] Talbot offered the name Basket Makers. No one was or has ever been impressed by that choice. As Richard told Talbot, "The Basket Makers . . . is more distinctive than anything I could have thought for a name but it does not convey an idea."[48] Later, archaeologist Charles Amsden would summarize the term Basketmaker as "an awkward and essentially meaningless term, for most of the world's peoples are makers of baskets."[49] Talbot's terminology, while unpopular, was common archaeological practice of organizing and making sense of the world. They labeled the people they chose to no longer see by the monuments they could not ignore. The East and Midwest had Mound Builders. First the West had Cliff Dwellers and now they had Basket Makers. Anthropologists and archaeologists could arrange them all in a neat and tidy order and watch the past prove their belief in cultural evolution.

They continued digging up the alcoves as they tried to make sense of the Basketmakers. Richard began culling the collection after the Cave 7 discovery. He notified Talbot: "I saved all the skeletons from the first cave as I thought you would want them for study, but I will not save any more; the distance is too great, but will save all skulls."[50] He was also making sweeping claims about the people he disinterred: "They are a larger race than the Cliff Dwellers. I have measured none of them, but I know from comparison."[51]

In March, Richard led the party back to Bluff and officially ended the first season of the Hyde Exploring Expedition. Largely they had stuck to Richard's recordkeeping strategy, photographing every site, assigning numbers to both sites and artifacts, and keeping additional records. To his credit, Richard wrote letters informing the world in a timely fashion of their discoveries. Even so, information would be lost over time. By the 1990s, archaeologists would summarize that "there is some ambiguity as to the exact number of burials found in Cave 7 by the Wetherill party." The number would range from 88 to 97 in the intervening years, demonstrating that recordkeeping still had some way to go.

As Richard wrapped things up in March 1894, there were other signs that the expedition had not gone all that smoothly. After receiving funds from Talbot at the end of March, he replied, "I am very glad to have received the money just now as I was getting in desperate circumstances. I would not have felt it so much but we lost $2,500 last fall, or rather didn't make it on account of an early frost."[52] Alamo Ranch was in trouble, and the Hyde brothers were showing a casual attitude to timely payments. And Richard had still not paid all his attorney's fees from the cattle kerfuffle of 1893.[53] Even amid his financial struggles, Richard found peace in the gulch, writing, "I am in the field where I like to work and have no thought for anything else, but it is necessary to have supplies."[54]

After returning to Mancos, he began working through the collection. It took until September to prepare the collection for transportation to New York. He wrote Talbot, "I shipped by express all relics except the bones of the 96 skeletons. The heads of these skeletons were all shipped." The rest of the collection was in storage in the granary. He expressed his gratitude to the expedition's patron: "I thank you very much for what you have done for me. You did me a great deal of good while here. I now begin to feel the effects of it."[55]

News of the discovery in Cave 7 spread around the world. Nordenskiöld stayed in touch, keeping Richard abreast of the Mesa Verde collection. Writing to Richard as "my dear friend," he told him of Europe's appreciation of their findings: "I have been in Spain one month and came just a few days ago back to Sweden. As I think I have told you my collection is exhibited there. I got a gold medal for the collection." As always, Gustaf wanted more. He concluded, "P.S. If you would strike some nice Navajo blankets send them to me."[56] With the Grand Gulch findings, Richard had something that would impress his aristocratic friend. He informed Gustaf, "I will be able to send you 12 or 13 skulls of the new race. . . . There is no money in sending them at the price you offer but I want you to have them."[57] And so the Indigenous diaspora continued under the false guise of archaeology.

Richard's interpretation of the Cave 7 burials made its way into local papers as well. The *Rocky Mountain Sun* reported on the expedition's "indisputable evidence of a third, hitherto unknown race which in lieu of a more suitable name has been called the Basket People." Botching Talbot's unpopular nomenclature, the paper continued, "It is thought by Mr. Wetherill that these Basket People were the ancestors of the Moqui and Pueblo Indians. . . . Little or nothing is known, however, from whence they came, and the deepest mystery covers the origin of the first inhabitants of America."[58]

FIVE

Whence and Whither

By 1894, John Wesley Powell had long grown tired of the questions asked by professionals and amateurs alike: Whence and whither came the Mound Builders?

He had been over it in 1879, when Congress appropriated $20,000 to the BAE. Despite the public interest in the Smithsonian-sponsored investigation of Ohio's mounds by Ephraim Squire and Edwin Davis, Powell could not find any practical justification to continue this effort. It seemed obvious to Powell that the ancestors of the modern tribes built the mounds, and he felt there had been "much unnecessary speculation" and "no reason for us to search for an extralimital origin through lost tribes." He acknowledged that "the tracing of the origin of these arts to the ancestors of known tribes . . . is more legitimate, but it has limitations" because ancestral tribes now "belong to several different stocks." Pursuing mound explorations to prove the existence of the mystery race "promise[d] but a meager harvest."[1]

He was focused on preserving the traces of the nation's living Indigenous peoples—that's why they called it the Bureau of American Ethnology, not the Bureau of American Archaeology. He had no time for the Mound Builders.

Plenty of others did, though. It seemed everyone had a suggestion for who had built the earthen monuments dotting the United States.

In a 1784 publication, historian and surveyor John Filson suggested that early Welsh immigrants built the monuments of Kentucky.[2] In

Ohio, those to receive credit included the Scandinavians of the *Vinland Saga*[3] and post–biblical flood shepherds from Asia. At this time, much of the world still believed that Earth was only a few thousand years old, making the biblical flood a thing of the recent past, though geologists were hard at work debunking that theory. Ohio's official history offered the theory that God himself built the Serpent Mound.[4] William Pidgeon, an archaeologist in Mississippi, also went the biblical route, suggesting the Bible's first man—Adam—as the original Mound Builder.[5]

Other suggestions supported more recent origins. Buccaneers of Seville and Spanish explorers received undue credit for Tennessee's ruins.[6] Still others proposed citizens of Atlantis, Antediluvians, Phoenicians, Irish monks, Egyptians, Aztecs, and Toltecs.[7] Basically, anyone and everyone.

Few agreed with Samuel F. Haven or Henry Rowe Schoolcraft. Both disavowed the existence of a Mound Builder race and credited the ancestors of America's Indigenous peoples with the construction of the mounds.[8] Vikings and Biblical protagonists seemed a more likely explanation to many.

This slew of opinions emerged from the power vacuum of Powell's disinterest, the absence of other coordinated professional efforts to address a question of public interest, and garden-variety racism. An author who published as C. Wetherill, presumably Clayt, called for explorations that would abolish the steady stream of "misrepresentation and nonsensical trash," concluding on the state of current knowledge, "What such theories are based on no one knows."[9] Years later, Al explained in the spirit of a conspiracy theorist, "Each of us is permitted his own theory because none can deny it."[10]

Once again, the void between the past and the people lay exposed, and archaeologists needed to bridge the divide with tangible evidence or surrender authority to the prowling charlatans and frauds.

The nineteenth century witnessed a cornucopia of archaeological hoaxes. There was the Cardiff Giant of New York, a ten-foot-tall "petrified man," who proved to be carved of a block of gypsum that retained tool marks. Professionals soon concluded the Giant was "a humbug."[11]

There were "discoveries" of the sixteenth-century Pompey Stone and the Calaveras Skull. Beginning in 1891, Michigan witnessed a slew of clay cups and tablets covered in a "jumble of ancient Oriental writing" and "bogus hieroglyphics." They were not only a lie, but with their tantalizing ties to the Near East of the Bible they increased looting. In one instance, a man dug into a mound "a greater depth than usual" and was killed when the walls collapsed on him. These forgeries had real impacts.[12] One professional mused:

> Why, you will ask, have not steps been taken to put so incorrigible a scoundrel as the manufacturer of these spurious objects in an institution where his ingenuity and skill may be expended in the service of the state, without opportunity to deceive or beguile? Under existing laws this worthy end would be difficult to compass. Now that pure-food legislation is making progress we may perhaps hope for national regulations which will make the manufacture of objects of archaeological interest as unprofitable as the adulteration of coffee or sugar.[13]

As always, change eluded the needs of archaeology. Thus, nineteenth-century archaeology accepted that "for the immediate future at least the principal weapons available for contending against archaeological forgeries must continue to be skill in detection and publicity regarding the operations of forgers."[14]

In Powell's defense, it was not as if the BAE had done nothing. There had still been explorations of mounds. Powell allowed one assistant ethnologist, Wills De Hass, to explore Ohio's mounds in 1879–1880.[15] But for De Hass and some conspirators, a year was not enough. They secretly petitioned Congress behind Powell's back, and Congress earmarked $5,000 of the BAE's precious funds for mound research in 1881. Powell let the underhanded De Hass have his day, for a time, appointing him head of the BAE's Division of Mound Exploration.[16]

Powell bided his time. His health was deteriorating, and WJ McGee was largely running the BAE. A self-taught anthropologist, McGee worked closely with Holmes and exchanged many barbs with the Paleolithic camp, arguing that it was his duty to publicly dispel archaeological inaccuracies, "harpies," "husks of fiction," and "the lotus of myth."[17] Though De Hass favored the mounds of Ohio, Powell ordered him to explore those of West Virginia and Kentucky. He defied Powell, who withheld half his salary, then refused to publish his Mound Builder report. And finally, De Hass found himself out of a job.

In his place, Powell appointed Cyrus Thomas in 1882. Thomas had worked as "a practicing lawyer . . . a Lutheran clergyman, an assistant on the geological survey of the territories, a normal school science teacher, [and] a state entomologist" before joining the BAE.

With this appointment, Powell signaled his desire to end the Mound Builder saga. With Powell's support, Thomas and his team set out to explore mounds across the country to determine "the origin of these curious erections."[18] And they knew just where to go.

Wisconsin held a reputation for intriguing effigy mounds in the shape of birds, bears, deer, wildcats, and turtles. But one stood out among the rest—the Elephant Mound. The idea of elephants roaming around with the Mound Builders implied that the ancient engineers established contact with the Eastern Hemisphere, or that more recent peoples built the effigy after European introduction of the elephant to North America.[19] Either way, the mystery of the Mound Builders would only deepen.

Wisconsin's southwestern neighbor Iowa had its own interesting clues about the Mound Builders. In the late 1870s, the state's Davenport Academy of Natural Sciences teemed with excitement. Excavations of two mounds produced three tablets: two made of shale, one of lime-stone. They depicted amazing scenes. One showed the "planetary configuration, the 12 signs of the Zodiac, known to all nations of old, and the seven planets, conjoined with six different signs."[20] A funeral pyre sat atop a mound on another tablet, while the third featured animals, including what appeared to be an elephant. To add further intrigue, the tablets appeared to show a text suggesting the Mound Builders were literate as well as globalized.

Thomas's team arrived in Wisconsin and studied the Elephant Mound. But things just were not adding up. The elephant seemed "to have no trunk at all." Consulting the previous drawings, the team noticed irregularities. Each sketch of the elephant mound showed "the trunk in widely different positions."[21] They leaned toward the conclusion that "if the appendage was not entirely imaginary it was never anything more than a sandhill piled up and shifted by the wind." Just like that, the elephant died. The team presumed the Mound Builders meant to craft a bear or similar mammal and plowing and natural processes took their toll. But the ancient engineers did not ride elephants to work, of that the BAE team was sure.

Across the country, Thomas's team's work gradually clarified the picture of the Mound Builders. Over three years, they excavated 15,000 specimens. Although America had a long history of mound excavation dating back to Thomas Jefferson, careful excavation was not the norm.[22] Thomas, by contrast, employed a strict, formulaic approach. When the team arrived at a new mound, one of the field assistants jotted down the area's topography, environment, and distinguishing features and described the size, shape, and character of the monument. Another assistant made maps and illustrations of the site. Then, they took an assortment of measurements and drawings. Only then could the digging begin. The team took detailed notes as they excavated. Field assistants recorded each layer of earth, its thickness, color, and texture as well as the discovery location for all individuals and objects. Detailed horizontal and vertical sketches were drawn of each significant item. Additionally, Thomas went to great lengths to maintain order in collecting artifacts. He assigned each specimen a number while digging and generated a corresponding artifact list for cross-comparison.[23]

Assessing the artifacts from the mounds, the BAE team discerned "many reasons for not going beyond the Cherokees and their fellow red men of Ohio and Mississippi to find the origin of these curious erections."[24] Thomas consulted historic records of the early European explorers and cited the absence of any mention of the alleged mystery race. Instead, he found that early Europeans wrote of Indigenous Americans near mound complexes. He also referenced accounts of Osage and Winnebago burial customs where mounds were erected over the deceased.[25] This multidisciplinary approach increased the quantity of data and offered a strong interpretive context. Of his methods, Thomas argued:

The questions relating to prehistoric America are to be determined not alone by the study of its ancient monuments, but by the study also of the languages, customs, art, beliefs, and folk-lore of the aborigines. Only by such a comprehensive study can the exact relations of the ancient archaeological remains to the historic Indian tribes be made apparent.[26]

His emphasis on ethnographic and anthropological evidence was BAE through and through. After surveying over 2,000 mounds, Thomas felt there was only one possible deduction: The Indigenous peoples of North America built the mounds that dotted the country. He published his argument in 1894. He took considerable effort to dispel the claims out of Iowa that the tablets proved a mystery race roamed America with elephants:

A tablet is taken from a mound under the very shadow of one of our leading scientific academies on which is an inscription of sufficient length to silence all doubt as to its being alphabetic, and immediately under it is the altar with the smoking sacrifice or burning body on it. Nay, more on the reverse is the figure of the elephant. Nor is this all: In the same mound is another tablet with markings for the zodiacal signs, a calendar in fact. But good fortune, not satisfied with this generosity, throws into the hands of the same individual two elephant pipes, so distinct that there can be no doubt as to the animal intended. To clinch this evidence and show that it relates to the true mound-builders, the fairy goddess leads the same hands to a mound which contains a tablet bearing figures of the veritable mound-builders' pipes and copper axe some of the letters of the other tablet and the sun symbol. Thanks to the energy of one person the evidence on all these questions is furnished, which, if accepted as credible, must forever settle them.[27]

With admirable sarcasm and contempt, Thomas closed the door on the mystery race theory. His conclusion gradually gained acceptance, though many continued to hold onto the mystery race theory. Thomas's report did little to improve the bias against Indigenous peoples. One newspaper called Thomas's conclusion "a theory which has much plausibility, and shows that probably Indians, instead of an earlier or different race, were guilty of the scarification which still disfigures much ground which otherwise might be good farming land."[28]

The damage had been done. If a mysterious race of extinct peoples first conquered the United States, then America was fair game. If God or survivors of the Flood built the Ohio mounds, then what right did the Shawnee have to live there? If Welsh or Scandinavian seafarers constructed mounds in Georgia, would that not make Anglo-Americans more likely descendants of the Mound Builders than the Cherokee?

The troubling relationship between early archaeological interpretations and manifest destiny provides an important context to early American archaeology. It also explains why this odd theory had caught on so strongly. People wanted to believe that they had a right to all of America's land, resources, and the promise of wealth and liberty afforded by the vastness of the continent. Most believed the Judeo-Christian God willed the colonists to win the Revolutionary War and it was their destiny to make something of their independence. In its infancy, archaeology gave credence to the Anglo-American's right to take occupied lands. Scholar Vine Deloria Jr. felt it fair to summarize: "Indians have been cursed above all other people in history. Indians have anthropologists. . . . Had the tribes been given a choice of fighting the cavalry or the anthropologists, there is little doubt who they would have chosen."[29] Dramatic words, but Deloria's sentiments offer some sense of the reputation of archaeologists in Indigenous communities.

Putnam resisted Thomas's conclusions. Five years after the publication of Thomas's report, he continued calling for "a suspension of judgement, while giving free expression to opinions, until the facts have been worked over anew and more knowledge obtained."[30] He implored, "Let us first clear away the mist which has so long prevented an understanding of this subject by discarding the term 'Mound Builder.' Many peoples in America, as well as on other continents, have built mounds . . . it is thus evident that a term so generally applied is of no value as a scientific designation."[31] He preferred to attribute the mounds to "an offshoot of the ancient Mexicans" and decried crediting the Indigenous peoples as a case of "not giving fair consideration to differences while overestimating resemblances."[32] Just as he had with the Paleolithic people, Putnam held on to past interpretations despite new evidence.

Perhaps it was the narrow perspective that led to his blindsiding with regard to Chicago. As the Chicago World's Fair ended, a considerable mass of archaeological artifacts, Indigenous objects, and ancient individuals remained in the White City. The professional community had anticipated this issue during the fair and had high hopes for the creation of a museum. Marshall Field wrote a seven-figure check, and the Field Columbian Museum was born.

Putnam thought he would be appointed head of the Field Museum. And he expected there to be a place for Boas, too. Boas was unemployed, anxious, and perhaps a bit depressed from the recent death of his child. Having done so much to make the fair a success and after preparing the fair collection for the new museum, Boas thought he had earned the gig. Then, he heard the whispers.[33]

Chicago did not want him or Putnam. They preferred another: Dr. William Henry Holmes. Rejected, Boas developed a grudge toward Chicago that would last a lifetime.[34] Putnam felt snubbed personally and on Boas's behalf. He had devoted years to the fair, and the Field Museum's collection was the result. Yet the powers-that-were simply took his goods and cast his opinions to the side.[35]

But as one door closed, others opened. The American Museum of Natural History (AMNH) offered Putnam the top job in 1894. He accepted and hired Boas as his assistant. In still better news, Putnam was able to award the United States' first archaeology doctorate to George Dorsey that same year.[36]

As 1894 ended, the AMNH was Putnam's to fill. By befriending wealthy patrons, he intended to stock every inch with the evidence of whence and whither.

SIX

Bonito, 1895

The summer sun hurtled toward Arizona's desert horizon, as the audience watched the priests in the plaza below. The Antelope Priests of the Hopi Tribe wore decorated white kilts and sandals with thunder clouds and lightning bolts painted across their chests. From their kiva, they walked in single file, solemnly imbuing the plaza with their sacred mission. Around and around they marched, chanting exhortations for the protection and welfare of the Hopi. Then came more priests awash in red: red kilts, red moccasins, red feathers. They wore red and black paint on their chests, arms, and legs. The Snake Priests' faces were painted white; the lower portion of their faces were black.[1]

The Snake Priests paired off and made their own procession around the plaza. They approached a tent, where a bag was proffered. One member of the pair reached in and pulled out a rattlesnake. He closed his eyes, opened his mouth, lay the venomous, twisting creature between his teeth, and bit into the dry, smooth scales. He kept his eyes closed. His partner acted for him, guiding him and the snake around the plaza once more. As the Snake Priests completed their laps, Hopi women dropped cornmeal on the ground. The head Snake Priest made his own ring of cornmeal. Completing their march, the Snake Priests let the vipers fall into the ring, where they hissed and squirmed. The Snake Priests dove into the melee, scooped up several snakes, and ran. They stopped when they reached the valley below, releasing the snakes in the four cardinal directions. All this to end the drought, ensure a bountiful harvest, and ultimately protect the Hopi. For their efforts, the priests were given a "powerful emetic," and all celebrated at a great feast.[2]

Richard, with Clayt, Julia's nephew Bert Cowing, and a recent visitor to Alamo Ranch, Dr. Mitchell Prudden, was just one of hundreds of Americans who played tourist at the Hopi Snake and Antelope Ceremony in Walpi, Arizona in 1895. As might be expected, the ceremony attracted throngs of anthropologists, ethnologists, and archaeologists. Their descriptions of the ceremony bore no evidence of objectivity or scientific caution. The Hopi Snake and Antelope Ceremony was "the most weird and yet interesting spectacle," a "strange ceremony,"[3] a "strange heathen rite," and "hideous rites" with the "lurid tinge of a nightmare."[4]

Was it?

Was it stranger than a talking serpent goading a naked woman into eating a forbidden apple, with the woman then punished with exile and the horrors of childbirth?

Was it weirder than the almighty ruler of the universe allowing his only son to be crucified by mere mortals to redeem all humankind?

Was it odder still for worshipers of that almighty and kin to convert their deities into bread and wine and then consume their saviors?

It would probably have sufficed to say that faith is a strange beast. But indeed, the Hopi Snake and Antelope Dance was stranger and more heinous to nineteenth-century scholars and tourists than their Christian theology. There was no comparison to Eden, immaculate conception, or transubstantiation. This was otherworldly. Cushing's replacement on the Hemenway Southwestern Archaeological Expedition, Jesse Fewkes, explained that the ceremony resembled an African performance, rather than an American ritual.[5] The ceremony was un-American, at odds with American civilization. Looking upon the priests, observers saw something inherently different from themselves, something savage, something barbarian, something inferior.

The Hopi, like so much of Indigenous America, were fighting for their very existence in 1895. Their lands had been under siege for some time. In 1894, the tribe wrote to the US government decrying encroachment on their territory.[6] The strangers who watched the ceremony used hyperbolic adjectives and their belief that "anthropology was a science that could be an agent of social reform"[7] to tell the world how the reservations, the massacres, the occupations, and the entire mission to civilize Indigenous peoples had failed. The Snake Priests circling the plaza sent their own message: the Hopi lived. And gods willing, they would continue to.

After the ceremony, Richard, Clayt, Bert, and Dr. Prudden departed Arizona. As often seemed to be the case, Richard had been away from Alamo Ranch for too long. Since the bad frost of 1893, things there had not improved. The summer of 1894 brought a dry spell that wiped out the crop yield and put the family in a precarious situation.

Richard requested a loan of $6,000 from the Hydes in the fall of 1894, but Talbot and Fred declined. Resourceful as ever, Richard continued to hock the Southwest's ancient artifacts for extra income. Meanwhile his brothers kept hoping for salvation from the gold fields.[8]

Sometime in 1894 or 1895, the Wetherills found a new haunt in Tsegi Canyon, Arizona. The canyon exhibited large, complex cliff dwellings in red alcoves. They found burial mounds, many unexcavated, until they shoved their hands inside. They also found "immense quantities of broken pottery ... a great proportion of which is red with black decoration." They opened one burial mound and removed over one hundred individuals and 400 pieces of pottery. All of this they transported back to Mancos with the help of a party of Mormons in Bluff, who charged $1.25 per pound.[9]

Money continued to move the United States' nonrenewable archaeological resources far from home. Richard wrote to Gustaf Nordenskiöld from Marsh Pass just before the Hopi Snake and Antelope Ceremony, sending more artifacts across the Atlantic: "Yesterday I shipped to you by express one piece of very rare pottery with black and white markings. I and Al wish to present you with this as a token of the many kind things you have done for us. ... This piece came from the head and to the right of a skeleton found in a burial mound."[10]

Gustaf never received the letter or the pottery. Like Richard, he stayed on the move. It was expected that the twenty-six-year-old would follow in his father's footsteps to become the next great Arctic explorer. Sadly, while traveling by train on June 6, 1895, he died from tuberculosis.

It's unclear when Richard received the news. Gustaf had been both a customer and a friend who shared his passion for the past. His sudden death must have been a considerable loss. And Richard was already awash in losses. Yet Richard continued to be pulled into the past, pushing away the present struggles, letting the future bring what it would.

While John, Al, and Win probably missed Richard and Clayt's help, there was rarely a dearth of people at Alamo Ranch. In addition to Dr. Prudden, the Wetherills hosted a family of Quaker musicians that summer—the Palmers.[11]

Sidney LaVern Palmer played a wide range of instruments and invented on the side. His wife, Elizabeth Ann Palmer, played and sang as well, and they taught their three children their talents. A photo shows the respectfully dressed family carefully posed, each holding a horn or trumpet. Sidney and Elizabeth's youngest children, Edna and LaVern Junior, sit obediently in front of them, while their oldest daughter, Marietta, stands to the side. The remoteness of the Southwest made any sort of entertainment a welcome event, so the Palmers traveled the Southwest giving concerts as they went.

Marietta, or Mamie as her nearest called her, was nineteen when the family pulled up to Alamo Ranch. It was an impressive sight, "everything neat and clean . . . just like you'd dream a farm should be."[12] Mamie's childhood had been filled with constant movement and exploration. She seemed to enjoy it. Certainly, she admired her educated, talented, and industrious parents. Looking back, she remarked, "With parents like mine, I ought to have made something of myself, but I didn't."

Mamie was short and plump with a round, full face, and large brown eyes. A childhood friend remembered, "Being the prettiest girl in school, she was a favorite of all the boys. We would gather up whisky bottles, sell them for a penny each, and buy solid gold rings that came around a stick of candy about a yard long, at a penny stick. Mamie's fingers were stiff with these rings most of the time."[13]

A talkative young woman, she quickly got to know her new hosts and they her. Mamie liked to tell stories. In one difficult-to-believe tale, she spoke of sitting alone at the family campsite when she was nine or ten years old. Suddenly, a group of Apache rode into view. One approached and asked her where the water was. She claimed he believed her to be a kidnapped Apache enslaved by White people, and he decided to take her with him. His fellow travelers did not want to be slowed down by her and convinced him to leave her at the camp. It was only later Mamie realized her would-be savior was the one and only Geronimo.[14] So said Mamie.

With astounding tales of independence and near misses, Mamie's stories caught the family's attention. Mamie remembered Marion Wetherill exclaiming, "You're the most unusual girl I've ever met. . . . You seem to have been so many places and are so interested in all the things we're interested in." Perhaps modest Marion meant more than she said. Mamie did not doubt the sincerity of her comment. She replied, "I was born a pioneer. . . . I've traveled all over the United States. I ought to know something because I've been learning all the time."[15]

Six years older than Mamie, the youngest Wetherill brother, twenty-five-year-old Winslow, called Win, was a natural companion. Win was short and thin like his brothers. And at least in an 1893 photograph he was clean-shaven. Mamie thought him a "pretty nice boy," and Win took it upon himself to "take [her] around a lot."[16] With her family, Mamie settled into the Alamo Ranch life, listening to Benjamin's tales from his agent days and stories of his sons' excursions into ancient ruins. There was always plenty of land to explore and books to read in the hammocks that swayed beneath the cottonwood trees. It was a cozy haven full of peace and curiosity.

One day, Marion sent word to the Palmers that her sons Richard and Clayt were expected home. She brightened at the thought of her boys' arrival and exclaimed, "We'll make a little homecoming party of it." The Palmers joined in the festivities. Richard, Clayt, and Bert arrived less than party-ready. The rough roads to Alamo left them covered in red dust. They "were dirty and travel-worn and had long beards on." Mamie had heard so much about these men and their discoveries. Possibly she envisioned more picturesque adventurers. But looking them over, she "wasn't impressed with them" and "was perfectly satisfied with Win."[17]

Soon, the Palmers gathered around the Wetherill dining table to celebrate Richard, Clayt, and Bert's safe return. When the men joined the table, they "were all cleaned up and looked quite different."[18]

The Palmers had come to Alamo Ranch to see the cliff dwellings of Mesa Verde, and they had been waiting for a tour from Richard. Never one for rest, Richard took the Palmer family out exploring the next day. They went to a ruin called Sandal House and dug around for fun. Mamie noticed that Richard was stand-offish. For one thing, he refused to tell anyone his age. Bewildered, Mamie asked, "Are you ashamed of your age?" But the thirty-seven-year-old cowboy could not be coerced. It was just as well as far as Mamie was concerned. There were younger cowboys in the canyons and of course that "pretty nice boy," Win. Still Mamie had to admit, Richard "was such a young, vigorous, quick, energetic, ambitious man that you never thought about his age. He didn't have any age."[19]

Then Richard took the family to Mesa Verde. They arrived on horseback and spent five days exploring the cliff dwellings. The Palmers enjoyed the tour, but Sidney was interested in seeing another ruin he had heard of.[20] It was in the northern portion of the New Mexico territory and called Pueblo Bonito. Rumors had circulated for a century over the area called Chaco Canyon. The Navajo lived nearest Pueblo Bonito. *Navajo* is a Spanish creation originating from the word *navahu* attributed to the people's penchant for large field cultivation. The Navajo refer to themselves as Diné. Nineteenth-century America equated civilization and assimilation with picturesque sedentary farming communities, so ostensibly the wealthy, agricultural Diné were good. But of course, assimilation and civilization were just acceptable guises for the true aim: colonization or extermination.

Western historians trace the Navajos' arrival in the Southwest from a fifteenth-century Canadian migration. Diné archaeologists Wade Campbell, Kerry F. Thompson, and Richard Begay offer another version of events:

Archaic hunter-gatherer maize farmers are ancestral to both Puebloan and Dine communities. Navajo culture then is a fusion of knowledge from among various pre-existing mobile groups in the

Four Corners region and an Athapaskan-speaking hunter-gatherer migrant population, as well as Puebloan groups who join this ancestral Dine core. . . . This framework emphasizes the validity of Dine clan histories, oral traditions, and ceremonial narratives as a basis for exploring Dine relationships with the places and other people of the ancestral Southwestern world circa AD 800–1400, including Chaco Canyon, Aztec Pueblo, Mesa Verde, and points farther afield.[21]

By 1846, the US government's opinion of the Navajo was clear. They promised the growing numbers of European-Americans in the territory that they would protect them, their livestock, and all their property from the raids and violence of the Diné. Following the historical pattern, the Diné entered a peace treaty with the United States in 1846. But peace did not follow. In 1849, echoing Lewis Henry Morgan, the provisional governor of New Mexico, Colonel John Macrae Washington declared that the Navajo and other tribes must give up following herds and crops and join "civilization." And so, Washington assembled his troops, a Mexican militia, and a detachment of Pueblo and headed into Diné land.[22] Along with this party rode topographical engineer Lt. James Simpson and his Mexican guide, Carravahal. When Washington's military campaign entered Chaco Canyon in 1849, Simpson and Carravahal christened the most impressive ruin Pueblo Bonito. Washington's campaign ended in a hail of bullets that killed an elderly, sick Diné leader, Narbona, and six other Diné.

Continued violence made the peace treaties of the 1840s redundant. By the end of the 1850s, the territory's governor, James Carleton, and his commanding officer, General Edward R. S. Canby, were ready to implement a solution. They appointed Kit Carson to take the lead, and he engaged Ute, Hopi, and Zuni informants. With their help, Carson launched the first of fifty-three forced marches from traditional Diné territory to a new reservation, Bosque Redondo, in 1863. Carson implemented an unrelenting war of attrition, destroying the Navajos' carefully cultivated fields and peach trees. The cruel climate and uncaring soldiers killed many along the way. The Diné who arrived at Bosque Redondo called it Hwéeldi.[23] It has since been called a concentration camp. As the Diné struggled to survive in captivity, Diné women reverted to their traditional looms and began weaving to protect their people from the cold, and perhaps themselves from despair.[24]

Pueblo Bonito remained geographically isolated and more rumor than ruin. In 1878, the Hayden Survey explored Chaco Canyon. Survey photographer William H. Jackson explained to the world that Chaco Canyon held "the finest examples of the numerous and extensive remains of the works of unknown builders to be found north of the seat of the ancient Aztec Empire in Mexico, and of which there is comparatively little known even to this day."[25] Richard likely had heard of Chaco Canyon and Pueblo Bonito before as an anecdote of archaeological myth. But certainly, the stars had not aligned for him to see the ruins himself. Now with the invitation of Sidney Palmer, and of course his guide fees, Richard could see what all the fuss was about. His decision was probably helped by the fact that the Hyde Exploring Expedition was on pause in 1895. Maybe the Hyde brothers had enough artifacts already. Or perhaps that loan request had complicated matters. In any case, the Hydes were not funding Richard's explorations that fall.

Richard grew close to the Palmer family, visiting them regularly. He would arrive on horseback with a bedroll, see how everyone was doing, stay for dinner, and talk around the fire until it was quite late. Respectfully, Sidney and Elizabeth would then ask if he would like to sleep over and Richard would. They would rise early, share breakfast, and then Richard would ride off again. Mamie, who referred to him only as Mr. Wetherill, thought "he was interested in us."[26]

They headed off on their journey to Pueblo Bonito. Richard drove "a light spring wagon pulled by two nice little jet-black mules." They stopped in Durango first for supplies. This was going to be a journey into remote roadless lands. From Durango, they moved south, stopping in San Juan County, New Mexico, at the Aztec Ruins. Built around 1100 CE, the Aztec Ruins consist of multistory great houses centered around an open plaza and kiva. But they moved on quickly. By October 1895, the *San Juan Times* was reporting, "Richard Wetherill is with the Palmer company showing them round the country. Mr. Wetherill . . . is a reliable and experienced explorer and guide."[27] And Richard needed all his experience to get to Chaco Canyon. When they stopped at the few trading posts in the general vicinity of the ruins, no one knew what they were talking about.[28]

Finally, they encountered a Diné man. Yes, he knew of Chaco Canyon, but no, there was no easy way to get there. Sidney Palmer hired this man as a guide, but no one thought to remember his name for posterity. Much as in Mesa Verde, the party found that it was a long, difficult, dangerous climb and descent made more difficult by their awkward, bulging wagons. But Sidney's wagon "had good breaks [*sic*] and good mules" and finally they fell into Chaco Canyon behind a ruin called Hungo Pavi.[29] At around 140 masonry rooms and one great kiva, the D-shaped twelfth-century ruin was covered in sand and brush and only a taste of what was to come.

Beneath the cliffs, the land leveled off into a large desert valley. Ponderosa pines and pinon trees brought bits of color to the otherwise overwhelmingly tan landscape. As the party came around Hungo Pavi, they saw Fajada Butte on their left. *Fajada* translates to banded or belted and describes the red and tan stripes that circle the 135-foot-tall tower of rock. What they could not see was the Sun Dagger, the rock art marker of the summer and winter solstices near the summit of Fajada Butte.[30]

They carried on to a place called Chetro Ketl and then at last under the same cliff they arrived at Pueblo Bonito. The ruin was rubble — huge sandstone blocks and collapsed timber beams falling on top of one another between massive masonry walls. But Richard could see below the centuries of accumulated sand what Pueblo Bonito was — a large, complex series of rooms and kivas. In fact, it had been the largest great house of them all, with nearly 700 rooms, 32 kivas, and 3 great kivas rising four stories above the valley. One day the early phase of construction at Pueblo Bonito would be dated to around 850 CE, but in 1895 it was just very, very old.

Richard disappeared. The Palmers did not know where he went, but he (and their Diné guide) had done his job. They had arrived at their destination safely. Hours later he appeared on the skyline staring down at the Palmers from the cliff above Pueblo Bonito. He had found water. They could stay.[31]

Richard and the Palmers settled in, making camp in front of a cave nestled between two boulders. Richard drew sketches of the ruins, and they all "did quite a bit of excavating." Elizabeth dug into a grave in the canyon and recovered "six or eight pieces of pottery." Mamie looked for pottery too and focused especially on the handles from jugs, starting a "handle collection." She estimated that collection grew to "over a thousand pottery handles." Richard set a lower bar; he only wanted to stay until he found forty pieces of pottery.[32] For Richard, who found peace in digging, the days in Chaco Canyon must have been heavenly. At night, the family would gather around the campfire to eat and watch the flames dance against the cliffs.[33]

Around three thousand years ago in Chaco Canyon, Archaic hunters built fires in stone hearths, where they cooked small game like rabbits and pack rats. They left the earliest evidence of humans yet found in the canyon. But they were nomadic. It took until approximately 500 CE for people to start settling on a more permanent basis in Chaco. These people built homes on the mesas above the canyon and crafted baskets, among other things. Two centuries later, people began moving off the mesa tops onto the valley floor. Slowly, they extended storage rooms into larger structures, then around 850 CE they added two or more stories to the buildings, gradually producing the great houses like Pueblo Bonito. They built roads and water control systems, too. Chaco Canyon flourished as a southwestern center of activity for a short while. But by 1150 CE, the great houses endured as testaments to a world that had been. The people had left Chaco Canyon.[34]

After a month or so, it was time for the Palmers to do the same. Richard probably could have stayed forever. Sidney had his mind on other ruins, and he convinced Richard to act as their guide once more. Richard agreed and they set off again knowing that the journey out promised to be as arduous as the journey in. Richard remained dependent on local Diné for directions. Just what could happen without Navajo aid became clear when they reached the San Juan.

They could see the river was high. Sidney had a heavy wagonload, though they were down to peaches and bitter chocolate for food.

Richard and Sidney stared at the high waves for a while, then Richard decided. They would wait until morning; maybe a Diné would pass by and tell him of a safer crossing. Morning came, but the Diné did not. So, Richard got on with it. They could not wait forever on a diet of peaches and chocolate. He readied a wagon and Mamie jumped in the passenger seat. But the water was even higher than they had expected. Mamie felt "the wagon starting to lift" almost immediately. As the water roared, Richard yelled, "I can't go straight across. I've got to go up the river. We have to be careful not to go downstream because we'll end up in a canyon, and then we'd be lost." He pushed the mules forward. Mamie sat tight, paralyzed by fear. Why had she jumped in?

The mules struggled. The water kept rising. Mules were not meant to swim these depths. But they were strong and with Richard's insistence they finally made it to the bank. But the water roared faster, and the mules could not make it up onto the bank. Richard "grabbed his rope from the back, ran out on the tongue of the wagon, jumped onto the bank, roped one of those mules and snubbed it against some driftwood there." The mules took in the fresh air greedily and then finally stepped onto solid ground.

At last, Mamie had something to be impressed about. The feeling was mutual. Richard signaled the other Palmers not to follow. It had been a risky mistake. Mamie still sat in the wagon. Richard asked, "Were you frightened?"

Mamie responded with the obvious: "Why sure, I was scared to death."

Richard asked, "Where do you put your fear?"

"I guess I swallowed it. I couldn't say anything."

Richard agreed. The always talkative Mamie had been unusually quiet throughout the episode. Then he asked: "Will you marry me?"

The timing was odd, if dramatic. Richard had told Marcia Billings long ago not to expect grand acts of romance from him. It was not his style. But with their adrenaline coursing as fast as the waves of the San Juan, Richard had made a rare decision about his future.

Nineteen and uncertain, Mamie replied, "I don't know. I'll have to think about it."

Richard knew. He explained, "I think we were meant to live our lives together. I'll do anything to make you happy."

It worked. Mamie gave in: "Well, then I will, I'll marry you."[35]

When word reached Win, he was furious. Perhaps he already had some inclination that something was going on between Richard and Mamie. Richard had been spending a lot of time with the Palmers, bedroll in tow, and then he had gone off on a months-long journey with the family. It is not clear that there was any sort of agreement, much less engagement, between Win and Mamie, but Win certainly felt his brother had destroyed his future chances of happiness. There could have been some underlying angst in their relationship before Mamie entered the picture. Win, the youngest, was frequently left behind, while the older brothers jetted across the Southwest exploring and seeing the world. He was stuck at home, at school, doing farm chores, going to Quaker meetings. However justified his annoyance at Richard's frequent absences may have been, seniority won the day. The family supported Richard and Mamie's decision, and Win was sent away to Iowa.[36] Only time would tell if Win could forgive and forget.

Richard spread the good news. He wrote to Talbot Hyde, "Not having anything important on hand this winter I have taken the opportunity to visit the ruins of New Mexico. . . . The ruins there are enormous . . . grass and water is plenty—wood is scarce. A wagon can be driven to the Ruins in 5 or six days from our Ranch."[37] The message was clear. Pueblo Bonito was accessible and ripe for the taking.

Although Talbot and Fred had not sponsored the Hyde Exploring Expedition in 1895, they remained engaged with American antiquity. In fact, they had joined the American Museum of Natural History (AMNH) as patrons. Putnam must have been excited to have two new deep pockets at the AMNH.[38] But then there was more good news. Putnam reported, "Messrs. Hyde . . . have not only given their collection to the Museum, but have arranged to continue their explorations in the southwest for several years, under the general direction of the Curator of the department, until the Museum is supplied with an extensive and authentic collection from the cliff houses, ancient pueblos, burial caves and mounds of the southwest."[39]

So, Talbot and Fred had big news for Richard too. The Hyde Exploring Expedition was to continue *but* under new management. Putnam would be in charge on paper and would "detail a man to superintend field work and work up the result during the next winter." Richard could stay on as a field manager. They felt it "essential to have [Richard's] cooperation."[40]

In Iowa, Win may have derived special pleasure from this turn of events.

SEVEN

Cacao and Turquoise

Putnam cast his eye around the AMNH and selected George Hubbard Pepper as his man on the ground in Chaco Canyon. Born in Staten Island, Pepper turned twenty-three in 1896. Thin with dark hair, Pepper was relatively new to archaeology. After high school, he enrolled in a "special course in anthropology at the Peabody Museum" in 1895. That same year he also excavated at Tottenville, Staten Island. Despite minimal formal training, he was appointed curator of the Department of the Southwest at the AMNH and sent off to Chaco Canyon to take over excavations.[1]

In April, Talbot Hyde traveled with Pepper to introduce him to the Wetherills.[2] Talbot did not stay for long, and the group settled into Chaco Canyon. Clayt left his name and the year 1896 on Hungo Pavi, indicating that he was there.[3] Orian Buck and E. C. Cushman were also there.[4] And the expedition hired local Diné men to dig in the ruins, too. There was some staff fluidity with the Diné workers heading home to their families regularly. But a few Navajo workers were mentioned more frequently in Pepper's diaries than others, including Juan, Agovita Tensia or Agapito Atencio, Thomacito, Charley, and Welo.

The infrequent use of last names makes it difficult to connect workers mentioned in various accounts of the Hyde Exploring Expedition. Mamie described a man named Tomacito as a "nice looking boy about my age with hair down to his waist," whom she met on her first trip to Chaco Canyon. She referenced Juan as her kitchen helper and as a ladies' man and Welo as an older gentleman who often pointed out new areas to explore.[5] But these brief descriptors are the only glimpses available of the Indigenous people behind the shovels.

Working on the excavation of Chaco Canyon may have been a complicated moral endeavor for the Diné archaeological fieldworkers. Navajo archaeologist Davina R. Two Bears writes, "For Navajos many 'archaeological sites' are recognized in Navajo oral history as places of clan origins and history, the homes of Navajo deities, and also feature prominently in Navajo religion and ceremonies. These special places were, and still are, taken care of by Navajo people."[6] Natasha Gambrell of the Eastern Pequot Tribal Nation offers another perspective on Indigenous participation in archaeological work:

> I started archaeology when I was 13, right after we got our federal acknowledgment taken away. I felt invisible, and I felt like we didn't exist. I was hurt, and I couldn't find any reason to continue fighting until I started doing archaeology. It gave me the passion that I needed to continue fighting for my people because no matter what anybody said I could prove we had been here with all the artifacts. It was a powerful feeling to know that I was touching the same thing my ancestors held; it rooted me to this land and ever since I've always wanted to learn more.[7]

For Juan, Agovita Tensia or Agapito Atencio, Thomacito, Charley, and Welo, it is likely that the excavation of Pueblo Bonito held multiple meanings. It was a financial opportunity, but one that required the invasion and desecration of a sacred, traditional place. On the other hand, it offered a chance to explore the material heritage of the region's Indigenous peoples. Each of the workers likely internalized these conflicting motivations differently as the summer progressed.

In May, Pepper's first season as head of the Hyde Exploring Expedition commenced. The focus was Pueblo Bonito.[8] The Diné did most of the digging, earning 50 cents per day plus board, and Richard did the supervising. Days in Pueblo Bonito proved long and arduous, Monday–Saturday.[9] Pepper concentrated his efforts on the expedition's records. He worked in a tent outside of the ruins, where the records and artifacts were also stored. On August 17, he wrote: "Got up half

Figure 4. Navajo laborers excavating Pueblo Bonito (American Museum of Natural History Library, 00411970).

past six and numbered pottery fragments until breakfast was ready." Another day, he recorded that he "got up and worked on potsherds." After breakfast, he "wrote for some time." Later he returned to the artifacts, "numbering and cataloging until noon then went to the kitchen and ate dinner."[10] Maintaining thorough and accurate records proved a time-consuming and monotonous task, but Pepper offered no complaints. He also spent time excavating in Pueblo Bonito and managed payments for the crew.

Perhaps these days of strict working and writing were not the stuff of great adventure stories, but Pepper hoped they might be the stuff of great archaeology.

On August 20, Pepper was doing his usual numbering and cataloging, when Richard came into his tent. He wanted the camera and told Pepper to "come out to room #28 if [he] cared to see something." Room 28 rose two stories on the northern end of Pueblo Bonito. The Diné workmen had removed burned rubble and found very little of interest. But then that morning, Juan "uncovered one of the most unique pieces of pottery." It was "cylindrical in form and stood a foot in height having a bottom diameter of about four inches." Richard took pictures of the odd jar and Pepper took the fragments of it back to his tent. He "got glue and then put it together," discovering that one piece of the jar was missing. Juan dug through the pile of dirt he had been dumping sand in and found the missing sherd. Pepper went back to gluing and Juan went back to digging.[11]

As Pepper finished reconstructing the jar, Juan "came over and told [him] he had made another find." Pepper returned to Room 28 and found that Juan had uncovered a second cylinder jar and three other bowls. Pepper did some more gluing. Then he joined Juan in Room 28, recovering shell beads and bowls. At dinner the men naturally discussed the spoils of Room 28 and what might come next. Richard and Pepper speculated that there "was probably a body under the pottery." Juan said nothing that night, but he was unsettled by the thought.[12]

Pepper rose earlier the next day at half past five. Richard was cooking breakfast. Pepper ate and then returned to Room 28. Richard soon entered laughing. Juan had evidently spent a sleepless night haunted by the thought of the people they might soon excavate. A specter of some sort appeared in his tortured dreams and Juan reported it "would climb up to him and grab him."[13]

Many Diné share Juan's concerns. Traditionally, seeing a corpse, improper burials, or disturbing the dead puts Navajo in danger of "supernatural retribution." The dead are supposed to be left to rest to avoid antagonizing the spirits. Those who lay eyes on disinterred remains are believed to have been exposed to "ghost sickness."[14] Juan was expressing his concerns about the sacrilegious nature of their work, and his views were likely shared by some of the other Navajo workers.

Despite the fears of the workers, they continued to excavate Room 28. They recovered a total of 174 ceramic vessels from the room including 111 cylinder jars. Pepper mended pots for days. As he poured glue onto the pieces of pottery and fitted the ceramic jigsaw together, he had no idea that his fingers were sliding across residue of cacao from centuries before. Pepper knew only that what he had found was unique. It took another 113 years for archaeologists and a nutritional chemist to find out something more about the cylinder jars of Room 28.

By 2009, it was understood that the cylinder jars dated to approximately 900–1030 CE. But Room 28 had a longer history that reflected the regular renovations of Pueblo Bonito's architecture. Room 28 had once been a place for "outdoor activities." It transitioned into a domestic space and then was possibly abandoned for a period. The room was altered, and a shelf was installed for the storage of the cylinder jars. During the 1000s, after all the jars and their cacao were stacked on the shelf, the room was set on fire, leaving a layer of burnt rubble to conceal the jars and the cacao. Ancient Latin America is well known for its use of cacao in ritual ceremonies. Thus, the traces of cacao in the cylinder jars and the deliberate and extreme nature of their disposal raises questions about the relationship between Chaco Canyon and Latin America and their shared use of cacao.[15] But this was all knowledge for another day. As they finished up their work in Room 28, Pepper had no idea that Juan had discovered something truly monumental and that he literally had his hands on the first evidence of cacao north of Mexico.

Archaeology is a long game, and the labyrinth that was Pueblo Bonito had many secrets yet to reveal. The north wall of Room 28 intrigued the group. There was a sealed doorway filled in with stones. They removed the stones and found sand, but they could see that there was an opening between the ceiling and sand in the western portion of the room. They cut a tunnel toward the opening and dug until they reached open space. Then they lit a candle and examined the room's contents.

Ceremonial sticks guarded one corner, and cactus spines were visible amid the sand. They could see another doorway along the western wall also filled with sand.[16]

As they made their way through the room, which they numbered 32 (numbers 29–31 had been excavated and terminated at the same time as Room 28), they found a grayware mug with black decorations, a white and black cylinder jar like those recovered from Room 28, a red bowl, a gray bowl, and several other ceramic vessels. They found one gray cylinder jar standing upright. Inside rested nine turquoise beads and two shell beads.[17]

They moved toward the southwest corner of the room, where they found human ribs mixed with wooden objects. As they pushed farther south, they found more human remains dispersed around the room. They began shoveling out debris that had fallen around the bodies and found a bird made of hematite inlaid with tiny pieces of turquoise.[18] The room was producing interesting pieces of art that the excavation had not seen before.

Pepper paused to sketch during the removal of the sand. He charted the "general stratification" of the room: Layer A, sand—3 inches thick; Layer B, soil, charcoal, etc.—5 inches thick; Layer C, sand—½ inch thick; Layer D, black soil—1 inch thick; Layer E, sand—3½ inches thick; Layer F, soil.[19] By recording the layers, Pepper was moving in the right direction. Nonetheless, to truly enrich his data and interpretations, he needed to slow down and excavate, collect, and record artifacts by distinct layers of stratigraphy.

When they finally reached the northwest corner of Room 32, they found hundreds of ceremonial sticks guarding the area. Pepper reported that collecting these sticks was "slow and tedious, as many of the specimens were quite soft, evidently from recent rains. The crossing and interlocking of the sticks, and the necessity of bracing the ceiling beams added new obstacles. It was, therefore, impossible to remove many of the sticks in a perfect condition, but it was possible to mend a goodly portion of them after they reached the museum."[20]

They continued to find many interesting objects before they found the western doorway of Room 32. The door measured only two feet high, but Pepper squeezed through it and entered Room 33. He lit a candle and peered inside. It was a much smaller room than Room 32. After noting the ceremonial sticks, they soon encountered the partial remains of an individual. Portions of the body were missing, and Pepper soon noticed that the room was exposed to rain, which he blamed for the disturbance of the bodies. In short order, they encountered two more skulls. Uniquely, these skulls were surrounded by hundreds of turquoise beads. As they moved through the room, they found twelve skulls interspersed with turquoise and shell beads and cylinder jars.[21]

After the twelfth skull, they came to a floor of wooden boards. They excavated beneath the floor and found the first intact individual. This person had been buried with at least 5,890 turquoise beads. Beneath this person lay another person buried with more than 6,000 turquoise beads. By now the room was awash in turquoise beads and pendants of all sizes.[22] As they sifted through the sand, they found one object shaped like a cylinder basket. Its exterior was covered with gum, and Pepper found that it had once been covered in a turquoise mosaic.[23] They also found animals carved from turquoise including tadpoles and frogs.

The widespread availability of turquoise in the present era may obscure the magnitude of the discovery in Room 33. Two of the bodies in Room 33 were buried with more than 37,000 ornaments. Southwestern archaeology was very much in its infancy in 1896, so Pepper lacked context to quantify the turquoise objects in Room 33. But to this day, more turquoise artifacts have been recovered from Room 33 than at all other archaeological sites in the United States combined.[24] They collected thousands and thousands of turquoise beads and inlaid objects despite lacking one simple, but crucial tool. They didn't use a screen. Today, most archaeologists dig and pour their soil into a mesh wire screen that has openings that measure somewhere between ¼ and ⅛ of a centimeter. When the screen is shaken, the dirt falls through and most artifacts stay in the screen, allowing for as comprehensive a collection as possible. The method of 1896 was more along the lines of dig—see—grab. Thus, some beads fell away as they packed the turquoise from Room 33 and shipped it off to New York.

Pepper considered the turquoise evidence of the individuals' high status and membership in the priesthood. He interpreted their burials within Pueblo Bonito "as a mark of respect and as a means of protecting their graves from possible spoliation at the hands of semi-nomadic tribes."[25] He was also aware of a place called Cerrillos Hills, located around 125 miles from Pueblo Bonito. Cerrillos Hills was a natural source of turquoise, and Pepper thought the turquoise might come from there. Subsequent studies with improved technology have demonstrated that the turquoise could have come from mines in New Mexico, Nevada, Arizona, and Colorado as well. Rather than a single mine, research suggests that an extensive turquoise trade network with many routes was in operation and possibly significant to relations between Chaco Canyon and ancient Mexico.[26]

Nor was this the only evidence of contact outside of Chaco Canyon. In Room 38, they found remains of fourteen macaws. Pepper thought two had died and been buried ceremonially, while the other twelve had been intentionally killed or had died in some sort of accident. Moreover, because the macaws of his time were common in northern Mexico, Pepper suspected that the macaws entombed in Pueblo Bonito hailed from Mexico as well.[27]

Pepper ended his first season in September 1896. He had to return to the AMNH, and the Hyde funds, while generous, would never support year-round excavations in Chaco Canyon. The work had been difficult and the results slower to appear at times than desired, but they had made great discoveries that first season. At a date unknown, Pepper expressed his passion for Chaco Canyon:

> Even now, at a time when the life blood has been sapped and the canon is but an echo of the past—where ruin, desolation, and bleaching bones now reign in place of life and gaiety, there is a charm, indefinable, but one that grips with a fascination all its own; and even in the realization of what may have been in the eternal yesterdays, one lives in the now—and the story that is locked up in these old strongholds fires the imagination and kindles a keen desire for the historical revelations that some day [sic] these old walled-in towns will afford.[28]

For Pepper, the 1896 season had gone better than most rookie archaeologists could hope for. Had they made mistakes? Yes. Even a very experienced archaeologist does, much less a novice excavating a new region. Laughing away Juan's concerns about the disturbance of the Pueblo Bonito's dead ranked chief among the season's shortcomings. They also made impressive discoveries, kept detailed records, and preserved an immense and complex collection to the best of their abilities. The Hyde Exploring Expedition was very much an undertaking of its time. It was focused on gathering as much stuff as possible in response to demands of eastern museums. In that regard it was a success. Richard Wetherill wrote to Talbot that "this collection is one worthy of your name."[29]

Richard had quite a few other things to say to Talbot once Pepper headed back to New York. He started on a humble note, "I wish to thank you for the opportunity you have given me for labor in my favorite work and the chance for perfecting myself in photographing." He quickly dropped the façade and got to the heart of his message: "Mr. P's records are o.k. also but I know the man better than you ever will therefore I know I will receive no credit from him unless I were in his presence." He continued dragging Pepper through the mud: "Nothing whatever was accomplished this year until I mutinied." He concluded with a suggestion: "I wish to say that if we go into the field together again that you could put one in a different footing." Clearly, Richard remained insulted by his demotion, and he preferred Pepper's feet stay well out of Chaco Canyon in the future.[30]

Richard had one other piece of news for Talbot. In October, he wrote: "I expect to be married about the 15th of next month in San Francisco." He offered no further information.

Wedding bells rang most of 1896 for the Wetherill family. John married Louisa Wade in March 1896. They would welcome their first child that December: Benjamin Wade Wetherill.[31] Win put Mamie Palmer behind him, marrying Mattie Pauline Young in September 1896. And still, Richard and Mamie remained unmarried. They had exchanged letters since their adventures in 1895. But in December 1896, Richard and Mamie reunited in Sacramento. Mamie and her mother found a dark red suit, black hat, gloves, and shoes, and Richard found a justice of the peace. Before Mamie's family they swore to be faithful until death did they part. They headed to Mexico City for their honeymoon, but the trip was cut short by a letter from Richard's father. Paying customers were waiting for him at Alamo Ranch eager to explore. So off they went.[32]

EIGHT

Return to the Grand Gulch

Having spent the summer playing second fiddle to Pepper, Richard longed to lead again. He was also set on pursuing archaeological work, rather than ranching or mining. He told Talbot: "My circumstances now are such that I am free to work, as I have lost all the property I had and this work is now all that I am fitted for. It has been the cause of loss but I can build up a better reputation for careful honest work . . . shall try for work at the academy of sciences."[1]

Richard may not have been aware of his own standing within the small world of archaeology, or the whispers of looter and charlatan attached to his name. But universities were now handing out doctorates in archaeology. The rules of the game were about to change. Have shovel; will dig—was no longer going to cut it.

Work at the academy of sciences did not materialize, and Richard chased other leads. "I learned that the Field Columbian Museum Chicago intended putting an Expedition in the field this winter to work in Grand Gulch and Southern Utah. Since you do not wish to continue the work this winter I shall endeavor to get work from them. . . . Failing in that I will put an outfit of my own there," he wrote Talbot.[2]

Richard had asked the Hydes to sponsor another round of explorations in the Grand Gulch. They declined. Instead, he met George Bowles, a Harvard student with cash to burn, and his tutor C. E. Whitmore, who needed to keep Bowles "occupied . . . with the idea of getting his money back at some time in the future."[3] Richard knew just the place. With Bowles's money, Richard organized another expedition to the Grand Gulch.[4]

This time a team of fourteen made the trip. Clayt was the only brother to join, though Charlie Mason came this time. The other men were Jim Ethridge, Levi Carson, E. C. Cushman, C. M. Thompkins, Hal Heaton, George Hangrove, Orian Buck, and Bert Hindman.[5] George Bowles, accompanied by C. E. Whitmore, assembled his gear at Alamo Ranch as well. Mamie decided to go along too, the first and only woman.

Around January 13, 1897, Richard marched the new team out of Alamo Ranch. They followed the route of the 1893 expedition, stopping in Bluff before heading into the gulch.[6] If the journey to Pueblo Bonito had been difficult, Mamie saw quickly that the Grand Gulch was much worse. She remembered, "It would break a snake's neck to crawl through that canyon."[7] No snakes lost their lives on their way into the gulch that winter, but all were not so lucky. Levi Carson and E. C. Cushman managed the pack train of more than forty animals.[8] As they moved down the narrow trail, their horses carried "pans, coffee pots, canned goods, and a keg of sourdough" in side boxes. Mamie recalled that the horses served a second purpose: extra meat in the event of insufficient game.

As they made their way along a narrow trail, Mamie suddenly heard a commotion. A horse scraped a rock, scared, and careened down the canyon. Soda crackers and a sack of grain flew with him.[9] A thump echoed through the canyon as the horse hit the ground. Waiting for her turn to pass along the same part of the trail, Mamie was terrified. Richard, a horse lover, sent Clayt down to put the horse out of its misery, if by some chance it still lived. Clayt eased down the canyon, but before he got to the horse, a two-year-old colt ran into another horse and fell to its death, too.[10] Another horse met the same fate.[11] Clayt returned with the supplies from the horses, and Mamie and the rest of the team made it down the trail without injury. But Mamie remembered, "I couldn't eat any supper that night. I just crawled into my bedroll and stayed there."[12]

They soon fell into the familiar routine. Richard remained committed to high recording standards. They measured every alcove, photographed the sites and artifacts. The larger crew meant they could dig more this time. "Jas. Etheridge, O. H. Buck, C. C. Mason, Bert Hindman, and R. Wetherill were in the excavation continuously, and all others whenever other duties pertaining to work did not interfere."[13] Richard put Mamie in charge of paper records, and she took the task seriously.[14] Once more, they were reminded that they were not the first visitors to the gulch. In one alcove, they found graffiti from Charles McLoyd and C. C. Graham from 1891 or 1892. Petroglyphs on the walls pointed to still older visitors. Rooms made of the sandstone blocks typical of cliff dwellings sat in the southern end of the alcove. This alcove was 700 feet long, 150 feet high, and 100 feet deep. Looking around, Richard saw not treasures ripe for the picking, but layers of feces.[15] There was also a different sort of ruin, a wattle-and-daub enclosure. Richard took in the scene: "This looks like a turkey pen."[16]

Richard ordered the team to dig into the site that became known as the Turkey Pen Ruin. If they followed their standard procedures at Turkey Pen, something happened to the records afterward. The records that exist do not include the standard sketch maps. They record a list of artifacts, which included a mixture of Cliff Dweller and Basket Maker sandals, six yucca brushes, three hide bags, three bone tools, pieces of an arrow shaft, projectile points, a ceramic pipe, an individual, and pottery, among other items.[17]

It was something, but Richard wanted more. He had discovered a new race of people and some ninety individuals in mere weeks the last time he entered the Grand Gulch. The yield at Turkey Pen Ruin paled in comparison. So, they kept moving. Mamie kept recording, and they kept assigning numbers to alcoves, objects, and bodies. In this way, they carried on searching for something as big as the Basket Maker discovery and coming up dry.

They kept moving camp further and further into the gulch, exploring every alcove they could. They continued to be frustrated by the work of previous diggers. In one alcove near a stream, they found someone had pulled individuals out of earthen pots (their final resting places), and scattered them about the alcove. "You couldn't walk in that cave without stepping on human bones they were so thick in there," Mamie recalled.[18]

They moved again, measured some more, and dug around, but a

body here and there was all they were getting. Richard and Mamie worked a series of alcoves one day without much luck. On the final alcove, Richard looked around, thought it would have made a poor home, but possibly a decent temporary camp. A large rock leaned against the alcove wall, intriguing Richard. He walked behind it and "thought it would make an awful good burial." So, he started digging. In no time at all, he found a coarsely woven basket. As he continued to remove sand, he realized it was quite a big basket. Mamie estimated that it was at least five feet long. Richard felt something important coming. He called Mamie and asked, "Would you mind getting on your pony and telling Clate [*sic*] to bring the camera?"

Mamie rode fast, but by the time she and Clayt got back to the alcove, it was too dark for the camera to be useful. But Clayt jumped behind the boulder to help dig, leaving Mamie to wait "in agony to see what was underneath it."

Richard and Clayt removed the first basket to find another basket. Under that basket rested a blanket made of turkey feathers and spots of bluebird feathers. Under the blanket was another blanket, also made of turkey feathers, but this one had spots of yellow bird feathers. Beneath the yellow-spotted blanket laid a final basket. Richard lifted it up and Mamie cried out, "Oh, she's alive!"[19]

Beneath the baskets and blankets, a woman was once put to rest. Someone in her world painted her body in yellow paint and her face in red paint. She had long hair and a necklace of shell beads. In this isolated alcove, behind a rock, they carried her into the grave cradled in another basket. Covering her in layers of baskets and blankets, her people must have thought she would be safe from all disturbance. But whatever peace she had had for centuries was over. Her body was no longer hers; it was no longer her people's. She belonged to George Bowles, C. E. Whitmore, Richard Wetherill, and the imagination of her discoverers. They named her "Princess."[20] And soon they found her "Prince" buried nearby.

That winter in the gulch proved much harsher than the winter of 1893–1894. It was a less pleasant working environment, and at times it made domestic arrangements difficult as well. Mamie woke one night to a worried Richard. It was snowing. "What would you like to do?" he asked his new bride. "Would you like to have them at your head, or at your feet?" By *them* Richard meant the individuals they had excavated from the alcoves. Bewildered and tired, Mamie chose her feet. Richard left their tent and returned with four mummified individuals, whom he placed at Mamie's feet.[21]

Dr. Wortman had counseled years before on how to store and transport excavated human remains. He wrote: "Number each skeleton and pack it in a separate box. . . . It will be found that the best material for packing is either soft paper, chaff, or very soft straw or hay, and after each layer sift the interstices *full* of sawdust or bran. This, if well done, will prevent all movement or shaking of the specimens." He thought this process would prevent "permanent injury to the specimen."[22] According to Mamie, they "wrapped the mummies in muslin in those long tarpaulin bags packed them with grass and snapped them all shut."[23] It was something, but not quite as secure as Wortman had suggested. Mamie was less worried about the security of the individuals and more about their smell. She remembered, "They sure did smell. Every time it was sunny I got our beds out and aired them."[24]

Figure 5. Mamie stands in the center of the expedition crew in an alcove in the Grand Gulch (American Museum of Natural History Library, 00338269).

Beyond the logistics or the economy of excavating ancient individuals lay concerns of descendant communities. Legal scholar Walter R. Echo-Hawk of the Pawnee Nation writes, "Regardless of the motive for expropriating Indian graves, the impact of this activity upon the affected Indians is always the same: emotional trauma and spiritual distress."[25] The crew in the Grand Gulch likely never intended to cause anyone distress; they were simply ignorant.

Sleeping with decaying ancient individuals, finding less than he hoped for, and still drowning in debt, Richard knew he had to end it. At the end of February, after a little more than a month, Richard led his team out of the Grand Gulch.

Although the Hydes had declined to sponsor this project, Richard still updated them. On February 15, he wrote to Talbot:

> We are doing our work here carefully and thoroughly since the value of these things consist[s] largely in the scientific data procured. . . . I was somewhat surprised to hear from you at this late date as I had written two or three times and not heard a word since last spring when you were here, (you may have said something in your letters to Pepper), so I did not know whether or not my work [at Pueblo Bonito] met with your approval. I fancied it had not.[26]

Perhaps it was the Grand Gulch's lack of goods, but Richard comes across as insecure and testy. His frustration at his demotion and Pepper's relationship with the Hydes remained a sore spot. Even with Pepper in New York and unassociated with the Grand Gulch work, Richard could not help taking a swipe at his rival. He informed Talbot: "My wife is in the party doing the work Pepper did last summer."[27] Never mind that it was the work that would make the difference between a worthwhile or destructive excavation; it was woman's work. And thus, inferior to Richard's own physical contributions.

In later life, Mamie shared another tale from the Grand Gulch. She claimed that one alcove could be reached only by descending from the mesa above, so she rode her pony up. She let her horse rest and laid down on the mesa, where two mountain lion cubs were playing. Then the mother mountain lion approached. After a standoff, Mamie retreated unscathed. She rode away and never told the rest of the team about the lion. Instead, she began sneaking bits of horsemeat away and taking it to the mountain lion cubs every day. On her return one day in March, she ran into five Paiutes. They kidnapped her. She was held for ransom with a man named Ben Bolton. Richard and Clayt had to return hastily to Alamo Ranch to raise thousands of dollars. And then one day, the Paiutes marched Mamie and Ben down the canyon to Richard and freedom.[28]

The team had left the Grand Gulch in February, raising questions about the March kidnapping. Richard's biographer later wrote, without citation, that the Paiutes kidnapped George Bowles and C. E. Whitmore.[29] Interestingly, available newspapers did not report the kidnapping in 1897. So, we are left to wonder if any of the party were kidnapped, or if these tales are just figments of the imagination.

Richard divided the team when they got back to Bluff to conquer different sites and ideally expand their artifact yield. He sent Charlie Mason, Orian Buck, and George Bowles 150 miles west of the Grand Gulch to Mysterious Canyon. Clayt, William Henderson, and Jim Ethridge were sent to Moqui Canyon. The rest of the party had been sent toward Marsh Pass.[30] Minus one. On their way back, Richard kept saying to Mamie, "You know, it would be kind of nice if you'd go back to Mancos and be with Mother." Was the honeymoon over? Their time in the Grand Gulch was probably the longest time they had spent together as a couple. Was Richard finding Mamie's company too much? It would be easy to see how Mamie could have become disenchanted with the Grand Gulch as the adventure turned into monotonous measuring and note taking. Had her purported independent excursions and taking of provisions irked him? Or was it an innocent suggestion made from concern for his wife's well-being? Whatever Richard's reasoning, Mamie wanted to carry on with Richard and see new sites. But then they had a nice dinner at the home of some Bluff friends of Richard's. She had her first bath in weeks, and she decided to stay, parting with her husband after just two months together.[31] At least that's the way she remembered it.

Richard left Bluff and ended up in Arizona, in Tsegi Canyon once again. Charlie Mason was there, too. As they dug around and filled their wagons with artifacts, they left their marks on the canyon. At a ruin called Keet Seel, Richard left his mark on a back wall, "R. Wetherill 1897." Charlie climbed to the ceiling and did the same, "C. C. Mason 1897."[32] From Moqui Canyon, Clayt "reported wonderful caves with many pot holes [*sic*] in them. But all entirely empty."[33] They had been beaten again. The three-pronged approach seems not to have reaped the rewards Richard had hoped for. They found artifacts, but nothing earth-shattering. George Bowles and C. E. Whitmore were not the Hydes. They were not going to fund the expedition forever. So as spring faded into summer, Richard knew he had only one option if he wanted to continue his pursuit of the past: back to Chaco.

The arrangements for the return to Pueblo Bonito exceeded those for the Grand Gulch. They bought "five hundred pounds of flour, one hundred pounds each of sugar and Arbuckle's Coffee, rice and tea, canned tomatoes, beans, peaches, asparagus . . . dried fruit . . . candy, crackers, vinegar . . . tents and cots." Mamie thought it was "just as if we were going to Africa."[34] They left Mancos on May 13 and arrived at Pueblo Bonito on May 22.[35]

When they arrived in Chaco Canyon, they established camp between Pueblo Bonito and the cliff behind the ruin. Mamie and Richard had one tent. Pepper returned from New York for another season of the Hyde Exploring Expedition and took the other tent, where they stored all the artifacts and records. They unpacked the provisions and stored them inside Pueblo Bonito. They dug a well to ensure sufficient water access during their stay.[36]

The Hyde Exploring Expedition had left Chaco Canyon in September 1896. Upon their return in May 1897, they found that while they were away others had played. In April 1897, Warren K. Moorehead arrived with a party to conduct his own excavations in Pueblo Bonito. There was nothing to prevent anyone who had read about the Hyde Exploring Expedition's discoveries from heading to Chaco Canyon for their own hoard. There were no permit requirements. No one had been delegated authority to permit or deny excavation. Everything was up for grabs.

Moorehead worked hard and fast. With a group of local farmers' help, he tore down walls to reach underground rooms he was interested in. Their digging seems to have been frantic and careless. They encountered an unknown number of burials, and the remains of these people were scattered across the burial chamber. In less than a month, Moorehead collected six hundred pounds of artifacts. The next year he began advertising some of the skulls from Pueblo Bonito for sale.[37]

Frustratingly, Pepper found evidence of Moorehead everywhere during the 1897 season. Excavations carried on much as they had the previous year. They cleared room after room, collecting and recording artifacts as they went. After discovering Moorehead's work, things got off to a slow start. They cleared rooms of rubble without finding any specimens. As they continued digging, the number of artifacts ticked up. In Room 44, they found "a large metate, a game stick, a stone slab, a broken bowl, and a canon walnut."[38] This quantitatively limited but functionally varied assemblage repeated itself in the next several rooms they excavated. While these items were information rich, they were less thrilling for the collection-oriented archaeologists who had recovered caches of cylinder jars and turquoise a year before. Put another way, these finds were not sexy. Excavating for wealthy backers put pressure on archaeologists to deliver aesthetically alluring artifacts, rather than information-rich data.

They had no choice but to confront the rooms worked by Moorehead. Pepper numbered the first of these Room 53. He noted in his field notes, "The northern wall had been completely torn down by Moorehead."[39] The Diné workmen cleared the debris that remained and uncovered an individual whose skull was missing. Two pitchers, a small bowl, and part of a cylinder jar were found nearby. The workers found the skull of child near a deposit of approximately 4,000 turquoise beads and thirty shell beads or pendants.[40] Perhaps it was the haste or merely their methods, but Moorehead's party had overlooked quite a lot of material in Room 53. With objects from Pueblo Bonito soon to be sold to the highest bidder, pieces of the Pueblo Bonito puzzle were falling into the unregulated antiquarian abyss.

They again encountered Moorehead's handiwork in Room 56. Pepper noted this room as "where Moorehead party took out two bodies."[41] Bones from the graves were "scattered throughout the dirt." The Moorehead party made such a mess of things that they could not determine how many people had been buried there.[42] Despite the fact that "the Moorehead party dug out the greatest part of this room," the Hyde Exploring Expedition still found "almost a complete skeleton."[43]

In Room 83, Pepper recorded the discovery of a copper bell. In the same room, they cleared away stones and sand to reveal a semicircular layer of stones that proved to be the outer wall of a kiva.[44] Richard wrote to one of the Hyde brothers that he had supervised the bell's discovery. He went for a drink, returned to the ruin, looked down and saw one of the workers "examining something, which proved to be the bell." It is unclear how Pepper and Richard got along in Chaco Canyon that summer. Pepper's diary and field notes are clinical documents of the excavation's progression. There is little to no sentimentality or personal information. Richard, however, continued to prod the Hydes for more authority: "You paid me for my time, but did not outline my duties, but I felt the success of the expedition depended on my efforts." He also wanted his patrons to know that "the find of Turquoise overlooked by Moorehead, I uncovered with my own hand in room #53."[45]

While continuing to demand credit for his efforts, Richard also acted as a strict manager of the workmen. He reported, "Seven o'clock in the morning every man was at his place, when I was in camp. They worked until noon, nooned one and a half hours, then worked until six p.m."[46] Richard offered "fifty cents a day plus room and board. The room would be their own sheepskin and their own saddle blankets on the ground anywhere they wanted them."[47] It had become clear to some workers that they could earn extra money from the artifacts in Pueblo Bonito, too. Arrowheads and turquoise beads began to wander off. After buying some objects from the men, Richard implemented a surveillance system. "Two men worked to the room, or as many as could to advantage, because there were so many more eyes to see, and less liability of them stealing."[48] Richard seemed to see no irony in preventing someone else from making a dime off the past as he had done for so many years. He maintained hypocritical standards and low tolerance: "Each one knew what I expected of him and where and how to work; failure in this meant the loss of their job, as also being late more than two mornings."[49]

Mamie became camp cook. It is unclear how her cooking measured up with John and Clayt's, but it didn't seem to matter. After a long day of hard labor, the Diné "were ready to eat anything."[50] Mamie could not say the same. In August, she found that "I couldn't stand the smell of food and I'd get up in the morning sick to my stomach." When she failed to get better, Richard took her to Alamo Ranch. Marion looked her over. "Don't you know what's the matter with you?" she asked her twenty-year-old daughter-in-law. "You're pregnant." Richard left Mamie in the care of Marion and returned to Pueblo Bonito.[51]

Richard was keen to report other news to the Hydes. While in Colorado, he "learned that there was no money in the bank and that Pepper was liable to prosecution by the angry holders of his checks."[52] Though Richard seems to have been eager to blame Pepper for anything and everything, he knew all too well how flighty a patron the Hydes were. He had struggled in 1893 and 1894 to get the brothers to send money on time and even had to disband the expedition at times due to insufficient funds. Pepper's imminent prosecution, while possible given the Hydes's inconsistent payments, was probably a wish of Richard's heart.

Somehow, they got on without Mamie as cook, but trouble emerged around the camp stove. Richard had been renting the stove from Welo; it seems he had done so in previous years, too. Welo decided he wanted the stove back, but Richard refused as he had already paid the month's fee. The situation escalated until Richard grabbed his six-shooter and drew a line in the sand. He allegedly said, "I'm sorry to do this but the first Navajo that crosses that line, I'll shoot to kill." Richard kept the stove.[53]

Richard was less concerned with what the Diné were eating than what they were drinking. The strict Quaker manager could not abide drunkenness. But Spanish merchants continued to import and sell liquor to the Navajo workers. Richard tried to kick a Spanish liquor salesman out of Chaco Canyon. But he scoffed and reminded him "he didn't own the canyon." Then one day, morning came, but the workers did not arrive at Pueblo Bonito.[54]

Suspecting that alcohol was to blame, Richard went in search of the workers. He found a group of Diné passed out drunk in a trench. He decided to leverage his knowledge of their spiritual and traditional beliefs against them. Disturbing the dead went against Diné beliefs. Richard poured sand on top of the sleeping men and gathered some of the skulls they had excavated. He placed them around the sleeping men.[55] One version of the story has Richard lighting candles inside the skulls. When they awoke, the men were terrified, believing themselves victims of disturbed spirits or murderers.[56]

The dramatic manipulation had the desired effect. Richard established who was boss of the canyon. He might not have owned Chaco Canyon, but he was in charge. Reflecting on what anthropology and archaeology contributed to Indigenous communities, Vine Deloria Jr. later wrote, "The total impact of the scholarly community on Indian people has become one of simple authority."[57] Instances of control by force fostered this unfortunate conclusion.

Pepper continued to record artifacts as well as traditional accounts of the land. There was one story the Diné told about Chaco Canyon:

Once a man named Nááhwiilbiihi or Noqóilpi arrived in Chaco Canyon from the south with a large turquoise talisman. He settled in with the Chaco locals, passing his days gambling on dice and footraces. It soon became clear that this was no ordinary man, but a god. He never lost a gamble and the people fell under his control as they forfeited all their possessions. Soon the people ran out of possessions and began paying their debts with their spouses, children, and labor. The Gambler, as he became known, soon had a slave force that he employed to build the great houses of Chaco Canyon. But as the Gambler enjoyed a luxurious life with all their possessions, the slaves grew resentful. They made a bet with the Gambler. If they won, they got all their possessions back. The slaves entered an alliance with the Holy People and rigged the game. The Gambler "lost everything except his home when the Holy People won the bet. He was very angry." The Holy People then made a weapon from a long reed and aimed it at the Gambler. "They said:

'We'll put you some place where you will have something good to start with again.'" They shot and the Gambler flew into the sky. He uttered something as he ascended beyond Chaco Canyon. It sounded foreign, and tradition has it that it was the first utterance of the White peoples' language in Chaco Canyon.[58]

As another season of the Hyde Exploring Expedition came to an end, the Gambler remained a star of the Diné pantheon, a tale of how the oppressed rose up and killed their oppressor, taking Chaco Canyon back for themselves.

NINE

The Trade

"There is no money to be made at archaeology, either as a scientific worker or a pothunter, and no future to one's efforts."[1] Al Wetherill offered this sobering summary years after he turned in his shovel, and for some reason, it has since been omitted from most Introductory Archaeology classes. It is a somewhat surprising verdict from a member of a family that earned so much money by selling artifacts around the world. Al explained that the amount of money they received was simply never enough to excavate and explore the way they thought was best. As if anticipating questions, Al wrote, "Although we seemed to harvest plenty of money, it was something like pouring into a bucket that had no bottom to it."[2]

With the pitter-patter of little feet on the horizon, Richard became more concerned with that bottomless bucket. Between stock market crashes, financial panics, frosts, disappointing gold mines, and bad harvests, the Wetherills had faced hard times for several years. Alamo Ranch remained in the red, but it was still the family home. Richard returned to the ranch and Mamie after the 1897 excavations at Chaco Canyon.

The truth of Al's view became all too clear that year. Richard still had thousands of artifacts and individuals from his trip to the Grand Gulch sponsored by Bowles and Whitmore. Despite his best efforts, he could not find an interested buyer at the prices he offered. Eventually, either to get rid of the artifacts or obtain any money at all, Richard went to the Hydes. He told them that Bowles and Whitmore needed cash and had "decided to sacrifice the Collection."[3] Richard wanted $5,500, of which he would receive half. The Hydes offered $3,000. He agreed to their terms, taking a loss.[4] The expedition he launched to assuage his hurt ego after his demotion to Pepper had cost him more than he expected.

Still, the family could not let go of the hope that the past would save them. Al dug around Pueblo Bonito and found a few things. He wrote to family friend Dr. Prudden to ask if he knew a philanthropist who might buy his artifacts. Prudden was shocked at the proposition. As he saw it, Pueblo Bonito's artifacts were now the concern of the Hydes. To sell them off to anyone else would be detrimental to the collection, to the understanding of Chaco Canyon's past, and to the Hydes' investment. So, his answer was no.[5]

To some the fiscal component of academic and nonprofessional archaeology casts a shadow. Cree-Metis archaeologist Paulette Steeves writes, "One difference between tribal groups who have pushed for protection of ancestral sites and burial grounds, and non-native archaeologists who have worked with them, is financial compensation. Tribal peoples traditionally were not paid to do the work to protect their heritage . . . it was a way of life, an honor, a duty, and a responsibility, but not a job."[6] The Hyde Exploring Expedition shows that Indigenous laborers accepted financial compensation for excavation, but this may have differed from traditional conceptions of avoidance and respect for which they were not financially compensated.

Al thought there was one foolproof way of making money. "It always seemed to me that if a person could start a trading store with the Indians—anywhere the financial part of worry would be settled." Accordingly, Al had opened his own trading post in Pueblo Bonito in 1895. Orian Buck was his partner. They "did a swell business as long as our stuff held out." Even so, the trading post appears to have closed rather quickly. Later, Mamie turned the post into a chicken coop.[7]

Richard decided it was time to give the trading post idea another try. During the 1870s and 1880s, many had opened trading posts and done well. One of the more successful traders was New Mexico native Juan Lorenzo Hubbell. He opened a trading post in Ganado, Arizona, south of Chaco Canyon and the Diné Reservation and east of the Hopi Reservation. Hubbell's original post evolved into a string of posts, freighting, and farming operations including a blacksmith, bakery, and school. Through trade with the Diné and other locals, Hubbell amassed a fortune that allowed him to build a 4,500-square-foot, seven-bedroom home. He served as sheriff and on the Council of the Arizona Territorial Legislature and the Republican Central Committee. In 1895, he was also named postmaster of Ganado.[8] It seems certain that Richard would have heard of the Hubbells and their fortune. Such fiscal and social prestige may have been on his mind.

Richard sent Al and Clayt to get everything set up. In Pueblo Bonito, rather than expend resources on new structures, they decided to make the best of what was already there. Their donkeys hauled stone and water in to make mortar, and the men built a one-story building onto Pueblo Bonito. They scoured the ruin for timber beams and then laid them across the top of the building as support for the adobe roof.[9] Although dendrochronology had yet to be invented, the timber beams holding up the trading post roof held critical information about the historic environment and when and how the great house was constructed. Moreover, Pueblo Bonito had stood undefiled for hundreds of years, but within just two years of contact with the Wetherills, its original footprint had been augmented for profit.

With the structure complete, the Wetherills threw all their energy into business. Richard started with stock valued at $1,200 including dry goods, cattle and farming equipment, tools, and candy. But the real money was to be made in acquiring the artistic crafts of the Diné in Chaco Canyon. Mamie pushed Richard to buy punches, hammers, tongs, anvils, and Mexican silver dollars that the Diné could use for silverwork. The Navajo made bracelets, rings, and necklaces sold by the trading post.[10] Like other trading posts, they also acquired Diné rugs and blankets as well as other "curios."[11]

Trading and craft were not new to the Diné. Prior to Kit Carson and the reservation, the Diné had long traded with other Indigenous peoples including the Yavapai, Hopi, Havasupai, Ute, and Western Apache. In the seventeenth century, the Navajo continued to create and barter with Spanish traders. As American settlers moved into the West, the Diné continued to exchange in this traditional manner.

The Diné's most popular trade items were woven goods, primarily blankets and rugs. Weaving is a practice imbued with sacred traditions in Diné culture and has been called a "cosmological performance." The Diné creation narrative includes an anecdote about Spider Woman, whom the Holy Twins encountered as she sat weaving a rug surrounded by her other completed rugs in Canyon de Chelly. According to this narrative, all knowledge of weaving comes directly from Spider Woman. Interviews with twentieth- and twenty-first-century Navajo weavers indicate that many women who weave view their work as a continuation of the Spider Woman's tradition. The item they create is not merely a product for sale, but an object with a story, experience, beauty, and reverence.[12] Suffice it to say, traders never saw anything more than pretty colors, fetching designs, and dollar signs.

George Pepper grew interested in the weavers of Chaco Canyon, revealing his own interests in ethnography and anthropology. He had apparently studied textiles collected from southwestern ruins and drew comparisons between the ancient weavers and those he observed: "From the evidence at hand we are safe in saying that prehistoric

Figure 6. Cylinder jars from Room 28, Pueblo Bonito, Chaco Canyon
(American Museum of Natural History Library, PTC-3521).

sedentary people of our own Southwest were also textile-makers of no small merit. But of their descendants we cannot say as much."[13] Although he deemed contemporary blankets "simple," he explained that the designs were "drawn in their entirety upon the kaleidoscopic mirror of the mind alone."[14] Pepper seemed to have learned some of the meaning behind the blanket from the women he watched. He explained, "In the rush and turmoil of our busy life we do not think of the story that is woven into those ever-changing strands, nor the tales of woe and suffering those bright and gaudy colors have beheld."[15]

Diné weavers became critical to the Wetherill Trading Post, as they were to trading posts across the Southwest. Newspapers advertised Navajo blankets across the country, and they proved popular around the world.[16] The demand for Navajo woven products weighed heavily on Diné women, who were also responsible for cooking, herding goats and sheep, and caring for their children.

To a limited extent, it was the nature of weaving, a very time-consuming art form. Pepper described the long process. Diné women managed their sheep and began the blanket or rug process by catching a sheep, which was then "thrown upon its side and hog-tied. . . . and then, with an occasional bleat of protest, the sheep is relieved of its coat." Naturally, the sheep gave the weavers white and black wool to work with, but if the women wanted to add other colors, they next had to dye the wool. Then "the wool is pulled apart and placed on the wool-cards . . . thin rectangular pieces of wood with handles. . . . With these cards the wool is prepared for the spindles. In the process the fibers are made to lie in the same general direction, so that the finished piece is of uniform thickness." Next came the "lengthening and twisting of the wool." Pepper emphasized the labor-intensive process, as he continued to describe the making of a Diné blanket: "Harder and tighter she twists it until after long hours of toil, she produces a strong, kinky, bristling twine whose little filaments will hold the woof-strands in a vise-like grip as the weaving progresses."[17]

Even as he admired the intricacies and labor of the weaving process, Pepper had criticisms. He wrote, "The uniform line is not always maintained. Work of this kind . . . detracts from the aesthetic appearance of the finished product; and as it seems to be attributable to nothing less than sheer laziness on the part of the squaw, it is being discouraged by those who are interested in the development of the art of the Navajos." The scheme of influence did not pan out. These women wove from a place of spirituality and creativity and were not so easily persuaded by the profit-oriented designs of the traders. Pepper conceded the point, noting, "The reclaiming of the Indian's art proved to be a task that necessitated untiring labor with results hardly sufficient to repay one for the time and money expended. . . . The Indian had been moving in a certain groove for years and did not appreciate innovations that tended to disrupt the work that had been brought about by the traders."[18]

Weaving did not make the Diné rich. As one anthropologist summarizes, "The more Navajos wove, the poorer they became." The same could not be said for the trader; the trading post economy ensured that outcome. One anthropologist estimates that Diné weaving resulted in "triple profits for the traders, which translated into a double loss for Navajos."[19] Southwestern trading posts were generally cash poor, and traders paid Navajo craftspeople through barter. Many Diné quickly found themselves indebted to traders in the same fashion as tenant farmers and sharecroppers.[20] Pepper described the situation:

> The squaw knows from experience what she should receive for her work, and therefore demands a certain amount as her just dues. The trader, hard-hearted and grasping, as a rule, takes from his money-pouch perhaps one-half the blanket's value in silver and throws it on the counter. The squaw realizes the injustice of the act, but knows full well that there is but one alternative and that is to ride perhaps a score of miles to the next store, and that too, without the slightest prospect of better treatment when she reaches it.[21]

The Wetherill Trading Post got off to a strong start. Richard reported they were making $20 to $60 daily.[22] Once more, Richard put all his energy into what he hoped would be his final financial salvation. It was clear that the debt weighed heavily upon him, and he felt dramatic change was necessary. Previously, he told the Hydes, "I want to save the home ranch as it is mortgaged."[23] But by the summer of 1898, he had washed his hands of such aspirations. "I left Mancos. I have left there for good. I had to get into something to make a living and had decided on this point for a store."[24]

Thus, it was crucial that the Wetherill Trading Post become a success. And when Fred Hyde visited Pueblo Bonito in 1898, he felt it had. Impressed, he invested $1,000 in the endeavor. The Hydes and Richard agreed to bring the trading post under the Hyde Exploring Expedition's umbrella. Richard promised the store would not detract from his responsibilities as manager of the excavations. He said Mamie would handle the store and he would carry on supervising the excavations.[25] Maybe, just maybe, Richard could begin to turn things around.

TEN

Digging Deeper

"A nine and a half pound boy came to the home of Mr. and Mrs. Richard Wetherill on Thursday last," announced the *Mancos Times* in March 1898. "'Papa Dick' has not regained his ruddy color, although insisting that his nerves are unshaken."[1] Richard and Mamie named their first-born Richard and soon returned to Chaco Canyon. They now made their first home in Pueblo Bonito. Literally. They cleared out intact rooms and moved in.

John and Louisa tried to keep Alamo Ranch afloat. They welcomed their second child, Georgia Ida Wetherill, that January. Things remained challenging at the ranch. Louisa later remembered, "The first year of farming was a failure. The whole wheat crop was ruined by frost. The second year was a year of drought. The third year brought rust."[2] With little ones to feed, the stakes at Alamo Ranch had never been higher. Richard's permanent move to Pueblo Bonito proved prescient, though all was not well in Chaco Canyon. A smallpox epidemic swept through the region around the winter of 1897, striking the Diné particularly hard.[3] Richard complained to Talbot, "I have lived in uncertainty all winter and it drives me wild almost." He disliked that his circumstances left him "so horribly dependent" on Talbot.[4]

Nonetheless, Pepper made the journey back to Chaco Canyon for the Hyde Exploring Expedition's third season in 1898. They continued numbering the rooms sequentially, measuring the walls and doors, and tallying up the types and numbers of artifacts in each room. By 1898, they had numbered and cleared over a hundred rooms in which they continued to find large quantities of pottery. These vessels were often large and decorated in intricate geometric designs. Pueblo Bonito could still surprise. Room 92 had been burned, but under the debris, they found a floor covered in corn. There was a bean bush in one part of the room and piles of beans. Pepper credited the dry conditions in the room for the preservation of this evidence of diet in Pueblo Bonito.[5]

When they opened Room 99, they found a floor full of ceramic pitchers. This room had been burned as well.[6] Although the parallels between Room 28 and Room 99 must have interested Pepper, his primary focus was on the chronology of construction at Pueblo Bonito. He made extensive notes on his interpretations of which rooms were constructed first as well as on the methods of construction. Nonetheless, other details of life at Pueblo Bonito crept in. In Room 102, they found several dog skeletons.[7] They also found two more copper bells in Room 106.[8] These seemingly random items offer a glimpse into the auricular landscape of Pueblo Bonito, a place where hundreds of years ago, dogs barked and bells rang.

The AMNH Annual Report declared the third season a success: "A large amount of interesting material was secured. Photographic views were made illustrative of the progress of the exploration of the ruins, and showing the objects in place as they were disclosed."[9] Pepper also remained positive. In 1898, he wrote, "We are having very good luck with the work, and have made some interesting finds; a new type of flute was found in a room that had been burned. . . . In another we found a beautiful shell trumpet."[10]

The AMNH's Annual Report also noted the progress of the first year of the Jesup North Pacific Expedition, financed by Morris Jesup, banker, philanthropist, and president of the AMNH. Franz Boas was still working at the AMNH as assistant curator of the Anthropology Department and with Putnam had pitched the structure of the expedition to its namesake. It was to be a six-year investigation spanning both sides of the Bering Strait. After chasing stone tools across North America in search of the origins of people in America, Putnam and Boas were now proposing a massive project to explore the theory that the first peoples to enter America crossed the Bering Strait from Asia.

The expedition split into two teams. Boas led one team on the Pacific Northwest Coast of America exploring the village of Bella Coola and studying the Indigenous peoples of British Columbia. German ethnologist Berthold Laufer, who was Jewish, led the second team in Siberia, studying the Indigenous peoples of Sakhalin Island under political tension from Russia's violent antisemitism. Boas never really got too involved with the question of the peopling of North America, focusing on collecting data on the cultural and physical attributes of different tribes instead. The expedition thus became a study in the mold of Powell and the BAE, as it focused on documenting the ways of life of peoples the anthropologists thought would soon disappear. The expedition also gave him the opportunity to rival the Field Museum, against which he still held a grudge. George Dorsey had replaced Holmes by this time, but Boas's anger remained.[11]

Working as curator of the Southwestern Collection for the AMNH kept Pepper busy throughout the year, but he still worked on the Pueblo Bonito finds. He presented a paper at the meeting of the American Association for the Advancement of Science's Section H, Anthropology in December 1898 on the turquoise mosaic objects they recovered in earlier seasons. For the modern archaeologist, a detailed report on the methods and context of each discovery would be preferable. However, this was an age when archaeological discoveries were conveyed via personal communication rather than professional journals or reports.[12] This means of recording and sharing information resulted in the loss of many archaeological records.

Standards were beginning to change. Boas and his fellow researchers published prolifically and quickly on the results of the Jesup North Pacific Expedition. In 1898, Boas published "Facial Paintings of the Indians of Northern British Columbia" and "The Mythology of the Bella Coola Indians." While it was not yet common practice, Pepper had the opportunity to disseminate more information about Pueblo Bonito but did not.

Although the Hyde Exploring Expedition had been conducted under his name for years, Frederic Ward Putnam had never seen Pueblo

Figure 7. George Pepper holding snake in Chaco Canyon (Middle American Research Institute, Tulane University, US_01_099_0532).

Bonito with his own eyes. That changed in 1899. Along with Fred Hyde, Pepper, and Professor Richard E. Dodge, Putnam made his way to Chaco Canyon. There, Putnam concentrated on the big picture. He was "devoted principally to a study of the facts relating to the antiquity of the ruins and to the cause of the desertion of this ancient pueblo by a once numerous and agricultural people, after so much labor had been expended in house building and in extensive irrigation."[13]

Professor Dodge focused on geology and geography "and a study of the geological evidence of the antiquity of the ruins with special reference to those in Chaco Canon."[14] He planned to correlate the geological data with the cultural data. Dodge described his methods:

> a detailed study of the comparative weathering of the different rocks used in the pueblo walls, particularly at the top and the bottom of walls which are standing to a height of three stories; secondly, a study of the deposits about the ruin to a sufficient depth to reach pure sand; thirdly, a study of the deposits in the large dump heap to the south of the ruin; and fourthly, a study of any traces of the deposits to be found on the walls of the exposed rooms.[15]

Based on the relationship between the cultural material and the layers of the earth, Dodge "was convinced of the great length of time in which the ruins were occupied."[16] American archaeologists were some time away from being able to tie chronologies observed in the earth to calendar dates. As the nineteenth century closed, they had to content themselves with relatively dating cultural materials to estimated timespans.

Unlike his older brother Talbot, it seems that Fred was never actually employed anywhere. Fred was tall and strong with a "restless energy [that] found manifold outlets."[17] He had a habit of showing up unannounced and roaming the world without any particularly clear intention. Mamie thought he was "a fine young man, but temperamental. He would work hard, then lay off for a long time."[18] He seems to have been doing more of the same that summer.

One other scholar joined the group in Pueblo Bonito. Dr. Aleš Hrdlička was born in Bohemia and immigrated to the United States in 1882, aged thirteen. Upon arrival in New York, he began working in a cigar factory while attending school at night. He graduated top of his class from the Eclectic Medical College of New York City in 1892. He began practicing medicine while still attending school at night. In 1894, he graduated from the Homeopathic College and accepted the job of associate in anthropology at the Pathological Institute of the New York State Hospital. He went to Europe to study anthropological methods in Paris, Germany, Switzerland, Austria, Belgium, and England. Based on these studies, in 1896 he launched "an ambitious program for detailed bodily measurements in large series of inmates of state institutions and for the systematic collection of human skeletons and autopsy material."[19]

Hrdlička's work followed in the footsteps of the phrenology movement. Phrenologists studied the size and shape of crania to determine cultural and intellectual traits. They analyzed skulls for information on cognition, stealing the heads of famously brilliant individuals like Francisco de Goya, Beethoven, and Mozart as well as unknown individuals from all walks of life. Samuel Morton led the nineteenth-century phrenology movement. Morton amassed at least 800 skulls by 1849 and published his landmark study *Crania Americana*. Like every other aspect of America, the racial differences in the melting pot permeated Morton's studies. He ranked crania by size, positing that Caucasians had the largest brains and were thus most intelligent. Indigenous Americans and Black Americans came last in this ranking system. Over time, Morton came to see the differences in crania to be not just indicative of race-based cognition, but evidence of distinct race-based species. His ideas were popular, and they stayed popular for a long time.

In 1897, Hrdlička testified in the criminal trial of Maria Barbella, an Italian immigrant who murdered her lover in New York and was subsequently sentenced to death. She was the second woman to be sentenced to die by the electric chair, and her case was up for appeal when Hrdlička became involved. He measured Barbella and "fifteen to twenty persons from the same locality and from the same social class." With this context established, Hrdlička noted that Barbella was of "subnormal stature, almost all the measurements of her head are subnormal ... the forehead of M. is particularly low." Hrdlička made an in-depth study of all superficial and medical characteristics of Barbella's family. Her legal defense was insanity based on epilepsy. Hrdlička noted, "There is no such thing as a *physical criminal type*, but no one who has examined criminals, and especially murderers, will contest that various physical abnormalities are not only very frequent with these individuals, but also, that these abnormalities are usually of a more pronounced character than the similar ones found in other classes than criminals."[20] Thus, Hrdlička's interpretation of how Maria's physical attributes revealed her mental fitness was literally a matter of life and death in 1897. Barbella was eventually released, but the calling of Hrdlička to the stand in this high-profile case highlights the importance society placed on this burgeoning field of physical anthropology.

In 1898, Hrdlička was invited on his first anthropological-archaeological expedition to Mexico. He evidently enjoyed the experience and demonstrated value to the field. Putnam offered him a job at the AMNH in 1899. Hrdlička's personality was one Richard might have been able to appreciate. The "skull doctor . . . never used tobacco or alcohol and led a rather frugal existence, granting himself no luxuries." Moreover, "his work was his hobby and his only and absorbing ambition was to advance the young science of physical anthropology."[21] As he joined the Hyde Exploring Expedition, Hrdlička hoped to do just that.

There was just one little problem. Hrdlička was interested in physical remains, and the Hyde Exploring Expedition had encountered very few buried individuals. There had been bodies in Room 33, and Moorehead had taken and damaged the remains of several other individuals. Despite Juan's fears after the discovery of the cylinder jars in Room 28, they found fewer burials than they expected. Pueblo Bonito and the surrounding great houses were massive architectural undertakings that likely required hundreds of hands to build. Coming up empty, Pepper conceded, "The inconsequential number of bodies found in Pueblo Bonito naturally prompts the question as to the general cemetery wherein were buried the hundreds who must have died there."[22]

Hrdlička was up to the challenge. One acquaintance wrote, "That man knew exactly where to go to scratch out bones, he had the ability to think himself into the state of being of people who had lived in an area years before."[23] Hrdlička quickly found bodies of the more recently deceased. In burned hogans, he uncovered the remains of Diné who likely perished from the recent smallpox outbreak.[24] Coming upon a similar scene decades later, Navajo archaeologist Wade Campbell described the preferred strategy of avoidance: "Two large sheep camp complexes in the main valley were noted to contain several . . . burial hogans. . . . Because such sites are traditionally avoided by Dine during everyday activities, Phase I work at the sites was limited to simple recording and the dendroarchaeological sampling of non-habitation features like shadehouses, corrals."[25] It was thus possible to conduct archaeology in a way that respected the dead and Indigenous beliefs, but that did not happen in 1900.

John Wetherill acted as Hrdlička's guide. They visited the Hopi, Pueblo, and Apache Tribes. At the end of the 1900 season, Hrdlička tallied up his results: "a little over nine hundred persons measured and examined . . . over five hundred negatives . . . and about fifty skulls and sketches."[26] This was only the beginning of Hrdlička's career, which would see him promote the idea of a common origin for all of humanity. For now, the search for the elusive burial ground continued. Putnam excavated on a knoll outside the ruin and discovered the grave of an individual buried with pottery.[27] But the massive burial ground that "must" retain the bodies of the hundreds who built and walked the rooms of Pueblo Bonito continued to evade the Hyde Exploring Expedition.

With the Hydes still committed to the project, there was time to address these and other questions. But time was not enough. As early as 1897, Richard began looking over his shoulder. He wrote to the Hydes, eager to get a collection of artifacts off his hands. He warned, "All work in Arizona in Ruins is prohibited. New Mexico is waking up to that point also."[28] Despite their differences, the future of excavations in Pueblo Bonito proved common ground. Pepper wrote to Talbot to explain their strategy, "I have made an arrangement with Richard whereby he will take an interest in the business . . . then by him staying here, we can claim squatters' rights, and in time, have a government surveyor survey the canon and by that means probably acquire a tract of land embracing Pueblo Del Aroza, Bonito and Chettro Kettle."[29] Pepper and Richard continued clearing rubble, secure in the knowledge that they had plenty of time to uncover the rest of Pueblo Bonito's secrets.

ELEVEN

Death by Committee

Even as the Wetherills concentrated their efforts on Chaco Canyon, the plunder of Mesa Verde continued. Al estimated that between 1889 and 1901, the family escorted "nearly one thousand people" into the ruins beyond Alamo Ranch.[1] Many of those who visited the ruins, with or without the Wetherills, took bits of archaeology home.

This looting tourism frustrated Virginia McClurg to no end. She was perhaps the only person who knew the cliff dwellings of Mesa Verde as well as the Wetherills. But she saw scientific merit, not fiscal fulfillment in the ancient structures. And she held a deep disdain for those who raided the ruins. She lectured against treasure hunting, telling audiences, "The joy of exploring and finding is supposed to be adequate reward."[2]

Virginia knew that looting was taking a heavy toll on the cliff dwellings, but she also knew the roots of the issue lay in ignorance. Rumors abounded that the ancient ruins of the West concealed piles of gold and silver. Although no one had yet made it big hunting this alleged treasure, a stream of hopefuls trailed through the West. When they failed to find gold and silver, they comforted themselves with consolation prizes from archaeological sites.[3]

Though her heart lay with the cliff dwellings, Virginia had begun spending more time on the East Coast to improve her son's health. She also toured eastern cities giving lectures on the history of the ancient Southwest. She made the events nearly cinematic, presenting slides of her pictures to packed audiences, who paid seventy-five cents for the pleasure. The pictures had not been easily acquired. One paper noted that she often encountered Indigenous Americans living in the pueblos who "object[ed] seriously to having photographs taken, on account of an odd superstition that some virtue goes out from them into the picture."[4] Nevertheless, she snapped away. The word *no* held little sway with Virginia McClurg.

Virginia balanced her lectures with history and concerns over looting. She argued that the federal government needed to protect the cliff dwellings as a national policy. She noted that were she to visit Italy, she would surely be stopped from pocketing artifacts from Pompeii because the site was "national property." If the US government would step in and establish these sites as parks under federal protection, she felt certain the ruins would at last be safe.[5]

Virginia sought an immediate solution by meeting with Ute tribal leaders Ignacio and Acowitz in 1899. Virginia offered to pay the Ute $300 a year on a thirty-year lease for ownership of Mesa Verde. The Ute could stay on as police. Ignacio was not opposed to the idea, but he wanted all the money up front. Virginia did not have $9,000, and it is unlikely she would have agreed to such terms anyway. So, she left Ignacio and Acowitz, and the ruins remained a looters' paradise.[6]

Virginia was not alone in looking to the federal government for a preservation solution. Alice Fletcher watched Mary Hemenway lead the battle for the protection of Casa Grande, but a visit to Yellowstone convinced her that the federal government needed to establish parks to celebrate archaeology and the country's natural wonders. Born in Cuba and raised in the United States, Fletcher began working as a researcher for the Peabody Museum in 1880. She had worked on mounds in Florida, Maine, and Massachusetts and helped Putnam save the Serpent Mound. She was the first woman of much of anthropology and archaeology: first to hold any fellowship at Harvard; first to chair a scientific section of the American Association for the Advancement of Science (AAAS).[7] In 1887, she brought the issue to the attention of the AAAS, whose permanent secretary, Frederic Ward Putnam, presumably took notes as Alice called for the government to "set aside certain portions of the public domain in the southwest territories in which are characteristic remains of former and present aboriginal life and holding them as national reserves." Sensing the coming conflict, Fletcher continued: "Many of the most remarkable ruins and dwellings are upon land little value to the settler, so that the claims of archaeology do not interfere with local prosperity . . . they are daily in more and more danger from the curiosity and zeal of traders. If they are not speedily preserved many will irrevocably be lost."[8] Matilda Coxe Stevenson joined Alice's cause, and in 1889 the AAAS selected them for the Committee on the Preservation of Archaeologic Remains on the Public Lands. They began working on a bill to preserve the nation's heritage.[9] Attorney and curator Thomas Wilson headed the committee, which also included Putnam and George Dorsey.[10]

In 1888, Fletcher and Stevenson gave a report to the Committee on the Preservation of Archaeologic Remains on the Public Lands. They prioritized several sites: Chaco Canyon, Canyon de Chelly, Canyon del Muerto, Walnut Canyon, the Ruin on Fossil Creek, and Ruins in Mancos Canyon. They drafted a bill that would allow lands to be withdrawn from public use and put under the control of the secretary of the interior, who would in turn prevent "injury and spoliation [of] all natural and archaeological curiosities."[11] But it all came to nothing.

The AAAS was not alone in pursuing legislation. In 1899, the Archaeological Institute of America (AIA) established a Standing Committee on American Archaeology. Putnam sat on this committee too, as did Franz Boas.[12] The AIA and the AAAS combined their efforts and submitted proposed legislation to members of Congress. The legislation drew on the fact that the government already exercised the right to set aside and reserve tracts of timber forests. The AAAS and AIA sought to give the same powers to the president for "any public lands upon which are monuments, cliff dwellings, cemeteries, graves, mounds, forts, or any other work of prehistoric, primitive, or aboriginal man, and also any natural formation of scientific or scenic value or interest, or natural wonder or curiosity together with such additional area of land surrounding or adjoining the same."[13]

The committee justified the need for such sweeping legislation by citing examples of artifacts leaving the United States. They specifically mentioned Nordenskiöld's escapades in Mesa Verde. They also told Congress how the Smithsonian's inaugural archaeological investigation under Squier and Davis saw the artifacts of the Ohio Mounds sail across the Atlantic to the Blackmore Museum in Salisbury, England. The committee further noted the laws of other nations.[14] The Papal States had cultural heritage legislation by 1819. France passed the Commission des Monuments Historiques in 1837, and Great Britain enacted the Ancient Monuments Protection Act in 1882. Yet it was still legal for anyone and everyone to ransack America's archaeological sites.

If the committee expected a proud, xenophobic reaction comparable to that of Mancos in 1888, they were quickly disappointed. Three bills were submitted to Congress. After review, the House Committee on Public Lands' chairman, John F. Lacey of Iowa, sent the bills to Secretary of the Interior Ethan A. Hitchcock. Hitchcock passed the bills along to the commissioner of the General Land Office (GLO), Binger Hermann. The commissioner found too many faults in the bills but agreed that there was a need to protect archaeological sites. He put forth a fourth bill, which Representative Lacey introduced to Congress on April 26, 1900. Representative John Frank Shafroth of Colorado introduced yet another bill that reduced reservations to 320 acres in Colorado, Wyoming, Arizona, and New Mexico.[15]

In this tangled web of preservation legislation, it is apparent that many members of Congress felt that there was a need for federal protection of archaeological sites. They disagreed on the extent of those protections and what constituted heritage. These bills reflected the discomfort some states had in restricting public use of land, and foreshadowed years of disputes to come. But none of that really mattered in 1900. Congress failed to agree on who should have the authority to reserve and manage public lands protecting cultural resources. All the bills died in Congress, and the past remained up for grabs.

As the archaeological alphabet soup lobbied for sweeping legislation to encompass all archaeological and natural sites, others zeroed in on single sites. This tactic had worked in the past at Casa Grande and the Serpent Mound. Edgar Lee Hewett moved to the Southwest in the 1890s to improve his wife's health. He quickly became intrigued by an area once worked by Adolph Bandelier and began regularly surveying and mapping cliff dwellings in Pajarito Plateau. In 1898, the Normal University at Las Vegas, New Mexico, selected Hewett as its first president. Hewett harnessed his professional acumen and began lobbying the General Land Office and President McKinley for the creation of a national park at Pajarito Plateau. His efforts paid off with the General Land Office, which reserved 153,000 acres of Pajarito Plateau.[16] It wasn't a national park, but it was a start. Hewett seems to have been energized by partial victory and to have recognized the value of friends in the right places. He set his sights on Congressman Lacey, who had introduced the failed bills that year, and began nurturing what he hoped would be a valuable friendship.

Hewett's concerns were not solely for Pajarito Plateau. He had also heard of the Hyde Exploring Expedition. As the *Santa Fe New Mexican* reported, "considerable work" was going on in Pueblo Bonito. "Over 100 people are employed and the company doing the work has a large freighting outfit which is busy freighting in supplies and freighting out relics."[17] Where the paper got the number of employees is uncertain, but readers like Hewett fretted over the unspecified number of relics leaving the Southwest once again. Hewett began lobbying for the protection of Chaco Canyon. His interests were not solely altruistic. As a leader of a western institution, he maintained concerns about eastern institutions hoarding the nation's cultural resources. The General Land Office was concerned enough to send out a special agent to investigate. Special Agent Max Pracht's investigation stopped short of Mesa Verde and Chaco Canyon, in Durango, just a stone's throw from Alamo Ranch. Unsurprisingly, the Wetherills' Colorado neighbors gave only favorable reports of the Hyde Exploring Expedition. In turn, Pracht's report raised little concern over the work in Chaco Canyon.[18] Pracht never made it to Chaco Canyon. Based on his journey in Colorado, he determined that a national park was justified, if cries of looting had become exaggerated. He reportedly stated:

I reported strongly in favor of establishing the proposed reserve. The cliff dwellers' country has a historic value beyond comparison. There is absolutely no end to the value of the relics which have been unearthed there, and are still to be unearthed. . . . There has been much said about the amount of plunder that has been taken out of the country. It is true that a great deal of value, that lies on the surface, has been tucked in the trunks of foreign scientists, and taken to museums in Europe, but the important things are still in the earth there. Ninety per cent, of the historic relics of the cliff dwellers remains to be unearthed and if the reservation is made, they will be preserved for the state of Colorado and the United States.[19]

The Hyde Exploring Expedition and everyone else were free to carry on.

Virginia McClurg decided to strike with or without Congress. She served as regent of a women's organization called the Colorado Cliff Dwellings Association (CCDA). At the CCDA's annual meeting, she asked members:

> "Why do we live?"
> "For what reason does the association exist?"
> "How shall we live unless we can control the ruins of Mesa
> Verde?"[20]

Like Hewett, Virginia wanted official park designation to protect Mesa Verde. Part of the issue in controlling Mesa Verde was that as much as two thirds of the proposed park sat on a Ute Reservation. The federal government could not hand over the reservation lands to the CCDA.[21] But wherever they were, Virginia and the CCDA were determined to control the cliff dwellings.

They ramped up their public relations campaign. Newspapers reported the goal of the CCDA was to "save the prehistoric ruins of the state from the depredations of vandals, and at the same time try to add to the world's stock of knowledge concerning those remarkable people, the cliff dwellers." The report continued, "They have had an accurate and comprehensive map made." And although reaching the cliff dwellings was dangerous due to the lack of roads, the CCDA believed "the difficulties and dangers only show how necessary it is to build roads and trails and a rest house, so that people with great enthusiasm but little strength may visit the ruins."[22]

In 1900, Virginia's friend Alice Bishop led a group of women on another visit to Ignacio and Acowitz. Things went better this time, and Alice left with a "tentative agreement" on the lease of Mesa Verde. However, when the secretary of the interior found out, he invalidated their lease because the women lacked the legal authority, as private citizens, to make a legal arrangement with the Ute. That was government business.[23]

The CCDA continued raising awareness even as they were stymied by bureaucracy. In 1901, the organization succeeded in raising enough funds to bring the AAAS to Colorado, where they journeyed to Mesa Verde. They understood the crucial difference between visiting these sites in person and flipping through someone else's photographs. They also lobbied political leaders for a law to prevent excavation and artifact collection in the cliff dwellings. Interestingly, the *San Francisco Examiner* quoted a member of the CCDA, Mr. Wetherill, who said that "if this [relic hunting] were permitted much longer everything of interest in the ruins would disappear."[24] No first name is given, but that any Wetherill of Alamo Ranch would complain about treasure hunting in Mesa Verde suggests an astonishing lack of self-awareness.

Despite the secretary of the interior's dismissal of their lease, Mc-Clurg and her vice-regent, Lucy Peabody, asked members of the CCDA to raise funds to buy the dwellings. Each woman was asked to raise 25 cents for the cause, but they joked to the public, "Wealthy individuals who have more than a quarter to spare will not be ruthlessly spurned, and even if the decimal should be placed after the figures, instead of before them, Mrs. McClurg will bear the news with becoming fortitude."

Hewett held on to the hope that someone might distinguish the Hyde Exploring Expedition's work in Chaco Canyon as looting rather than archaeology. He continued lobbying everyone he could. Reports from Chaco Canyon indicated that the expedition was removing timbers and taking out entire rooms from Pueblo Bonito to send to the East Coast.

In between these acts of destruction, the Wetherills were allegedly sell-ing artifacts to any market they could find.[25]

With preservation an unresolved issue in Congress and rumors swirling, the General Land Office sent Special Agent S. J. Holsinger to get to the bottom of the accusations. Unlike his predecessor, Holsinger would not stop until he reached Chaco Canyon.

TWELVE

Anni Horribiles

The word "loot" derives from the Hindi word *lūt*. Some also associate it with the Sanskrit *lōtra* or *lōptra*, meaning "booty" or "spoil." The roots of the words, *lup* and *rup*, translate as "to break" or "to rob." In English, loot is generally defined as "goods (esp. articles of considerable value) taken from an enemy, a captured city, etc. in time of war; also, in wider sense, something taken by force or with violence." The word "loot" entered the English lexicon only as early as 1788 in an Indian vocabulary book,[1] as the European nations amplified their colonization of the Eastern Hemisphere. Thus, the entire concept was both foreign and new as America's archaeological community called for federal protections against looting, and diggers kept digging.

The Wetherills readily admitted that their early work in Mesa Verde fell short of archaeology. Al explained, "We had started in as just ordinary pothunters, but, as work progressed along that sort of questionable business, we developed quite a bit of scientific knowledge by careful work and comparisons."[2] The Wetherills felt they had evolved into scientists and better-than-average stewards of the sites they worked.

That is the rub. There is a subjective element in defining loot.

The Wetherills did not consider large-scale clearing of rubble, timbers, or artifacts from Mesa Verde, the Grand Gulch, or Chaco Canyon acquisition by force. Nor did they consider the procurement and trade of artifacts particularly lucrative. They saw themselves as cowboy-scientists-traders-etcetera just trying to get by. Archaeological sites, ancient ruins, and nonrenewable artifacts were just interesting means to an end.

The AMNH was filling up with those means. A row of cases on the second floor of the museum held artifacts from the Grand Gulch expeditions as well as turquoise ornaments from Pueblo Bonito. But even as the cases filled, the museum reported that "only a very small portion of the Hyde expedition material [had] actually [been] placed on exhibition."[3] Included in that vast material being stored away in New York were the skulls Hrdlička, Pepper, the Wetherills, and the Navajo laborers had removed from the ruins. Hrdlička was working on "an elaborate memoir on the physical characters of the peoples of the southwest" based on those bones.[4]

Owing to the renewed investigation, excavation in Chaco Canyon was on hold by federal decree. Trading was not, so Richard and Mamie carried on with the business side of things. They had no choice. Early in 1900, Mamie gave birth to the couple's second child, a daughter named Elizabeth Ann.[5] The trading posts continued to expand across the Southwest. There were Hyde Exploring Expedition trading posts at Tiznatzin, Raton, Ojo Alamo, Escavada, Sautells, San Juan, Farmington, Thoreau, Little Water, Two Grey Hills, Manuelito, and Largo.[6] The Wetherill brothers and their wives were crucial to the enterprise. In 1900, John and Louisa opened the Ojo Alamo Trading Post.[7] Win took over Two Grey Hills in 1901. Clayt helped Richard at Pueblo Bonito. Only Al remained at Alamo Ranch.[8]

With the exception of the ranch, things seemed to be going well. In 1901, the *Western Liberal* reported that the expedition had a blanket worth $1,000. It "had been the property of a Navajo chief who lived over two hundred years ago. In the center of the blanket [was] a worn place where the cloth was folded to wrap around the shoulders of the Indian, otherwise it [was] in perfect condition and the bright colors show no sign of fading."[9] Placing public price tags on items of such antiquity can only have added to the mounting concerns of the nation's preservation community. Still, reports continued to cast Richard and the Hyde Exploring Expedition in a largely positive light. The paper concluded: "The Indians call Mr. Wetherill 'Anasasie' [*sic*] which means

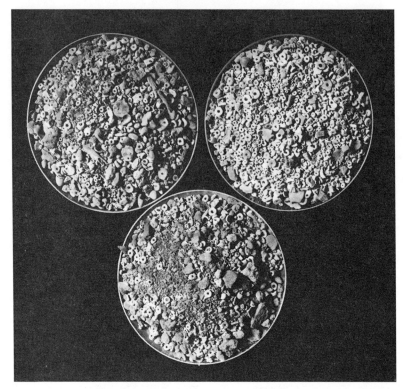

Figure 8. Turquoise recovered from Room 33 (Middle American Research Institute, Tulane University, US_01_099_0426).

'the old people.' . . . The Navajos are devoted to Mr. Wetherill and his word is law among them."[10]

During the nineteenth century, southwestern law lay largely in domineering personalities like Richard Wetherill, authoritative men and women with visions, unafraid to take charge and make demands of others. But as the United States settled into its new territories, it did so with the intent of making the West less wild. Laws and law enforcement followed. And the days of gentlemen's agreements, vigilante justice, and open ranging faced their end.

Agent S. J. Holsinger embodied this new arm of the US government as he rode toward Chaco Canyon. He was accustomed to both being on the road and enforcing federal law. In 1897, the Interior Department made him a special agent charged with investigating "fraudulent land claims and the preservation of public lands and timber."[11] Timber was a high priority for incoming homesteaders and the federal government. The nation's cultural resources, though nonrenewable, were farther down the list of priorities. But Hewett and the Santa Fe Archaeological Society's persistence paid off. So, in April 1901, Agent Holsinger pulled up to Pueblo Bonito to investigate claims of rampant looting and misuse of the ruins.[12]

But Agent Holsinger had other claims to assess as well. Richard first filed a homestead claim in Chaco Canyon on May 14, 1900, for land known as Section 30, where one ruin, Kin Klizhin, sat. Months later, he withdrew that claim and resubmitted a claim for nine lots of Section 12, which included Pueblo Bonito, Chetro Ketl, and Pueblo del Arroyo.[13] To Holsinger, this seemed to indicate that Wetherill's interest was not merely in establishing a permanent home for his family, but in controlling the ancient ruins.

The Wetherills argued that their intentions were to protect the great houses from trespassers. They were then acting in the same manner as Hewett, McClurg, and Putnam, taking private control over vulnerable antiquities, where the federal government had failed to act. But Hewett, McClurg, and Putnam were not simultaneously running a trading post off Pajarito Plateau, Mesa Verde, or the Serpent Mound. Looking around Pueblo Bonito, Holsinger documented the family home, the store, a stable, a warehouse, a blacksmith shop, a boarding house, the employees' quarters, a windmill, the Blanket Room, a ten-acre horse pasture, and two acres of planted corn. He valued the property at $10,500. Richard had reported a property valued at $3,000.[14]

Agent Holsinger did not confine his investigation to the Wetherill home. He traveled around Chaco Canyon, documenting a multitude of ruins including Tsin Kletsin, Kin Klizhin, Kin Bineola, Casa Rinconada, and Kin Ya'a. He noted irrigation systems, stairways, and ancient roads connecting the great houses. He took pictures of Navajo hogans surrounding the ruins.[15]

After a month, he filed a report with the General Land Office. It was clear that he took issue with the extent of the excavations in the canyon. Holsinger recommended that Chaco Canyon be reserved. He called for the federal government to protect the ruins from homesteaders. But his recommendations went further. There were extensive ruins lying outside the boundaries of his recommended 750-square-mile reservation and they warranted protection, too.[16] Anticipating the outrage of the Wetherills, Holsinger outlined the significance of Chaco Canyon, as he saw it:

> The lands are only valuable as an indifferent stock range; for the extensive prehistoric ruins and as the home of numerous Navajo Indians. . . . No interest would be injured by reserving the lands or by the establishment of a National Park, unless such reservation would exclude the Indians. What is of no practical value to the white settler for agricultural purposes is ample for the Indians and to deprive them of the land would be robbing them of that which in all its humbleness and poverty is very dear. As a National Park, I take it that the presence of the Navajo would not be detrimental to public interests and they would not only add picturesqueness and interest to the park but protection to the objects of scientific interest to be preserved.[17]

Holsinger clearly saw the Wetherill homestead as a threat to the preservation of these sites. He sent a letter to Commissioner Hermann sharing some confidential information he had received. An employee of the Hyde Exploring Expedition, "who does not desire that his name be used," reported to Holsinger that despite the government banning excavation of the ruins during the investigation, "Richard and one of his brothers were violating the Government's order."[18]

Some local press balked at suggestions of impropriety in the ruins. The *Albuquerque Citizen* pushed back against "the scarehead display and editorial comment indulged by the press throughout the country, relative to the despoilation of Aztec ruins in New Mexico by the Hyde Exploring Expedition." The paper claimed that "the homestead entry of Richard Wetherill did not cover or include any ruins whatever." False. The report then asserted that "F.E. Hyde Jr. has for the past two years been the prime mover through congressional influence, towards inducing the government to assume full charge of all rules in the Chaco canyon, and to absolutely forbid any excavation work except under the

direct supervision of the government." It seems likely that Virginia Mc-
Clurg, Matilda Coxe Stevenson, Alice Fletcher, and Edgar Lee Hewett
would have taken issue with this characterization. The paper concluded
with a ringing endorsement: "The true facts of the case are, the Hyde
Exploring Expedition have done more towards preserving these valuable ruins than all other factors combined, and what excavations were
made by them were done solely in the interest of science, and the relics
unearthed donated gratis to government institutions."[19]

The Wetherills braced for impact as the GLO considered Holsinger's
report.

In 1901, Congress gave McClurg and the CCDA permission to treat with
the Ute. As McClurg celebrated the CCDA's mandate for the protection
of Mesa Verde, she declared: "We have entered upon a work of vast
importance and no little difficulty. . . . It demands much more money
than the average work undertaken by organizations of club women. We
are on trial before the world, but we shall not fail!"[20]

Lucy Peabody assisted McClurg. Lucy was in her late thirties and
had previously worked as a secretarial assistant for the BAE. In 1900,
she also joined Section H of the AAAS.[21] In 1902, Lucy's brother-in-
law became governor of Colorado. Lucy soon leveraged this new tie to
influence state politics, while simultaneously using her contacts from
around the country to influence the national agenda.[22]

There were roads to be built, and the CCDA still wanted official park
designation. The *San Francisco Examiner* reported that the CCDA's
plans included "an act positively prohibiting all digging and carrying
away of relics from the ruins."[23] Crucially, this protection applied to the
ruins of Mesa Verde, not all archaeological ruins in the United States.
The CCDA was not joining the archaeological community's push for
comprehensive preservation legislation. Virginia saw an archaeology
hierarchy. She explained, "To me the interest of the work and its value to
posterity are vastly greater than the preservation of the big trees of the
California missions, of the Palisades, or the Indian mounds of Michigan
and Wisconsin—laudable as are these endeavors, to which we wish a
'God speed!'"[24] The CCDA concentrated on Mesa Verde.

Virginia's stance was a shame because she was a preservation sensation. She was well connected. Her husband was tasked with planning Colorado's Quarto-Centennial Jubilee of Statehood in 1901. The guest of honor there was the vice president of the United States, Theodore Roosevelt. Surprisingly, the notorious adventurer did not visit the cliff dwellings. He later reportedly told the Wetherills "that he was not interested in the past, that the future was what he was trying to keep in touch with."[25] Nevertheless, Virginia and the CCDA gifted him a bowl from one of the monuments. How the acquisition of this artifact differed from looting is unclear. But he thanked her for it: "Oh! How the golden mystery of the west that has gone, of the west that has vanished with vanished sunsets, must strike chords in the hearts of all who have themselves, the lift-upwards within them!"[26] He also told McClurg to "write direct to him personally in any case of need of government aid." Alas, Virginia's interests lay only in Mesa Verde and the archaeological community went without that direct line to Pennsylvania Avenue.

Still, archaeologists continued to press for the protection of the nation's ruins. A new character emerged in 1902: biblical archaeologist Reverend Henry Mason Baum, who headed the Records of the Past Exploration Society. Hewett gave Baum a tour of Pajarito Plateau that year. Baum subsequently argued for national park designation for Mesa Verde, Chaco Canyon, and Canyon de Chelly, but strangely not Pajarito Plateau. In the first issue of his journal, *Records of the Past*, Baum outlined what he wanted in a national preservation law: "first, that the antiquities be placed under the control of the Secretary of the Interior; second, that the institutions of the country shall have an equal right to excavate the ruins; and third, that all excavations shall be prohibited without a permit from the Secretary of the Interior."[27] All he had to do was get Congress to ratify his ideas.

Hewett gave a far more important tour in 1902 to Representative Lacey, the archaeological community's key ally. He introduced Lacey to the ruins of the Pajarito Plateau, which can only have reinforced the representative's commitment to preserving the continent's past. Lacey returned to Washington, DC, but Hewett headed across the Atlantic, moving to Switzerland to pursue a PhD at the University of Geneva.

American archaeology weathered an additional loss in 1902 with the death of Major John Wesley Powell. As head of the United States Geological Survey and the BAE, he profoundly influenced American archaeology in the nineteenth century:

> The monument of Major Powell is the Bureau of American Ethnology, where in his spirit and with his zeal for the ends he loved, the ablest men of science have labored and will continue to labor to solve the problems given birth to by the presence of the Red Man upon the twin-continent of America. Investigator, teacher, soldier, geologist, anthropologist, philosopher, the genius of the man dwelt within no limited bounds. His individuality, his personal magnetism, his thoroughly scientific frame of mind, impressed themselves upon all with whom he came in contact. To have met him was to keep the memory of a good man and a great.[28]

The issues inherent in building an agency off the back of the "personal magnetism" of a single man emerged rapidly.

Marion Wetherill paced frantically around the living room of Alamo Ranch. Fred Hyde stood nearby, dirty, having wandered in unannounced as usual. Marion stomped her foot and begged her daughter-in-law, "Mary, *make* him do it. *Make him do it.*"[29]

The him in question was Al, the last son remaining at Alamo Ranch. His father had passed away in 1898. The mortgage had not been paid in some time, and their creditors' patience had run out. The family had expanded their land holdings far beyond their capabilities, but Al also thought the new branches on the family tree were to blame. "If we could have all hung together, we would not have hung singly. When the boys and girls married off, the union, broken up, never got on its feet again."[30]

Fred Hyde offered to pay off the mortgage. Marion was desperate for Al to accept, but Al declined the offer because he felt they "would have just been a sort of a hired-help." Al reminded Fred that the Hyde family would never give him enough money for the ranch. Ever full of surprises, Fred pulled out seven thousand dollars from the toe of his shoe. It was more than they needed, but Al still refused. Instead, they "lost everything."[31]

On February 24, 1902, Alamo Ranch was sold at public auction.

The General Land Office was not swayed by the pro-Wetherill publicity campaign. In March 1902, it issued a formal notice for the permanent end of excavations in Chaco Canyon.

Talbot and Fred Hyde had to end things, too. At first, the Hydes tried to play it cool. The AMNH's annual report read: "Owing to the large amount of work to be done on material collected by this expedition in former years, in order to get it catalogued and ready for exhibition, field work in the Southwest was largely suspended."[32] No mention of any federal injunctions.

Richard had some inkling that the Hydes were losing faith in the operation. In 1901, he wrote almost goading Talbot with gossip he heard in New Mexico: "The Hyde Exploring Expedition will not last very long as . . . Mr. Hyde's father objects to his investment here."[33] He knew the ground was shaky and he tried desperately to hold on.

The Hydes kept face. In March 1902, just as the injunction became permanent, a Hyde Exploring Expedition exhibition opened in New York. A Brooklyn newspaper clarified, "The title is calculated to cause confusion. The expedition is primarily a scientific enterprise financed by two young capitalists of New York, but is likewise a philanthropic, commercial and educational combine." The paper praised the work of the expedition in salvaging the Diné's traditional weaving practices and "inducing them a good price for their work." It also advertised the "magnificent display of Navajo blankets and rugs at the show, as well as a remarkably large and interesting exhibit of other work by the Indians and curious and valuable relics of the race, some splendid representatives of which are in attendance."[34]

By March 1902, Richard had grown impatient. He wrote to Fred Hyde, "Have had no letters from you. What is the matter[?]" Richard had heard that Talbot was no longer officially connected to the expedition, but not from the brothers themselves. He blamed the brothers' advisors and resigned himself to the inevitable. "It seems to me that I am to stand alone . . . that is all right; You will find me here at the Old stand, trying to do business. Of course I know that we have made mistakes — and things are not in the shape they ought to be."[35]

Early in April, Richard headed for New York to try to address the situation. As he left New Mexico, he told reporters he knew "nothing of being deprived of his homestead in Chaco canyon, and [said] he took it out in good faith, expecting to make it his permanent home."[36] As he headed east, it may have occurred to him that this was just how the Hyde Exploring Expedition began with Julia Cowing in New York in 1893. Things had changed so much in nine years. But this trip changed nothing. By April 16, he was back in New Mexico, trying to sort out his homestead claims.[37]

Talbot and Fred had to face facts. The federal injunction looked bad. The preservation movement was gaining steam. And they were losing a lot of money. The GLO report marked the end. By July, a formal notice appeared in several papers:

> To all those with whom the Hyde Exploring Expedition has had commercial correspondence, and to all whom it may concern: Take notice that the business (including any and all partnership) heretofore conducted under the name "The Hyde Exploring Expedition," in New Mexico and elsewhere, has been dissolved, the said business and all its assets being now the sole property of the undersigned, Benjamin T. B. Hyde, and all business connection, whether by way of partnership, agency, or otherwise, between the undersigned, or any two or more of them, has been ended by mutual consent. By special agreement, Richard Wetherill has specific authority to collect certain specified book accounts now on the Putnam books, as may appear by writing in his possession signed by the undersigned Benjamin T.B. Hyde. B and Frederick E. Hyde Jr., will organize a corporation under the name "The Hyde Exploring Expedition," of which more detailed notice will be given hereafter.
>
> Frederick E. Hyde Jr., Benjamin T.B. Hyde, and Richard Wetherill, July 12th, 1902[38]

It was all over.

The collapse of the Hyde Exploring Expedition hit Richard, Mamie, Al, John, Louisa, Clayt, and Win hard, but they had been hit hard before. If nothing else, the Wetherill family excelled at adapting to new hardships. So, they reached for their bootstraps once more and gave them a pull. Richard and Mamie still had a lot of trade goods and the post office, so they decided to run their own trading post. The store had so much stuff to sell that people were "slipping on each other the store was so full."[39] Things were bad, but they had never been great. But with no home to run back to, a tsunami of debt rushing toward him, and his main source of income scuttled, it became uncertain if Richard could pull off another resurrection.

In August 1902, he ordered overalls, pants, and cloth for the trading post for $693, including shipping. Three months later, the bill had not been paid and the manufacturers, Tootle, Wheeler & Motter, filed against Richard in court.[40]

George Pepper remained an employee of the AMNH and had other excavations and projects to attend to. Nevertheless, the summer of 1902 saw him still sorting out the administrative aspects of the Hyde Exploring Expedition. He reported to Putnam, "We have a balance of $23.91 in the bank which leaves a balance of $340.20 to be met by Mr. Hyde."[41]

Hrdlička cut ties and moved on more quickly. In 1903, he and the Hyde Exploring Expedition entered into a formal agreement. He turned over all the remains of individuals that he had collected for the expedition to the Hyde brothers as well as the photo negatives. He turned over all his field notes and publications to Putnam. The agreement also outlined permissions necessary for publication of any of the materials collected during the expedition.[42] Hrdlička was not just breaking up with the expedition; he had become close with William Henry Holmes. Professor Holmes was back on the East Coast, having taken the job as head curator of anthropology at the National Museum in Washington, DC. The National Museum had long complained about the Army Medical Museum's monopoly on skeletal materials. And in 1903, Holmes hired Hrdlička to take over a new division of physical anthropology in the National Museum, where he could manage the newly transferred individuals and their remains.[43]

American archaeology would not miss the Hyde Exploring Expedition. In 1900, the *American Journal of Archaeology* published a review of the past ten years of archaeological achievements in the United States. This account recognized that the Hyde Exploring Expedition had succeeded in collecting "a large amount of valuable material." That was all, a prolific exercise in accumulation. But what had Americans learned about the ancient world from the Hyde Exploring Expedition? From the expedition, it was known that the people of Chaco had pretty jars, lots of turquoise, a couple of bells, some corn, some beans, and an elusive cemetery. This information was available to very few people, and it left a lot to be desired.

When was Pueblo Bonito built? How? Why?

Did people live there? How?

Did people worship there? Why?

What was the relationship between the great houses and the Chaco environment?

What relations did the Chaco world have with other people and places?

All these questions remained pertinent and unanswered. The Hyde Exploring Expedition was perfectly in keeping with the archaeology of the nineteenth century. It was collections oriented with less emphasis on data accumulation, analysis, and interpretation. In fairness to Wetherill and Pepper, the materials they collected and the records they made remain of use to archaeologists working to reanalyze and interpret Pueblo Bonito's material record. They also concluded that ancestors of the Pueblo Indians built the ruins of Chaco Canyon. No mystery race was needed to explain the presence of the ancient monuments. But the expedition showed no respect for Indigenous communities' concerns for these sites or the buried individuals. The whole affair was insular, isolated, and too aligned with profit to maintain scientific objectivity. Juan, Thomacito, and Welo were working right in front of the Pueblo Bonito team. Had they been treated as equal partners in the excavation, or their opinions given the same merit as Pepper's and Wetherill's, perhaps the buried individuals would have been treated with more respect. Likewise, had the trading posts not been attached to the archaeological expedition, the results of the survey might have been better received.

There is no evidence to suggest that Pepper, Wetherill, Putnam, or the Hydes ever intended to cause harm. They were fascinated by the past, and they loved Chaco Canyon. They wanted to understand the ancient world, and, in some respects, they lacked the technology to fully grasp the evidence they discovered. They had fit the mold of their time, but they were entering a new era with new expectations.

The *American Journal of Archaeology* recognized that the most important archaeological work had been accomplished by the Jesup North Pacific Expedition. Its datacentric anthropological approach to understanding the past was to influence future research in the United States. Many old questions still plagued American archaeology. Who first peopled the Americas? Did the Vikings ever reach the continent? Did Paleolithic peoples walk there?[44] American archaeology intended to improve its methods of exploring these questions.

Back in Chaco Canyon, the Wetherills kept trying to turn a profit. A letter from 1903 showed their salesmanship: "If you were pleased with the other ring you will have fits and spasms over this one if you think you have too many you might give one away or not just as you wish." The unknown Wetherill brother who wrote this letter had other news: "Richard writes that he has gone out of the trading business entirely. I don't know who he unloaded on." He added, "The H.E.E. [Hyde Exploring Expedition] will now sell the Farmington store to any one [*sic*] who will buy."[45]

It was an astonishing change of tactics for Richard and Mamie. But Richard wanted to focus on the livestock. This was not the only big change in Chaco Canyon. On September 11, 1903, William T. Shelton arrived in New Mexico to lead the nascent Shiprock Agency. Shelton, born in North Carolina, had worked for the Indian Service for a decade, specifically with the Cherokee and Havasupai. As the Shiprock Agency's head agent, he had a long to-do list: "bring peace to the northern borders of the Navajo Reservation, to be an advocate for his charges in settling disputes with neighboring Anglo and Indian elements, to limit habits — alcohol, gambling, polygamy, fighting, and some religious practices . . . and above all promote work ethic that would lead to economic development and prosperity."[46]

As he got to know the area, Shelton began to hear stories about the Diné's off-reservation neighbors, including the Wetherills. The Wetherill trading posts had been no stranger to disagreements with the Diné. In 1902, Win managed the Two Grey Hills trading post. A man named Charlie Bit-cil-li took a silver bridle and belt to Win to pawn. It was valued at $51. After paying off most of his pawn, he returned one day to give Win the final $11.25, but Win was not there. Someone told him that his stuff was with Richard at the Pueblo Bonito trading post, so he headed there. Richard didn't know what he was talking about, he said. But then in walked a Diné woman with Charlie Bit-cil-li's belt on. She said she gave Richard twelve sheep for it, but she felt bad about the situation and gave it back to Charlie Bit-cil-li. Richard later saw Charlie Bit-cil-li wearing his belt and took it back. Charlie Bit-cil-li reported

Figure 9. Unnamed Navajo worker, Orian Buck, George Pepper, and Richard Wetherill sifting through dirt for turquoise (American Museum of Natural History Library, 00411912).

Richard to the local agent. The agent wrote Richard a letter, but Richard ignored it.[47]

Also in 1902, Orian Buck tried to water a herd of goats at the Chico Trading Post, north of Pueblo Bonito. The watering hole Buck chose belonged to a Diné man who denied the goats water. Buck pulled out his gun and shot the man in the chest. Fortunately, the man lived. Buck paid 100 goats and avoided the courts.[48]

Shelton could not have liked what he heard about the Wetherills or their associates. But there was little he could do. His authority lay on the reservation. Richard was off reservation. And there he intended to stay. There was no Alamo Ranch to run home to. No new ruins to raid. Chaco Canyon was home; there was nowhere else to go.

THIRTEEN

All's Fair . . . St. Louis, 1904

Mamie was scared. It was eleven o'clock at night when she stepped off the train in St. Louis, Missouri. She "had never been in the city alone before." Her three children followed her, six-year-old Richard, four-year-old Elizabeth, and two-year-old Robert. Richard had gone ahead with Win for the World's Fair. They had put a year of preparations into their exhibit, overseen largely by Mamie. "We'd been around enough to know we needed to have a lot of small items for people to buy. The Navajo women made literally hundreds of those little pillow squares I originated and the little table runners. We also sold the larger rugs . . . baby carriers, bows and arrows . . . dozens of moccasins . . . rings and squash blossom necklaces, earrings, and bracelets."[1]

A lot of the goods had been acquired from Al Wetherill. Al and his wife, Mary, were running the Wetherill Navajo Indian Blanket Store in Denver. Al agreed to loan his savings to Richard and Win, and they took all the stock from the Denver store to St. Louis, leaving Al with a stack of promissory notes.[2]

Mamie's trip to St. Louis had been tumultuous. She had taken a longer route, stopping off to visit with family. Flooding, sudden storms, and rerouted trains delayed her arrival and exhausted her travel funds. She arrived in the strange city with three little children, no money, and no idea where to find Richard.

Though the family had high hopes for the fair, Mamie had not wanted to go. "I was never enthusiastic about going. I liked my home, and I had these children, and I'd had a baby that died and I felt badly over that.

Mr. Wetherill thought I should go so I finally worked myself up to it,"[3] she remembered. A sympathetic police officer helped Mamie find a hotel for the night, and she left the children there as she combed the fair for her husband the next day. On 1,240 acres in Missouri, the United States was orchestrating a display of the nation's prominence and progress for an audience of 62 nations and 43 states. Through the crowds, Mamie spotted rugs she recognized and approached the exhibit. "There wasn't one that was more beautifully arranged and colorful then [sic] ours," she reminisced proudly. Richard and Win had brought sixteen Diné to showcase. Mamie saw those familiar faces first and then she spotted her husband.

"My dear, where have you been?" Richard asked.

"Looking for you," Mamie answered.[4]

They settled into their usual routine, selling the Diné's goods. Mamie also claimed they were selling artifacts: "We had to have a lot of that ancient pottery to sell, so the Navajos dug those little shallow burial mounds and probably got a carload of that ancient pottery."[5] Little Richard remembered the Apache, Alaskan, and Pima baskets for sale. But he didn't get to spend that much time at the exhibit. "I remember my parents put us kids, when they didn't want us around, in this . . . playground* . . . and when a parade would come by I'd climb over the fence . . . The cops would pick me up and take me back down there and put me in the yard again,"[6] he recalled.

There were plenty of familiar faces to be seen, for better or worse. According to one uncited anecdote, George Pepper and his wife were taking in the sights of the fair when he ran into Richard and Mamie. Distance had not made the heart grow fonder. Going through the Pueblo Bonito collection, Pepper had found letters in which Richard disparaged him to the Hyde brothers.[7] Mamie maintained a low opinion of Pepper. "He was a queer little man," she declared. "The less I hear about him the better."[8]

Pepper remained at the AMNH and close to Putnam and the Hydes. Talbot had been at the fair before Pepper and notified him that George

* Richard was likely referring to the Children's Building, where parents could leave kids in the care of nurses for hours or a full day.

Dorsey was getting all the best artifacts for the Chicago museum.[9] In 1903, Putnam had left the AMNH to work for the University of California. Pepper wrote his former boss on June 28, 1904, to introduce a new acquaintance, Mr. George G. Heye.[10] Heye was also an heir of a wealthy New York family. After studying engineering at Columbia and Hamburg, he moved to Arizona to work on the railroad, encountering Indigenous peoples and their material culture for the first time. He returned to New York, did a stint on Wall Street, and when his wallet was full enough, he left the work world to pursue the life of an antiquarian.[11] Understanding the value of supporters with deep pockets, Pepper began helping Heye find acquisitions. Heye's first big buy was of pottery from New Mexico in 1903. In 1904, Heye sponsored the first season of "field collecting," paying Frank Utley to bring back artifacts from Puerto Rico. Pepper returned from Michoacan, Mexico, with pottery and burial goods for Heye's consumption.[12]

In their own ways, each of the major players of the Hyde Exploring Expedition had moved on from Pueblo Bonito, but not the past.

Just as in 1893, the St. Louis World Fair brought America's archaeological corps together. The loss of Powell remained apparent two years after his death, and leadership of the BAE had proved a contentious subject. WJ McGee had been heir apparent. As Powell had grown weaker with age, McGee took on additional responsibilities until he was practically running the BAE. With Powell's death, McGee expected to be named director. After Powell's passing, he wrote to the man who could make this happen—Samuel Langley, secretary of the Smithsonian, and coincidently the ex of McGee's wife, Dr. Anita Newcomb.

Langley did not think much of McGee professionally and perhaps there were personal hard feelings as well. Langley's preference for the directorship was McGee's partner in the Paleolithic wars, William Henry Holmes. Holmes refused the position out of respect for McGee. But Langley persisted.[13] Holmes finally accepted the post. He proved a humble choice, requesting a lower salary than Powell's and a change in title, preferring to be chief rather than director.[14]

McGee's response to Holmes's selection was less than gracious. He started a letter-writing campaign decrying the appointment. He complained to the press about the lack of transparency in the appointment process, and he publicly attacked Holmes as unfit for his new position.[15]

McGee did not fight alone. Franz Boas was in his corner. In 1905, Boas fell out with Jesup and the new leader of the Jesup North Pacific Expedition. He resigned without ever finishing his summary report. He moved on to Columbia University, establishing a legendary anthropology department where Margaret Mead, Zora Neale Hurston, A. L. Kroeber, and Edward Sapir studied. He had been in McGee's shoes a decade earlier when the Field Museum chose Holmes over him. In this bond of bitterness, Boas declared that "according to all the principles of good government, [McGee] should have been advanced to the position of director." He did not support the change in title, arguing that it made the Anthropological Division of the US National Museum and the BAE one and the same, rather than independent agencies. He wrote, "No severer blow could be dealt to the anthropological interests of the country than the subordination of the bureau to museum interests, and no means could be devised to hinder the development of the US National Museum more effectively, than its subordination under the bureau." He also took aim at Langley's decision-making process. "Personal inclination of the appointing officer has once more outweighed the principles of continuity and stability, which are indispensable for the welfare of scientific institutions."[16]

In the end, McGee's campaign failed. Holmes took charge of the BAE but asked McGee to stay on. McGee did not want to, but he soon had no choice. Financial concerns from the time of McGee's oversight emerged, and Secretary Langley launched an internal investigation. McGee was asked to stay in town. The investigative committee found evidence of inadequate fiscal management and suggestions of misappropriated funds. The day the committee concluded its work, McGee resigned. All charges against him were subsequently dropped. The scandal scarred his professional and personal lives, unofficially ending his marriage, too.[17]

Two years later, McGee, Holmes, and Boas all found themselves at the St. Louis World's Fair. They brought with them different visions for what anthropology and archaeology could and should be. McGee was the fair's anthropology director, but as head of the BAE, Holmes organized the collection of archaeological materials. The displays were charged with representing the "mythic symbolism of various tribes as embodied in their decorative arts."[18] His ethnologists and archaeologists set out to collect relevant materials. Jesse Fewkes brought back some of his finds from Puerto Rico. Ethnologist James Mooney collected shields and tipis embellished with what he termed heraldic symbols from the Kiowa and Cheyenne in Oklahoma. And Matilda Coxe Stevenson returned from New Mexico with Zuni baskets, textiles, and pottery.[19] States also sent artifacts. Tennessee sent a series of ceramic bowls and vessels crafted with intricate human and animal details. These objects had been recovered from graves by various individuals and acquired by the state's leading antiquarians.[20] In all several hundred objects went on display.

McGee needed the fair to be a success to restore his reputation. He organized an anthropological display like Putnam's Indigenous village in Chicago, with people from twenty-nine places. They came from Central Africa, Patagonia, and northern Japan. Roughly 200 of these people belonged to Indigenous tribes in the United States. They were there to give the audience a firsthand look at their "traditional" clothing, language, food, appearances, and general culture. McGee made sure they did so by restricting their interactions with the world outside of the fair and their access to modern goods.[21]

Some faced more restrictions than others. Geronimo, for one, was a prisoner of war. Mamie recalled seeing Geronimo standing all alone at the exhibit: "almost blind, the picture of misery." She introduced herself: "I put out my hand and he put out his hand and we shook. 'You don't remember me,' [she] said in Navajo." She explained to him that he had tried to take her from a camp when she was a little girl. She claimed that Geronimo responded, "You do know me. You are my friend from a very long time ago."[22] That was Mamie's story.

McGee organized the people by race to represent cultural progress as defined by Lewis Henry Morgan. Under McGee's leadership, Morgan's cultural evolution was also tested during the fair's Anthropology Days. McGee ran an Olympics of sorts that compared the athletic abilities of people he labeled savages, barbarians, and civilized.

Visitors could be forgiven for feeling a sense of déjà-vu. Criticisms abounded about how far American archaeology had or had not come. American archaeology had accumulated lots of stuff, but method and theory were stagnating.

At the fair, Boas and McGee gave speeches at the meeting of the International Congress of Arts and Science. In his speech on the history of anthropology, Boas emphasized four subfields. Other scholars had defined such subfields before him, but Boas typically receives credit for defining them as physical anthropology, ethnology, linguistics, and archaeology. As for archaeology, Boas characterized American archaeology up to 1904 thus: "Two great problems have occupied the attention of archaeologists, the origin and first appearance of the human race, and the historical sequence of races and of types of culture."[23]

For Boas, archaeologists did not go far enough in interpreting ancient cultures, and their work was built on an inherently flawed theoretical foundation. Boas believed the world's various peoples were far too diverse and complex to travel along a single continuum of evolution. Each community and society were unique with their own historical progression. If commonalities existed between cultures, he argued that cultural distinctions were diffused through various processes of interconnectivity, interaction, conquest, or exchange. His theoretical paradigm would be coined cultural or historical particularism. Accordingly, he also urged professionals to rid their interpretations of cultures of bias and understand traits and customs from the point of view of the culture itself. In short, Boas was demanding scientific impartiality in anthropology.

St. Louis was also the setting for an archaeological reckoning on preservation legislation. In the winter of 1903–1904, Reverend Baum succeeded in getting Representative William August Rodenberg to introduce his legislation. The Public Lands Committee and preservation community gave it largely favorable reviews. But Holmes, the BAE, and the Smithsonian objected to the provision of the bill that would place all antiquities under the authority of the secretary of the interior. They thought the Smithsonian was the rightful steward. They prepared an alternate bill to that effect, and it was also introduced in the Senate in February 1904.[24]

Baum's bill had more congressional support and advanced more quickly. It passed the Senate and was sent to the House the day before the congressional session adjourned. They were so close; Baum could taste it. The Smithsonian frantically sent lobbyists to Congress to prevent the passage of the bill. And once more, preservation legislation died. Congress adjourned without any new protections for the nation's cultural resources.[25]

Frustration penetrated every corner of the preservation community. The Archaeological Institute of America (AIA) met in St. Louis, too, in May 1904. The AIA created a committee—the Committee on the Preservation of the Remains of American Antiquity—that included Boas, Fletcher, Dorsey, McGee, Peabody, Putnam, and Holmes among other archaeologists and preservationists. The committee met again in St. Louis on September 22. They created a subcommittee to lobby Congress for the passage of preservation legislation. The AIA's president concluded, "Abundant encouragement is offered for our work, but as in every other undertaking, unremitting diligence is necessary if our proper end is to be attained."[26]

Not to be left out, the American Archaeological Association (AAA) also renewed its efforts. They appointed Hewett as a liaison of sorts to reenergize the push for a preservation law. The GLO had also commissioned Hewett to compile a report on archaeological sites in the Southwest that outlined what America stood to lose without preservation protections.[27] Under the auspices of the AAA, Hewett embarked on the unenviable task of consolidating the requirements of government agencies, the professional archaeological community, and passionate activists into one bill.

Hewett's job would have been Herculean in any era, but recent events within the CCDA added to his challenges. In 1904, McClurg and Peabody split over the future of Mesa Verde. After pushing for Mesa Verde's establishment as a national park for years, McClurg suddenly changed her mind. She began to advocate for a state park instead, run by the CCDA or more simply by McClurg herself. Her position was highly personal, and the battle became personal as well. Lucy Peabody maintained that the best method of protecting the ruins was through national park designation. The two were at an impasse that ultimately divided their organization. The feud also went public. McClurg was forced to deny that she had ever disparaged Peabody publicly, while maintaining that Peabody had vilified her in newspapers. Privately, Peabody certainly did not hold back. In notes kept by Hewett, she called her rival "Mrs. Flora McFlimse McStingee."[28] Their split proved irreparable.

During the 1904 congressional session, Representative Lacey once again introduced preservation legislation based on the input of Hewett, relevant government agencies, and the professional community. Congress mulled it over and America waited.

Mamie estimated they made a thousand dollars a day in St. Louis. But the Wetherills reported the fair as a bust. The family agreed to sell a collection of artifacts to a German museum and the Field Museum, but they never received the money. Win and Richard took a loss on Al's goods, forcing Al out of business. The family left St. Louis on the brink of bankruptcy.[29]

There was only one thing to do: return to Chaco Canyon.

They were fortunate to be able to do so. Not all the Indigenous actors in McGee's human exhibition left the fair alive. As curator of physical anthropology, Hrdlička made the most of this tragedy. He collected the skulls and brains of those native people who perished, conducted autopsies on others, and left the fair with over 200 new additions for the museum.[30]

Despite their financial despair, Richard continued to bring on new employees. Joe Schmedding was one. He remembered that Richard made "no fussy inquiries, no investigation of my record, no demand for pedigree." He just gave him a job and a list of things to get done.[31] Schmedding vividly recalled his first views of Chaco Canyon and Richard's office:

> From the nearly total darkness that reigned outside, I passed into a brilliantly lighted interior that had none of the features usually associated with an office. Instead, it appeared as if an Indian museum

had been combined with a collector's den. The room itself was rather large, rectangular in shape, and low-ceilinged. Heavy timbers, exposed overhead, supported the roof and ceiling. . . . The sturdy beams of cedar, pinon, and pine had been salvaged from excavations of the Pueblo Bonito ruins. . . . The walls of the office . . . were virtually hidden under a large assortment of specimens of Indian handicraft and the pelts of wild animals. There were priceless "Chief" blankets; fine old bayetas; marvelously woven antique Navajo rugs . . . squaw dresses; Hopi belts; Katchina dolls; dance masks; gourd rattles; mountain lion and fox pelts; Indian drums; water-color reproductions of Navajo sand paintings; turquoise-inlaid ornaments; ancient Pueblo pottery; Mexican ollas; silver-mounted headstalls; buck skin-braided lariats; medicine baskets; Hopi plaques, bows and arrows in fringed quivers; soft leather saddle bags beautifully decorated with beadwork, made by Ute Indians; and a great variety of other interesting things that dazzled and dazed the beholder.[32]

Whatever his bank balance said, Richard still had something left to hold onto.

Another "lean, sunbaked" man in his mid-twenties also came to Alamo Ranch looking for work. He wore a Stetson, chaps, boots, spurs, and a six-shooter slung low. Schmedding remembered how the stranger looked him over before introducing himself: "I'm Bill Finn." Schmedding pointed him toward Richard's office and Finn rode off to gain employment.[33]

Agent Shelton was still trying to improve the lives of the nearby Diné. By working with Navajo elders, he had begun to curb gambling as a pastime. He also tried to clamp down on the illegal whiskey industry, punishing offenders with days of hard labor. Other behavior proved more difficult to control. Rape of Diné women occurred chronically, but even in cases where the rapist was arrested, he often evaded justice because of racial politics. White taxpayers balked at paying to incarcerate non-White rapists. In February 1905, a young woman was riding home alone, when her uncle, reputed to be a serial rapist, rode up. He pulled her from her horse, tied her hands, and raped her. She survived, and the news led Shelton to lobby for the creation of an agency jail and a Diné police force. Both were approved and Shelton set about bringing a new era of justice to the Shiprock Agency and its surroundings.[34]

Chaco Canyon continued to witness other novelties. After the fair, Fred Hyde drove his new Buick toward the canyon. They made it to Albuquerque and then a little bit farther to Corrales before they broke down. Try as they might, they could not fix the car. They hitched a team of mules to it and pulled it the rest of the way.[35] But no one ever got it up and running again. Richard, Elizabeth, and Robert got a new toy for the place little Richard remembered fondly: "as unique a playground—as could be found."[36]

FOURTEEN

An Act for the Preservation of American Antiquities

In December 1905, the AIA and AAA held their annual meetings jointly. Hewett, the secretary of the AAA's preservation committee, updated the assembled professionals on the ongoing quest for preservation legislation. Congress had ended 1904 without ratifying any of the archaeology bills, and 1905 was poised to end much the same.[1] After listening to Hewett's newest version of the bill, the committees of the AIA and AAA unanimously endorsed it.[2]

Hewett then submitted the bill to Representative Lacey on January 9, 1906. Lacey had it introduced as House Resolution 11016.[3] The archaeological community held its breath as had become its annual tradition. Months passed and nothing happened.

In May, the Senate passed the bill by voice vote. Then on June 8, 1906, President Theodore Roosevelt signed the Antiquities Act into law. Years of combined efforts by scores of archaeologists, members of the public, government officials, and congressmen came to fruition in under 500 words. Congress gave the president the power "to declare by public proclamation historic landmarks, historic and prehistoric structures, and other objects of historic or scientific interest that are situated upon the lands owned or controlled by the Government of the United States to be national monuments." The act's first section established fines and imprisonment for taking or destroying artifacts without permission. The final section of the act required permits for excavations on federal lands and that these excavations be carried out by individuals who met professional standards.

While many contributed to the drafting and passage of the Antiquities Act, archaeology maintained a blind spot. Indigenous legal scholar Rebecca Tsosie notes, "Importantly, the Antiquities Act does not speak of tribal interests at all, nor does it give effect to tribal laws, customs, or beliefs as to the appropriate care of such sites. The act is thus completely unresponsive to tribal concerns and merely furthers the interests of professional archaeologists in having access to the sites unimpeded by amateur pot hunters and looters."[4] Archaeologist Joe Watkins elaborates,

> Beginning with the passage of the Antiquities Act in 1906, archaeologists (perhaps unintentionally) began to co-opt the American Indian's unwritten history and material culture. The United States government deemed archaeological and historical sites of past cultures in the United States as worthy of protection for the benefit of the public, but it ultimately developed a permit system that centered protection of the past within the scientific community rather than in the hands of those whose ancestors were responsible for its creation.[5]

President Roosevelt made quick use of his new powers, creating a total of eighteen national monuments. All were in the West, with New Mexico, Arizona, and California ceding the most territory to preservation and conservation. Some were well-known monuments, but archaeologists also brought new sites to the executive branch's attention. Archaeologist Byron Cummings's report on natural wonders in Utah led Roosevelt to create Natural Bridges National Monument.

Hewett's work was not complete. As he lobbied for the Antiquities Act, he also urged the creation of a national park at Mesa Verde.[6] The issue at Mesa Verde remained its location and the absence of a reliable map showing where each cliff dwelling lay in relation to the Ute Reservation. Twenty days after the Antiquities Act was signed into law, President Roosevelt signed the bill creating Mesa Verde National Park. Lucy Peabody and those women of the CCDA who had supported her played just as big a role as Hewett in preserving Mesa Verde. For her efforts, Peabody has been remembered as the "Mother of Mesa Verde."

It quickly emerged that there was a problem. Congress had set aside approximately 40,000 acres for the new national park, but almost none of the cliff dwellings of Mesa Verde lay within that acreage. Hewett went to survey the park and drafted a plan "by which all of the ruins could be included within the jurisdiction of the park without injustice to the Indians."[7] Once Hewett submitted his survey, Congress agreed to change the park boundaries. But it would take several years of negotiations between the US government and the Ute to establish the modern boundaries.[8]

In establishing Mesa Verde National Park, the US government withdrew 70,000 acres from the Ute Reservation. It offered them substitute lands, but they proved less ideal for grazing. This land withdrawal also split the reservation occupied by the Weeminuches, resulting in yet another geopolitical identity infringement that ultimately resulted in the creation of the Ute Mountain Ute Tribe.[9]

Not to be outdone, Virginia McClurg orchestrated her own legacy. McClurg oversaw the removal of a million pounds of precontact ruins from southern Colorado. Workers placed the remnants of the cliff dwelling on trains bound for Manitou Springs, where they were crafted into a replica cliff dwelling. The woman who railed against looting of ruins apparently saw no contradiction in these actions. A contemporary brochure for the site focuses on the site's authenticity: "Only the ignorant or malicious minded will tell you that a visit to these Ruins is not worthwhile because the prehistoric Cliff Dwellers did not build them here personally!"[10]

Virginia's stance is difficult to understand. She clearly felt passionately about the past and had great concerns about looting. Her passion morphed into some sort of obsession with control, rather than mere preservation. She once quoted a ballad that read, "And when I lie in the green kirk yard, With turf upon my breast, Say not that she did well or ill—Only—'She did her best.'"[11] But for those who pull off Highway 24 and into Manitou Cliff Dwellings, it is fair to ask who this faux ruin is best for. Archaeology? The public? Indigenous Americans? Or just Virginia McClurg?

A year after the Antiquities Act became law, Hewett led a field school in Colorado. In January 1907, he was also appointed director of American

Figure 10. Virginia McClurg and other members of Colorado Cliff Dwelling
Association put on a performance inside a cliff dwelling in Mesa Verde
(History Colorado, Denver, Colorado, 10046618).

archaeology under the Committee of American Archaeology. In his first
report to the committee, he complained about the rules federal agencies
were implementing to ensure compliance with the Antiquities Act. He
wrote, "Exceptions were taken to these rules on the ground that they
placed upon scientific research harmful and unnecessary restrictions."
The committee had subsequently worked with the War, Interior, and
Agriculture Departments to draft acceptable rules. Hewett was enthusiastic about ongoing research and the Southwest. He was particularly
pleased that Congress allotted funds for Jesse Walter Fewkes to lead
excavation and repair work at Mesa Verde. Hewett concluded:

> It will be obvious that the amount of research work possible to the
> Institute, through its numerous Societies, is large and will grow to
> greater proportions. It would seem that the most efficacious way of

handling this work and keeping it on a high lane of efficiency is that already inaugurated, namely through cooperation with American universities, thus bringing into the work a large number of students already trained in the methods of scientific research.[12]

It was time to end archaeology's amateur hour once and for all and concentrate efforts in the universities and professional societies.

On March 11, 1907, President Roosevelt created Chaco Canyon National Monument. The issue of Richard and Mamie's homestead remained unresolved. Richard reduced the size of the land and resubmitted his claim, but new issues always seemed to arise. In August 1907, their homestead claim was challenged because of coal discovered on the land.[13] That same month, Mamie welcomed a daughter, Marion, after previously suffering two stillbirths.[14] With their home still unofficial, Richard and Mamie remained in Chaco Canyon, relying on the stock, and raising four children.

In October 1907, stocks crashed. It was the first major panic of the twentieth century. Despite efforts to quell alarm, banks and New York trust companies experienced runs. After the suspension of one major trust, Knickerbocker's, runs on trusts spiraled out of control.[15] Richard had weathered bank panics before, but this was the big one. Joe Schmedding thought so, at least: "The Panic of 1907 inflicted losses from which he never recovered, financially speaking," he wrote of his boss.[16]

William Shelton had opened the doors of his new reservation school on February 8, 1907. One hundred and six students walked through the doors, and Shelton set his sights on enlarging the school and class sizes. Roosevelt issued an executive order in November 1907 that expanded the geographical range of Shelton's responsibilities. The Navajo Reservation now encompassed Chaco Canyon including all the ruins and the Wetherill homestead. Shelton was now within legal bounds to deal with the Wetherills.[17]

Shelton did not always trouble himself with strict adherence to legal boundaries. Discord rolled through the reservation when Shelton imprisoned two Navajo men in his new jail after a violent confrontation.

The Arizona Supreme Court ruled in 1908 that Shelton had unlawfully imprisoned them. Shelton quickly gained a reputation in Diné land for overbearing authoritarianism.[18]

Congress passed one additional piece of preservation legislation, officially incorporating the Archaeological Institute of America. It has been seen as a recognition of "the importance of citizen participation in archaeological programs."[19] It had taken decades of organization by private citizens, public awareness campaigns, surveys by professionals, the creation of seemingly hopeless and redundant committees, drafting and redrafting of proposed legislation, and lobbying of elected officials, but American archaeology had finally won some protections for the past. The process was messy, contentious, chaotic, frustratingly slow, and fractious. It was democratic through and through. Since 1906, presidents have established over 120 national monuments that stand as testaments to what the United States' imperfect democratic process can achieve.

FIFTEEN

The Race for
Rainbow Bridge

Life at Chaco Canyon tended to quiet down in the winter. Still, Richard and Mamie strove to make Christmas a festive occasion. There was a Christmas tree, and Mamie and two Diné maids spent days cooking cakes, plum pudding, cookies, bread, turkey, tomatoes, corn, sweet potatoes, mashed potatoes, cranberry sauce, mince pie, and pumpkin pie. Richard and Mamie generously distributed gifts to their children and employees. Mamie gave the Diné maids clothing and "inexpensive pieces of jewelry." Richard handed out presents to the cowboys. "There were spurs, hand-braided rawhide quirts, imported Mexican reatas with buckskin-bound Hondas, silk bandanna neckerchiefs, gauntlets, work gloves, warm woolen socks, and a number of other things calculated to gladden the heart of a cowpuncher." In return, the cowboys gave Mamie some dishes and Richard "a fine single-barreled shotgun, especially bored for long-range shooting."[1]

The world busied with the return of spring, though the children kept things raucous enough. Little Richard remembered how he, his siblings, and cousins spent their days running around outside, playing with the many animals around the homestead, and getting into mischief. He recalled that they would sneak into the store to get candy and cans of syrup. One day an Indigenous man caught them and took the candy. According to Richard, the children "sicked the dogs on him. There was this big snubbing post in the middle of the corral. This old Indian climbed up the post to get away from the dogs . . . we went to gathering wood and building a fire around him. We were gonna burn him at the stake . . . someone finally heard him and rescued the poor guy."[2]

Richard put his men back to work repairing fences and windmills, branding livestock, conducting roundups, and selling stock.[3] It took a considerable amount of work to keep the Wetherill homestead afloat. With the Wetherill finances ever-worsening, that work was all the more important. A court case in 1909 revealed the state of their fiscal affairs. Richard had borrowed $263.41 from a man named Harrison Hill in 1892, but never repaid him. After a long struggle in the courts, a judge ordered the sheriff to take $607.10 from Richard's bank account to settle the debt and pay damages. The bank informed the judge that Richard had insufficient funds to cover the fine: $515.38. The judge lowered the penalty to $505.38. Richard now had only ten dollars in the bank.[4]

These were desperate days. The trading post business had always involved extensions of credit and pawning, so Richard turned to collecting alleged debts to stabilize his own financial straits. A man named Ch'ii'is-chili accused Richard of threatening to murder him with a butcher knife over unpaid debts.[5] Richard sent cowboys like Joe Schmedding and Bill Finn on debt-collecting trips. Schmedding remembered, "The boys looked upon those collection trips with longing eyes. The tour was considered a sort of vacation; it would break the routine of ranch chores." Schmedding acknowledged, "Of course, we carried no authorization papers or power of attorney, but nobody ever questioned our right to act for the boss."[6] Perhaps no one questioned the debt collectors directly, but they certainly complained afterward.

When Richard sent his cowboys out to collect debts, he did not stipulate that they should notify the debtors of the collections made. Thus, Diné would find their property gone without explanation. Some felt the action amounted to stealing. A Navajo man named George was one of the offended. Richard claimed that George's wife was in debt to him. One day while George was away from home, Richard came by, took seven cows, and then sold them. George claimed his wife was not indebted to Richard, but neither of the men could prove their side of the story. George's wife had been dead for four years.[7]

According to Richard and his workers everything in Chaco Canyon was on the up-and-up. Schmedding declared:

Every trading transaction was a battle of wits, but none was allowed to have recourse to unfair means, to cheat, falsify weights, or in any other manner take advantage of the illiteracy of the Indian. Fair play was the rule of the game, and each deal had to leave a pleasant taste in the mouth of everybody concerned. The Indians were our hosts as lawful occupants of the reservation, they were our good neighbors.[8]

Nevertheless, credit and debt collection continued to spark tensions. Much as with George, Richard had ordered his men to round up some ponies of a man he said owed him money. His workers diligently returned with the ponies, branded them with the Wetherill mark, and sold them. The owner of the ponies arrived at the Wetherill homestead with a posse of family and friends. According to Schmedding, they were all armed and the man's tone evolved into a "menacing denunciation." Richard adjourned the meeting without resolving the situation. The next morning the man and his supporters returned to Richard's elaborately decorated office. Over the course of an hour, Richard's cowboys slowly entered the office alone or in groups of two or three, arranging themselves strategically. With his own men assembled and heavily armed, Richard told the aggrieved that what was done was done. Surrounded by heavily armed men, the offended owner came "to see the affair in a different light."[9]

Richard was proving difficult for federal agents to manage, too. He continued to graze his stock where he pleased and showed a hypocritical intolerance toward those who did the same. Ch'iii'ischili reported that Richard was known to kill livestock that strayed onto his land. Ch'iii'ischili alleged that Richard would slice the dead animals open and pour poison inside their carcasses to kill scavenging coyotes.[10] Years later, little Richard remembered poisoning animals as one of his chores. He caught mice in the trading post and recalled, "Everything that I did as a little kid, if I did work I was paid for it . . . so much for mice, so much for chipmunks, so much for rats. By the time I was eight years old they gave me strychnine. I'd poison coyotes, bobcats and foxes and skin them out. For the coyotes in those days they paid a bounty of $2.00, so my dad would pay me and the bounty he'd take off his county taxes."[11]

Poisoning was not always easy money, though. Little Richard remembered one particularly challenging incident. He had been quoted $8.00 an ounce for skunk musk. He killed and poisoned a bunch of skunks but could not figure out how to bottle the musk. His parents were out, so he "got the frying pan, cut all those musk bags up, put them in the frying pan and put it on the stove." When Richard and Mamie returned, they were furious at their stinking home. Little Richard got a "licking," a "scrubbing," and they made him bury his clothes. Mamie was usually the children's disciplinarian and she "didn't spare the buggy whip." Little Richard preferred his father handle the lickings—"he was lenient." But Mamie, he remembered, "Oh, God, she was terrible." Still when Richard caught his son smoking, he made the boy smoke a whole cigar until he was sick. Richard thought of his father fondly: "Father was good to us, but he didn't have too much time."[12]

Through the tension and financial uncertainty, the Wetherills maintained a sense of community in Chaco Canyon and found ways to entertain themselves. There was a constant marksmanship contest. Richard, Win, Fred Hyde, and Bill Finn were particularly good shots. And they held dances. Mamie remembered that one of the Hyde brothers was a good dancer and she "loved dancing with Finn." Richard abstained from dancing for religious reasons. Mamie remembered her husband would "come and stand with his hands up on the door on each side of the casing where we were dancing and say, 'I've missed a lot, I see.'"[13]

Despite all their troubles and the challenges of life in Chaco Canyon, Mamie felt, "life was good enough."[14]

John and Louisa Wetherill were living a similar, but different life. In 1906, they moved to a remote corner of Utah, where they opened Oljato Trading Post. Diné brought "wool and goatskins and blankets to sell, bringing silver and turquoise to pawn." In turn, John and Louisa sold "leathers, velveteens, calicoes, sugar and coffee."[15] But as Louisa saw it, there was none of the conflict of Pueblo Bonito at Oljato. Instead, "to the trading post . . . came friends."[16]

While Louisa managed the day-to-day business, John often traveled for work. He continued to explore the archaeology of Tsegi Canyon.[17] He also guided scientific enterprises around the Southwest. In 1909, an old customer sought John as guide for a new expedition.[18]

Professor Byron Cummings was a New Yorker, who earned an MA from Rutgers. He first arrived in Utah in 1893 to teach Greek and Latin at the University of Utah. In 1905, he was selected as dean of the College of Arts and Sciences.[19] But his entry to archaeology came later, and he only began his first excavation in 1906.[20]

In August 1909, John led Cummings and his students to a handful of ruins that appeared not to have been excavated before.[21] John also took the party to explore Tsegi Canyon, where so many Wetherill parties had stopped off, collected pottery, and left their names.[22] Leaving Cummings to excavate, John headed to Bluff. He would come back to Tsegi later and continue guiding the Cummings party. But in Bluff, he learned that Cummings's work was being contested by William B. Douglass.

Douglass hailed from Indiana, where he had worked as a lawyer before transferring to the GLO as US inspector of surveys.[23] Douglass was there to explore Natural Bridges National Monument. Cummings's survey of the area had been the premise for the creation of the park. Douglass had conducted the resurvey of the monument and was less than pleased to hear that Cummings was returning, too.

Under the Antiquities Act, Cummings needed a permit to excavate in a national monument. He had one—sort of. Hewett had gotten a permit to excavate in Natural Bridges National Monument and given Cummings permission to use it. Cummings's name did not appear on the permit, so technically he was in violation of the law. Douglass planned to press that technicality. Through the GLO, Douglass decided to halt Cummings's work and take possession of anything removed from the monument. John failed to dissuade Douglass and headed back to Tsegi Canyon to give Cummings a heads-up.[24]

John and Cummings shared interest in another bridge. Many talked about it, but no White people had ever seen Rainbow Bridge. If they could find Rainbow Bridge, John and Cummings might be able to spur the creation of the next national monument. Although keen to stop Cummings, Douglass also wanted to find Rainbow Bridge. A Paiute man named Mike's Boy had told him about the ruin. He decided to launch a rival expedition just as John and Cummings were about to set out to find the bridge. The only problem for either party was that neither knew where they were going. John felt it imperative to hire a native guide. He had met Nasja Begay, who claimed to know the way to Rainbow Bridge.

Having grown up the middle child among his ambitious and stubborn brothers, "John Wetherill's job had always been that of peacemaker."[25] He saw little to be gained from these competing expeditions. He planned for both parties to meet at Oljato Trading Post, come to an understanding, and proceed on the hunt for Rainbow Bridge together. Louisa summarized John's position: "We can explain what we are doing; we can show that our work is scientific and under proper direction. Then, since we are both hunting the bridge, we can hunt together."[26] Cummings's group arrived at Oljato as planned and then they waited. They waited and waited and then suddenly Douglass appeared with his team.[27]

The rival parties combined, with Douglass's informant Mike's Boy leading the way. The group made their way slowly toward Navajo Mountain. Too slowly, it would seem. John had been counting on Nasja Begay to find Rainbow Bridge, but when the party arrived at his home, he was gone. Nasja Begay's father told John what he knew of the way to Rainbow Bridge, and the party carried on accordingly. But the terrain and conditions were rough and after only two days, the expedition was suffering. To ease the burden on their horses and mules, they started dumping gear.[28]

There was another issue. Mike's Boy did not know where Rainbow Bridge was. Like many, he knew of Rainbow Bridge, but the expedition was on an uncertain path without Nasja Begay. Conditions and morale plummeted as they faltered along under the desert's summer heat with no shade for even a second of relief. The rival groups found something they could agree on three days in: the trip was a disaster. They gathered around the fire for a dinner of boiled rice, canned corn, Dutch-oven biscuits, and tea, where the idea of giving up and going home circulated as a not ideal, but reasonable conclusion to the ill-fated trip.[29] As they despaired, they suddenly heard a horse moving toward them in the dark. In the glow of the campfire, Nasja Begay emerged. The camp was elated to see him, even more so when he told them they would be at Rainbow Bridge by lunchtime tomorrow, if they kept going. All assembled went to bed with hope that they would be making a discovery of some renown in mere hours.[30]

On Saturday, August 14, 1909, Douglass awoke feeling like a child on Christmas day.[31] Nasja Begay led the way and as promised around eleven o'clock in the morning, Rainbow Bridge came into view. Cummings and John were on their feet carefully leading their horses up an incline. Douglass remained mounted and hellbent on being the first White man to reach Rainbow Bridge. He quickened his pace. John, perhaps out of loyalty, urged Cummings to beat Douglass to the bridge. "I don't want to be rude," Cummings said. John jumped onto his own horse. "Then I'll be rude," he said, and charged after Douglass. John easily passed the less experienced rider and "stood alone beneath the great span of rock."[32]

They found Rainbow Bridge, but celebrations were short-lived. They were all so tired, hot, and hungry that victory tasted pretty unsatisfying.[33] Their return journey was equally challenging. Having shed so much of their supplies to make it to Rainbow Bridge, they ran out of food on the way back. On the night Douglass finished his survey, his team also finished their provisions. Every man received a biscuit and a few beans.[34]

Just after John rushed under the arch of Rainbow Bridge, a Paiute warned him "against bringing tourist parties to Bridge country, threatening him with death if he returned." But John knew a good opportunity when he saw one. He ignored the threat and started leading tour groups to Rainbow Bridge just like the ones he had led to Mesa Verde for so many years.[35]

Though their own relations with local Indigenous peoples remained largely peaceful and hospitable, John and Louisa certainly heard of others' troubles. In November 1909, a Diné man named Zhon-ne robbed the Four Corners Trading Post on the Navajo Reservation. He waited for the trader Charles Fritz to walk outside and then opened fire, killing Fritz. The next day, William Shelton had Zhon-ne in custody, confessing to the murder.[36] Fritz was one of more than twenty traders murdered by Navajo between 1901 and 1934.[37]

Although John and Louisa sometimes found life lonely and difficult at Oljato, they had no plans to change. They seemed to enjoy the "struggle for life in a hard land."[38] Cornering a remote landscape could have its benefits. John knew the land well. In 1910, John was selected as the administrator of Rainbow Bridge National Monument. His official designation meant that his stewardship of the past was no longer a mere hobby or pastime. By bringing this knowledgeable individual into the fold, archaeology gained an expert and converted him to their cause, rather than excluding a passionate protector of the past.

Life remained busy for John and Louisa. John often found himself racing across the desert as he juggled archaeological investigations, the trading post, scientific expeditions, and preservation of national monuments. So that he could be found racing east in the summer of 1910 was no real surprise. Except for the fact that everything had just changed.

He was back in Tsegi excavating with Dr. Prudden when a messenger burst into the canyon.[39]

Richard Wetherill was dead.

SIXTEEN

"On the Borderland of Hell"

Young Richard wasn't supposed to be there. He had been told not to look. But curiosity and the magnitude of the situation pulled him to the back porch. There was his father. "He was just swelled up and busted. . . . Half his head was shot away, his brains were all over and the worms got in his head. . . . Kept swelling up and swelling up and blood all over," Richard remembered.[1]

He kept returning to the man who had always been so hard to catch. Of his father Richard remembered, "He didn't have much time, too many other irons in the fire, always had something going." Now with no time left at all, father and son could finally be together. Thirteen-year-old Richard periodically pulled back the shroud atop his father's corpse to "look at him and try to get the worms and flies off of him."[2]

On paper it all started and ended June 22, 1910. But the seeds of that bloody day were planted years before, though all involved would dispute who sowed and who reaped for years to come. Chis-chiling Begay, a Diné man in his early thirties, more or less saw the start of the troubles. Begay was married with five biological children and one adopted daughter, all under the age of sixteen. He lived in the Chaco Canyon area with his family. He was working in a cornfield on June 22, when trouble kicked off at the hogan of his brother-in-law, Antonio Padilla.[3]

There was a horse at Padilla's hogan. The Diné consensus was that a Navajo man had either sold the horse to Richard or was planning to, and somehow the horse was not where or how it should have been. Details are fuzzy. Richard sent Bill Finn and another worker to get the horse from Padilla's home, but when they arrived, something about the horse's condition set Finn off. Finn attacked Padilla in the doorway of his home. Finn landed a punch and then took out his pistol and struck Padilla again. Padilla collapsed in a pool of blood. Finn rode off. Begay either saw the assault occur from the cornfield or responded to his sister's cries for help. Either way, he found himself trying to wake Padilla. Sadly, he concluded that his brother-in-law was dead.[4]

Begay rode to Tsaya, entered the trading post, and reported Finn for the murder. He bought ammunition from George Blake, the store owner, and then headed back to Pueblo Bonito to avenge his brother-in-law. When Begay arrived, Finn was not there. He hid his gun, joined a group of Diné gambling, and waited. In the meantime, George Blake rode out to Padilla's hogan. He found the man under a shade tree. Blake poured cold water over Padilla, and the dead man awoke. He was severely wounded, and Blake sent for medical help.[5]

As he gambled, Begay seems to have shared his story. Certainly, the other men would have been outraged at Finn's treatment of Padilla. And many probably understood Begay's desire for vengeance. Nonetheless, they urged Begay not to kill Finn. After hours of waiting, Begay's temper cooled, and he consented. However, he does not seem to have received the news that Padilla was in fact alive.

Welo was one of the men there that day. He had known Richard for a long time, having loaned him that stove when he first moved to Chaco Canyon. He was no stranger to Richard's mercurial nature and was probably not all that surprised to hear of Finn's behavior. Around six o'clock that evening, Finn rode into view with Richard by his side. Richard spotted Welo's horse and a rifle stored astride the animal. Here accounts differ. Welo either removed the gun from the horse and Richard grabbed it from him, or Richard took the gun from the horse himself. What happened next is more certain. Richard disposed of the ammunition in the rifle and then slammed the rifle against a nearby fencepost, breaking the weapon. Richard, the Quaker who never swore, then unleashed a torrent of verbal abuse on Begay and threatened to fight him.

Begay must have been confused. His quarrel was not with Richard, but Finn. It is worth questioning what Richard knew of the day's events at this point. What had Finn told him of the confrontation at Padilla's hogan? Was Finn the aggressor or the victim in that account? Did he claim self-defense? Whatever Finn told Richard, it had placed a target on Begay's back.

Begay asked Richard if he was going to kill him.

Richard reportedly responded: "I want to get your head."

Coming from the man who had spent years removing human skulls from the great houses of Chaco Canyon, Richard's statement struck Begay as a desire to add his skull to his shelves of relics. His earlier rage resurfaced; he promised Richard: "I'll get yours first."[6]

Richard and Finn rode away, dismissing the feelings and concerns of their Indigenous neighbors and the rightful inhabitants of the federal acreage as they always had. Begay refused to be ignored. He rode back to the place where he had hidden his gun and headed out to find Richard again.

Begay found Richard and Finn on the road to Pueblo Bonito. They saw him, too. According to Begay, Richard and Finn charged their horses towards him, yelling curses and threats over the pounding of the hoofs. Begay sat in his saddle until Richard and Finn were within twenty-five yards of him, then he jumped off and raised his gun. He fired six shots at Richard, who fell from his horse and hit the hard desert floor. He fired two more at Finn but missed. Finn took off.[7]

Richard lived. Begay stood over him and asked if he still planned to kill him. Then he fired one last shot straight into Richard's head.[8] The fifty-two-year-old father of five died on the land of his obsession.

Confusion gripped Chaco Canyon. Many heard the shots ring out, but only Richard, Begay, and Finn knew what was happening. Finn sped toward the house at Pueblo Bonito. Seeing the fleeing man, some local Diné assumed that Finn had harmed someone else. They tried to apprehend him, and Finn opened fire. According to one account, one of his bullets hit a man named Hastiin Tsoh Bik'is. Finn kept moving until he reached the Wetherill homestead.[9]

Fear set in. Begay knew he had committed a crime. He headed to a trading post near his home and asked the trader to help him compose a confession. So, Begay narrated his version of events. But not everyone remembered June 22, 1910, the same way.

Mamie arrived home at the end of June 1910 from a hospital in Albuquerque with a newborn daughter, Ruth. She was still recovering and settling back into Pueblo Bonito on the 22nd. According to Mamie, there was no previous or pending sale of a horse. Rather, a man named Hosteen Nez Begay had stolen a three-year-old colt from the family.[10] It was Elizabeth's horse, and Begay had beaten it, wrote Eleanor Quick, the Wetherill children's teacher.[11] Finn went to retrieve the horse, and Begay emerged from his hogan. Finn sat in his own saddle and asked about the wounded animal. Begay claimed to know nothing and pulled on the bridle of Finn's horse. The animal reared back, Finn drew out his gun, and hit Begay with it. The man collapsed, and Finn rode back to the Wetherill homestead.[12]

Richard was in the family's sitting room with Sheriff Talle, who was leasing the Wetherills' north pasture. Mamie felt he was the real cause of discontent in the canyon. Many Diné had complained about Talle bringing large groups of cattle to graze on their limited lands. Richard blew them off. He needed the money; the Navajo could graze elsewhere. Mamie remembered Talle leaving his pistol in her sitting room that day.[13]

Later, Richard was working in his office. Mamie placed herself there, too, when Finn came in. Finn told of the morning's events. Either then or later, Finn reportedly said: "I oughtn't a done that but he made me so damned mad when he took hold of the horse I just saw red. . . . I guess maybe I hit him harder than I ought to have but there was no blood so I guess he wasn't seriously hurt."[14]

Richard did not seem to blame Finn. They set out to round up some cattle, and Richard told Mamie they might be a little late for dinner. Mamie's account also has Begay buying ammunition from George Blake at Tsaya, but she maintains it had nothing to do with Finn's assault. In her view, Begay wanted to stop Talle's cattle from grazing in Chaco Canyon.[15]

In Mamie's telling, Richard and Finn stumbled across Welo, who was allegedly angry about Talle's cattle, too. Richard took his gun and broke it—for Welo's own good, Mamie claimed. Richard told him, "You come up to the store when I get back and I'll give you a new twenty-two. You're a good neighbor and you need a better gun than this to kill rabbits. I'll throw in a box of cartridges."[16] Richard, who had been on a merciless debt-collecting spree, was suddenly all generosity and calm.

Mamie put Ruth to bed and started making a roast, she recalled. Begay and the other Diné, all allegedly angered by Talle's livestock, hid in the brush in the arroyo. Richard and Finn rode into the trap. Begay jumped out and fired his gun. The first bullet tore through Richard's right hand and kept going, striking him in the heart. Mamie was checking on Ruth when she heard shots. She looked outside and saw clouds of dust and horses flying, but she couldn't make sense of what was going on. Suddenly a man charged toward the house, leaning over one side of the horse. It was Bill Finn, who screamed, "Where are your children?"

"I don't know," Mamie replied.

"Get them in the house," Finn yelled as he rode off for more weapons.[17]

Eleanor Quick also heard gunshots. She stood in the doorway of the Wetherill house and watched Finn emerge from the chaos. Quick saw Mamie at the door waiting for Finn with a box of ammunition, having deduced that he was out.[18] Mamie rushed out to the children's play area armed with Talle's gun. It is at this point in her story that Mamie accused a man named Joe Hosteen Yazzi of jumping out from the blacksmith shop and trying to shoot her. She shot back. She remembered, "I shot to kill him."[19]

When little Richard got home that day, he found his mother, Finn, and Miss Quick inside and armed. Richard got a gun himself and began to get his own version of events. According to Richard, after Begay fired the shot into his father's heart, the Diné performed "some kind of dance around the body," and then a second man, Pesh-la-ki, fired the bullet into Richard's head. In this version, the murder was a carefully laid-out ambush by a group of people, rather than the action of one man.[20]

Richard remembered putting blankets on the windows to impair anyone's attempts to shoot in. He recalled Navajo stalking the house: "We expected them to make a charge anytime . . . expected they were gonna kill the whole family," he said years later.[21] By then, Finn had told Mamie that her husband was dead. Mamie says that she demanded to collect his body and that everyone told her it was too dangerous.[22] At dusk, Miss Quick rallied a few Mexican laborers to help her recover Richard's corpse. Dr. Prudden praised her for acting as "the main stay of the household in the troubled hours which followed."[23]

Despite the family's worst fears, no attack by the Diné ever occurred. As the dust settled, blame swirled, and divergent accounts multiplied. Mamie seemed to recede into despair. She later confessed, "I was confused mentally. I couldn't sleep." She believed she saw Richard in the days after his death and that he spoke to her: "He stood there right in that doorway with his hands up. . . . 'I'm sorry to leave you with all these children and when you know how things are you'll know why I'm feeling so sorry. I won't see you anymore,'" she heard him say.[24]

In her grief, Mamie saw only one explanation: "The Indian agents, both white men, killed him. They wanted control of Chaco Canyon." When the police arrived, she repeated her accusations. The police were caught off guard. After all, Begay confessed almost immediately. There were witnesses. The police asked to see Richard's body, and when they failed to remove their hats while observing him, Mamie blew up. "'Look, you scum of the earth,' [she] said. 'Get out of my house and off my premises and don't let me catch you here. I'll shoot you if I ever see you again.' . . . I could have killed him right there on the porch where Mr. Wetherill was. I've always regretted that I didn't, such a cur as that. That's the kind of man that the government sent out to train the Indians to be white people."[25]

Days later, they laid Richard to rest in a small plot between Pueblo Bonito and Chetro Ketl, where Richard's Uncle Clayt and several Wetherill babies had been buried. They buried Richard with his family between the ancient ruins. Al, John, and Dr. Prudden arrived and struggled to make sense of what had happened. Al started a poem as he so often did, but he could never finish it. He wrote that they had buried Richard "on the borderland of hell."[26]

Richard's murder made the news nationwide, and the press tried to sort out what happened, too. Many accounts seemed to hold Richard responsible. A report from Utah explained that the Diné accused Richard "of stealing and branding their cattle," leading to an altercation that escalated to murder.[27] In Texas, a paper reported: "It is said Wetherill had trouble with the Indians because of their assertions that he had taken advantage of them in trading."[28] The *Albuquerque Morning Journal* was more sympathetic to Richard but summarized, "It is said that there had been bad blood between Wetherill and a bunch of Indians for some time past, and that a shortage of water owing to the drought resulted in a dispute which ended in a killing."[29]

Less than a month after the murder, Mamie committed to her theory that agents had conspired to kill her husband. One of her letters appeared in several papers:

Dear Friend: By this time you have heard the terrible news. It was beyond all doubt an organized attack, and judging from past events, at least, indirectly instigated by others. All that I need of ask of my friends is that they assist me to see that justice is done, as I know it will not be if they do not help me. I have employed Attorney Jones. . . . I will write you all the particulars as soon as I am able.[30]

Samuel Stacher was on vacation on June 22, 1910, and rushed back to Pueblo Bonito. He was superintendent of the Eastern Navajo Extension, the portion of the Navajo Reservation that now encompassed Chaco Canyon. This was now his mess, and he was one of those Mamie blamed.

It seems fair to say that Stacher was not that sad to see Richard go. He had spent most of 1910 documenting Richard's transgressions and trying to find ways to get rid of him, with the equally exasperated Agent Shelton. At the beginning of the year, when Richard had been suggested as a census enumerator on the reservation. Shelton immediately made his opposition clear: "Mr. Wetherill's presence on this Reservation in any capacity would be very undesirable. His conduct and business dealings with the Indians in the past have been such that I respectfully request that you do not send him onto this part of the reservation." Shelton pressed the point: "You could not select a more undesirable person to be on the reservation for this purpose than Mr. Wetherill."[31]

Stacher's and Shelton's opinion only hardened. In March, Stacher wrote, "It will give me the greatest satisfaction for me to see him in the pen where he richly deserves to be."[32] Shelton and Stacher both suspected that Richard lay at the root of another issue on the reservation—the illegal whiskey racket. They could not directly tie Richard to bootlegging, but they had caught those affiliated with him. Still, they suspected the teetotal Quaker, who had scared his drunken laborers into submission, of running an illegal liquor enterprise. Stacher commented, "In all my experience I have never come in contact with a trader whose influence has retarded the progress of Indians as much as this Wetherill."[33]

Bill Finn had been on Stacher's radar as well. In April 1910, Finn allegedly stole a stallion from a man named Hostine-tin-de-goos-be-nulla. Finn castrated and branded the horse. Stacher had several such reports on Finn. He wrote, "I am endeavoring to work up a couple of cases against him and hope to land him and some others where they belong."[34]

Where Richard Wetherill and his cowboys did not belong was Chaco Canyon. Of that Stacher, Shelton, and their associates were sure. One employee of the agency wrote to the commissioner of Indian Affairs to get Richard fired from his job as postmaster. "Undoubtedly the Post Office Department would not wish to have a man of this character as an employee in this responsible position if they knew the true character of the man."[35]

There was some personal drama between Stacher and the Wetherills as well. The Wetherills had rented a home outside of Pueblo del Arroyo to the Stacher family when they first moved in. Eleanor Quick boarded with the Stachers, teaching both the Wetherill and Stacher children. But after two weeks, according to an affidavit, Quick moved into the Wetherills' home at Pueblo Bonito.[36]

She swore she had wanted to move there for some time. She complained that Stacher asked "impudent questions" about Richard Wetherill's business. He "began to insinuate that [Richard] . . . had stolen for years the Indians' horses, cattle and sheep." He even mentioned an incident when little Richard had stolen a calf.[37] As Mamie saw it, the biggest problem with Stacher's accusations was that Miss Quick repeated them at the Wetherills' dining room table. Mamie remembered Miss Quick airing Stacher's comments on a school he wanted to build for the Diné in Chaco Canyon. Richard wanted no such school. "He didn't want the Navajos coming in there with their sheep and horses running all over the ruins stirring up dust." But Stacher insisted Chaco Canyon was the best place for a school. Miss Quick relayed his insults to Richard. Mamie was not pleased. "Miss Quick came back to our table and told us what Stacher said and made her own little additions. She was good at that. I disliked her." Mamie later disparaged Miss Quick, saying, "But I'll say this in a whisper, her company came through the window."[38]

It would seem Chaco Canyon was not without scandal in 1910. Miss Quick testified that in February or March, "there was a very scandalous happening" at the Stachers' rented home.[39] Richard asked Stacher to move out in 1910, but the reasons why are not clear.

Thus, as Stacher set about dealing with the murder of Richard Wetherill, there truly was no love lost. Stacher sent a letter to the commissioner of Indian Affairs, outlining the version of events he had been told, which was broadly similar to the others, though many of the details varied. Stacher reported that the coroner's jury had charged Begay with the murder of Richard Wetherill and deemed four other men conspirators: Thomacito, Thomas Padilla, Billy Williams, and Pesh-la-hi. Bill Finn was arrested and faced two counts: "assault and battery . . . assault with intent to kill." Neither Stacher nor Shelton stood in the way of these men being indicted or arrested, and it was clear where Stacher's sympathies lay:

> While we deeply deplore the fact that such a crime has been committed on the reservation, we firmly believe that had Mr. Wetherill and Mr. Finn treated the Indians justly and with consideration this killing never would have happened. Your Office has been acquainted with the character and conduct of both Richard Wetherill and Will Finn in a number of letters from this agency and in reports of several inspectors. We further believe that Will Finn's assault upon Hosteen Nezbega was the immediate occasion of this trouble.[40]

As the trials progressed, the enmity between Mamie and the agents only worsened. Finn's case was resolved first. He pleaded guilty to simple assault and paid a fine. No body, no crime.

Mamie and her family hired lawyers. Mamie said the cost was twenty-five hundred dollars. "I had to sell everything I could get my hands on to pay them," she recalled, while also claiming ignorance about the family's finances. "Mr. Wetherill never told me about our financial condition, never said anything to me about it all." In the days after his death, Mamie quickly learned that they were broke. She said Fred Hyde wrote that Richard had taken out a life insurance policy for twenty thousand dollars. Mamie followed up with the company, but she found out that Richard had borrowed from the policy, and it too was empty. Al gave her a twenty-dollar gold piece. But Mamie relied on selling anything she could get her hands on.[41]

In turn this created a new set of problems. Stacher was sure Mamie was selling Navajo livestock. When he intervened, Mamie got an injunction preventing Stacher from interfering with "Mrs. Marietta Wetherill in the discharge of her duties as administratrix of deceased husband's estate." It must have looked bad from the court's end to prevent a White widow and mother of five from collecting anything she deemed necessary to feed her brood. But Stacher and Shelton worried about how these attorneys and the anger Mamie was stirring might impact the Diné headed to trial. Shelton wrote in July, "I am sorry to trouble you, but if some one does not get up evidence to protect the Indians, a number are going to be unjustly punished." Shelton argued that all he wanted was "to secure for [the Diné] a fair and impartial trial."[42]

This was no small feat in an era when Indigenous Americans were not considered American citizens and therefore were barred from juries. There was no legal way for Begay to be judged by a jury of his peers. It was a foregone conclusion that twelve White men and one White judge would decide his fate. Begay needed all the help he could get.

So did Mamie. One of her strongest supporters was Dr. Prudden. He launched a writing campaign against the agents, accusing them of "public slander and vilification."[43] Prudden wrote to the commissioner of Indian Affairs: "The unbridled talk of Stacher has been such that the Navajos could not help believing that he Stacher, would be pleased if Wetherill were removed."[44] Casting Richard as the Thomas Becket to Stacher's Henry II, Prudden went on to reveal his deeper biases in later writings. He slandered the Diné: "The Navajo is still at heart a barbarian. . . . He is an inveterate gossip, and dearly loves a scrap when other actors than himself are concerned. He is at heart a coward. . . . The Navajo is a natural thief and a born liar."[45]

Prudden's attack on the Diné departed from the family line. Prudden felt the whole affair had been grossly unfair to Richard. He claimed that Richard was "unarmed; he never carried a gun, never felt that it could be necessary for him to do so."[46] This claim differs with reports of Richard receiving a gun for Christmas, entering marksmanship contests, and the basic requirements of life in the Southwest. Prudden went on to claim that even if Richard got a bit rough sometimes, it was necessary. "Within bounds, and dealing with crafty and illusive barbarians . . . the letter of the law must be subservient to its spirit."[47] Prudden's comments are indicative of his commitment to clearing his friend's name and of the way many wanted to see the world.

Mamie proclaimed that she could not fathom a world in which any Diné would want to hurt Richard. Mamie and Richard worked closely with the Diné and spoke Navajo, but they never saw their neighbors or customers as their equals. They referred to them as children and took a paternalistic attitude toward them. Mamie and Richard knew what was best for the Navajo and they acted in their "best" interests with or without their consent. From this perspective, Mamie's attitude toward the Diné and her certainty that Stacher and Shelton orchestrated everything make more sense. Mamie later summarized: "I've had people question my sanity for loving the Navajo after what they done. I can't condemn them all for one accident of wrath. I never blamed the Navajo for what happened to my family."[48] Mamie could not blame the Diné because to her they were not real people with desires and egos of their own. Stacher and Shelton were greedy, ambitious, evil men in her view. Begay was just a wayward child. How could she blame him?

Little Richard made the same argument. His father "always had good relations with the Navajo." So, he "never did feel anything against the Navajos." He concluded that Begay "was a little mentally off and got talked into it. He wasn't too smart."[49] There was just no way Begay could have been furious enough about the violence of the day to want vengeance.

The jury not of his peers found Begay guilty of manslaughter and he was sentenced to 5–10 years. He had already served two years in prison at the Shiprock Agency by the time of his conviction. Begay was released, because of an illness, after serving three additional years. Combined with the time served, Begay had fulfilled the minimum sentence. However, those who believed Mamie's claims saw this as a very convenient ending. They claimed Begay showed no signs of illness and continued to believe in a conspiracy.

Richard Wetherill lived a life many would have envied. Roaming across the Southwest, he clambered through places of antiquity that most would be lucky to see in pictures. His fascination with the past resulted in the collection of massive amounts of materials and records, even if his methods and profits left much to be desired. He was a faithful Quaker who strictly abstained from vice. Money troubles plagued him throughout his days, exacerbated by his ambition and penchant for overextension. He was not a man of his time, but a man of a false promise, the promise that the West would provide opportunity and wealth for those who would come and work hard. Richard worked hard all his life, but it was never enough. The economy, the environment, and his own ego constantly thwarted his efforts at domestic and fiscal stability. As the challenges of his life compiled, his desperation grew. His treatment of the Navajo always drifted along a spectrum of paternalism and exploitation. Undeniably, he behaved cruelly and predatorily toward the Indigenous people whose land he wanted. Even so, neither he nor his family deserved his violent end.

Mamie soon learned that the sword of suspicion cuts both ways. Many believed there to be something romantic between her and Bill Finn. Despite igniting the spark that ultimately killed her husband, Finn stayed close to Mamie afterward. Eventually, Mamie decided to move the children out of Pueblo Bonito. Finn went with them. "We got established at the house. House chores and children were below Mr. Finn," Mamie said. But Mamie denied any impropriety: "I was fond of him … but not in that way," she maintained. A year after Richard's death, Mamie had settled into this new life, when baby Ruth died. "I thought I couldn't take it, it was just too much. But I did."[50]

Not everyone felt Mamie was entitled to much sympathy. A new conspiracy emerged that charged Finn and Mamie with designing the entire plot to get rid of Richard. Clayt had reportedly warned Mamie to guard her reputation in the days after Richard's death: "You are in trouble now. Your husband has been killed and everybody will torture you all they can. You'll be gossiped about. They'll accuse you of things. Do you know that you're a very attractive woman?"[51]

Speculation mounted when it was alleged that Bill Finn was Joe Moody, a criminal on the run from Texas.[52] But Mamie maintained that there was nothing to any of the rumors of an affair and that she had known about his real identity all along, as had Richard. Finn continued living with her until his death in 1918. Two years later, the census recorded that Elizabeth and Marion were living with a thirty-eight-year-old boarder, Peter Ward, and their thirty-seven-year-old mother, Marietta Finn.[53]

SEVENTEEN

Where the Red Rocks Run Under

In the summer of 1914, the Wetherills' two latest clients pulled up to the Kayenta Trading Post in the northeastern corner of the Navajo Reservation. Samuel Guernsey was the older of the two at forty-six. Born in Maine, he grew up fascinated by artifacts he found near his home. He moved to Boston to work as an artist, where he met Frederic Ward Putnam. Putnam hired Guernsey to make models for the Peabody Museum.[1] While Guernsey's path to archaeology followed that of many of nineteenth-century archaeologists, his companion's trajectory represented the shift toward academic archaeology.

Alfred Vincent Kidder was twenty-eight that summer. Though born in Michigan, he had been raised in Boston and considered himself a Boston man. He earned an AB degree and then excavated under Egyptologist George A. Reisner. Reisner's classes in archaeological field methods proved critical to Kidder's professional development. He then earned a master's and PhD in anthropology from Harvard in 1914.[2]

Guernsey and Kidder were in northeastern Arizona to explore "the immensely fertile archaeological field." They credited Byron Cummings for bringing the area to professional attention. And as representatives of the Peabody Museum, they had asked his permission before starting their journey west. Cummings gave his blessing. In keeping with archaeological tradition, their study was funded by wealthy East Coasters including Mary Hemenway's son, Augustus.[3]

Guernsey and Kidder arrived at Kayenta Trading Post via Shiprock, New Mexico, and established their headquarters there. John and Louisa

Wetherill welcomed them, and Guernsey and Kidder soon came to see Kayenta as a refreshing "little oasis of civilization."[4] Clayt Wetherill served as their guide into the ruins of northeastern Arizona. Guernsey and Kidder found Clayt to be "cheerful and intelligent" and relied on his expertise. A student from Farmington, New Mexico, Charles Amsden, joined the party, and they headed into the field in June.[5]

Clayt led them north to Monument Valley. They rode through a flat desert interspersed by cedar and piñon and spots of oak and cacti. The land was dry and "barren," and they saw no "permanent springs or streams." They did notice Navajo families herding their sheep and goats and cultivating their patches of corn. It was clear that they were not headed toward a Mesa Verde or Pueblo Bonito. They were in a land more akin to the Grand Gulch, where they would likely find small one- or two-roomed structures in the mouths of alcoves.[6] But neither Guernsey nor Kidder seemed fazed by the smaller scale.

The first site they explored was a cliff house in an alcove. They estimated that the house had once contained six or eight rooms, but it was mostly stone rubble and timbers by 1914. They noted dark stains on the walls and attributed them to smoke from fires long extinguished. On the surface, they found wooden digging sticks, bone awls, and a small corrugated jar. Other rooms contained corncobs, charcoal, and additional signs of life. They found a kiva and, looking west of it, they spotted a drawing on the alcove wall that appeared to be a mountain sheep. Following the wall, they found more drawings of "men on horseback hunting deer." Approximately twenty feet in front of this scene, they encountered a mound covered in potsherds and broken stone tools. They excavated this cliff house, mapped it, made plan drawings with north arrows, scale bars, and clear labels, and then they were ready to move on.[7]

They moved about two miles west to a place the Diné called Sayodneechee. Louisa Wetherill translated Sayodneechee as "Where the red rocks run under."[8]

One of the party spotted the next ruin, but it took the party some time to figure a way inside the alcove. They tied two poles together and pushed to the edge of the alcove opening. Guernsey, Kidder, and Amsden steadied the poles by pulling tight the ropes attached to their ends. Clayt made the first attempt. He scaled the makeshift entrance with "much daring and great skill" and then installed hand ropes for the others to follow. As they entered the alcove, Guernsey and Kidder were certain that they were "without question, the first people to enter this cave since its final desertion by the occupants."[9] Inside, they found a cliff dwelling and a small number of objects, including a red jar filled with squash seeds and corn kernels, greyware ollas, and black and white jars with stone lids. They diligently made their maps, plan drawings, and notes and moved on.

Back below the second ruin, they found a mound with pottery like that of the cliff dwellings, but not much else. Just a hundred yards away, they found their next site, a one-room cliff house. Along with smoke stains on the roof, they interpreted the bones on the surface as evidence that people had lived at this cliff dwelling and not used it for storage or ritual purposes. They packed up their gear once more and followed the cliff deeper into the canyon. They had not gone far when they looked up and saw serpents, mountain sheep, and handprints in white paint adorning the cliff.[10]

They made their way across from the second ruin, looking for a good place to take a panoramic picture. That was when they found the circular "watchtower" on a butte. Guernsey and Kidder posited that it was probably a "lookout place or a shrine." They continued past the watchtower and spotted a narrow alcove. They didn't see any cliff dwellings or evidence of domestic life, but the alcove roof was stained black from smoke. Then someone found a burnt human jaw, so they decided to excavate.[11]

Conditions were unpleasant. The first three to four inches of the alcove proved to be "closely compacted" sheep dung. Once they peeled away the excrement, they found a layer of soft, red sand that was 12–18 inches thick. Critically, Guernsey and Kidder recorded and reported the earth in stratum. They were excavating and interpreting based on the law of superposition. The law of superposition is a geological principle that holds that the lowest layer of the earth formed before the upper layers of the earth. The lower strata should thus represent an older period than an upper stratum, or the surface of the earth. By excavating by stratum and recording finds by stratum, Guernsey and Kidder were practicing a very different type of archaeology than that of the past. It was a much more scientific and informative way of digging.

There was some charcoal, organic material, corncobs, and animal bones mixed in with the red sand, but nothing else. Next, they encountered a layer of red hardpan. They found this very difficult to shovel through. But they kept digging until they came to "jar-shaped cavities." They labeled the first cavity Cist A. Inside the three-foot deep cist, they found a "rotted textile fabric" covering the body of a woman wearing a string of stone beads. Below her, they found the bodies of three other adults and three children. Many of these people had been buried with stone beads or shell pendants. But Guernsey and Kidder found few other burial goods, except for remnants of baskets.

They found Cist B behind Cist A. Inside lay the bodies of approximately nineteen people. Guernsey and Kidder noted that they had been laid inside carefully and theorized that some sort of epidemic could have plagued these people. They again recorded stone, shell, and bone beads and "traces of baskets" with the individuals interred.[12] Cist C contained the bodies of four people buried with Olivella-shell beads and one or more baskets. Cist D contained the bodies of two children, who had also been laid to rest covered in baskets.[13] They excavated the entire alcove to the layer of hardpan but found no additional cists or bodies.

As they took stock, Guernsey and Kidder were aware that their findings might be of considerable significance. The skulls they removed from the cists were not flattened as was typical of bodies removed from cliff dwellings. And then there were the baskets. It was unusual to find people interred with baskets on top of their bodies in cliff dwellings. But there had been one other discovery of such burials in 1893 in the Grand Gulch. The discovery of the Basket Makers by the Hyde Exploring Expedition had not been taken seriously in the subsequent two decades. As Guernsey and Kidder noted: "The claims, put forward by the commercial collectors who discovered and named the culture . . . had been received by archaeologists with more or less incredulity."[14] Their discoveries brought the question of the existence of the Basket Makers back to life, but they were scientific professionals and proceeded with caution.

Misfortune struck mid-season when water failed in Monument Valley. The team returned to Kayenta, where they ran into Cummings. He suggested they try the Marsh Pass region for the rest of the season. They did so. They found no additional suggestions that they were in the land of the Basket Makers that summer. They found instead artifacts and dwellings consistent with the Cliff Dwellers. The land continued to present challenges, though. They came upon an alcove with an entrance blocked with stones and lintels. They removed the stones and entered to find an array of Diné objects, "whose contents were not examined as it was thought best to leave the cache untouched rather than risk incurring the ill-will of the Navajo, with whom the party were on very good terms."[15] Exploring adjacent rooms, they came upon a wall covered in white handprints and then etched in charcoal: "Richard Wetherill and _ Billings, 1895."[16]

The names on the wall represented the enduring legacy of archaeology's past. But archaeology was moving away from the collection obsession embodied by the Hyde Exploring Expedition. Guernsey and Kidder were confident enough to conclude that the cists in the alcove in Sayodneechee represented those of a people distinct from that of the Cliff Dwellers and that they shared similarities with the people Talbot Hyde named the Basket Makers. But Kidder and Guernsey couched their findings in caution: "It of course goes without saying that we need more data before we can attempt to draw any certain conclusions as to the affinities of the Basket Maker culture."[17] Taking no risks, they added: "It should be remembered, however, that our knowledge of the Basket Maker culture is still far more scanty than our knowledge of the Cliff-dweller. Further field work may prove that some of the stated differences do not exist; it will also probably add others not now recognized."[18]

Guernsey would be back for another season of fieldwork to try to get to the bottom of the Basket Maker question. Their work brought professional attention back to the Basket Makers and led to much needed professional discourse. For some, their work also represented a revolution in archaeological method. In excavating, recording, and interpreting stratigraphically, they recovered artifacts at specific geological levels. If artifacts from a specific period, such as a specific pattern of pottery, were identified in one of these levels, they could begin to piece together the chronologies of the different cultures they studied. Alas, the first excavation did not offer this opportunity. They were "unable to find any such case of direct superposition." Nonetheless, they could apply these methods at another site, perhaps with better luck.

Who deserves credit for introducing stratigraphic excavation to American archaeology is a subject of historical debate. Some other candidates include Mexican archaeologist Manuel Gamio and Danish archaeologist Nels Nelson.[19] William Dall has also been credited with the first stratigraphic excavation in the United States.[20] Richard Wetherill has been given credit by some generous observers. A review of Richard's work shows that he understood the importance of documenting differences in levels of the earth, and he did interpret the cultural material in the Grand Gulch stratigraphically. However, he did not excavate or record stratigraphically. His work was concentrated on what they could find, not what they could find out.

Uncertainty about where to place credit for the first stratigraphic excavation persists. *Firsts* bring prestige and make for a fine line in an obituary. But *firsts* mean nothing without seconds, thirds, and so on. While it's unfortunate that the first archaeologist to excavate stratigraphically lost their claim to fame in the shuffle of time, what really matters is that Kidder, Guernsey, Gamio, Nelson, and Dall *all* excavated stratigraphically, and today it is standard archaeological practice.

Other changes were afoot in the Southwest. Andrew Ellicott (A. E.) Douglass was an astronomer, not an archaeologist. But as Guernsey and Kidder worked in Monument Valley and Marsh Pass, Douglass was kicking off what would be a fifteen-year effort to develop a method to date archaeological specimens with tree rings. The timbers Douglass used to analyze and cross-date tree rings came from Aztec Ruins, Pueblo Bonito, and Tsegi Canyon, among other southwestern ruins. The beams from Tsegi Canyon came from Cummings officially, but it is suspected that John Wetherill did the collecting.[21] While archaeology was moving toward the day where they could *relatively* date artifacts based on stratigraphy and artifact typologies, Douglass's work was leading toward a day when they could *absolutely* date artifacts to a calendar date.

Throughout the Southwest, archaeologists began implementing

seriation or ordering data into time sequences. A. L. Kroeber collected potsherds from the ground and began to see patterns. He found black-on-red sherds at sites where Zuni lived in the seventeenth century, but black-on white sherds or white sherds at sites without a seventeenth-century occupation. From this relationship, Kroeber deduced that he could date sites with black-on-red sherds to the seventeenth century or later and sites with black-on-white or white sherds to before the seventeenth century. Others refined seriation, incorporating statistics and accounting for sampling, and the technique began to be applied to other types of artifacts. Means of relative dating sites continued to expand.[22]

Circumstances beyond American archaeologists' control would disrupt this progress. World War I demanded that even archaeologists of certain ages and fitness enlist and head to Europe. Kidder ended up in France. George Dorsey enlisted in the Navy and found himself in Spain and Portugal. The Peabody Museum gave one floor to the military to use as a radio school and another to the Army Training Corps for a classroom. Finding his homeland to be public enemy number one must have been difficult for German immigrant Franz Boas. He remained a staunch supporter of Germany even though his own sons were deployed as American soldiers. In 1919, he accused at least four American archaeologists of using their profession as a cover for spying. Fueled by patriotism and righteous indignation, Boas wrote: "A person, however, who uses science as a cover for political spying, who demeans himself to pose before a foreign government as an investigator . . . prostitutes sciences in an unpardonable way and forfeits the right to be classed as a scientist." America's anthropological and archaeological corps responded with outrage at his potential endangerment of professionals many thought of as patriots and heroes.[23]

At the American Anthropological Association, Neil Judd introduced a resolution to censure Boas. Jesse Fewkes, Talbot Hyde, Judd, Kidder, and Guernsey among others all voted to censor Boas. Nels Nelson, Charles Peabody, and others voted against censorship. The final tally was 20 to 10. Boas was censured and lost his National Research Council membership.[24]

John Wetherill knew what it felt like to be silenced in the world of science. He wrote to Talbot, frustrated with continued doubts about the existence of the Basket Makers. He found Kidder's misgivings particularly annoying. "Kidder questions the existence of the basket people, because he knows nothing about it or that he is jealous of Sam Gurnsey's [*sic*] finds." He urged Talbot to "hang on" to all the materials they had collected from the Southwest because "the University of Utah and Dr. Edgar L. Hewitt, are going to claim all the discoveries and work done here." He dismissed criticisms and the struggles of archaeologists to duplicate the work of the Hyde Exploring Expedition. Defending his brother, he wrote, "He did his work so thorough, that in the ruins where he worked there is very little of value left, except the ruins."[25]

To some extent, that was precisely the problem. Today, minimally intensive excavations are preferred, as they allow archaeologists to gather sufficient data but leave enough intact data for future archaeologists to confirm previous findings and/or reassess sites with new technologies and methodologies. The Hyde Exploring Expedition's legacy was the ruins that remained, and the artifacts lying on museum shelves and tucked away in museum storage. Throughout all their years of digging, no one in the expedition had published a report on their findings. Pepper published a few short, informative articles, and there were the initial articles on the discovery of the Basket Makers in the Grand Gulch. Some of the records compiled by Richard, Mamie, and Pepper would eventually be recovered and prove useful to archaeologists. But there was no room-by-room report with maps, drawings, and pictures. As time passed, the expedition's legacy faded into oblivion.

Time was of the essence. Frederic Ward Putnam died on August 14, 1915. One colleague wrote, "He left behind him friends, but not an enemy; he harmed no man and helped innumerable; he placed anthropology in America upon its present foundation; he fulfilled all his capacities; and he leaves a rare memory, not only as a scientist but as a man."[26]

EIGHTEEN

Back to the Gulch, Again

"Procrastination"

Haven't done a thing today but fool my time away.
Don't know a single thought to write, nor anything to say.
My head, it sure gets hazy. I guess it needs a boss.
Nothing doing in its empty rooms; its rent a total loss.
Some other day, with brighter skies and sunlight shining 'round
Some high-brow stuff will come to me and then I'll write it down.[1]

It is unclear what inspired Al Wetherill's procrastination blues. Perhaps they resonated with George Pepper as he contemplated the unfinished business of the Hyde Exploring Expedition. The expedition had talked a big game when it came to reporting, but the sudden and dramatic collapse of the enterprise seems to have derailed any report on their years-long excavation of Pueblo Bonito.

Pepper pointed to another reason. He had held on to "the hope that further work could be taken up at the ruin and that a more exhaustive study of the cultural problem of the Chaco could be prosecuted."[2] Nearly two decades after the Hyde Exploring Expedition (HEE), Pepper had yet to find his way back to Chaco Canyon. He had moved on. In 1909, Pepper left the AMNH for the University Museum at Philadelphia.[3] He took "98 barrels and boxes" from the HEE collection and another collection with him.[4] Pepper took the artifact catalogs and parts of the expedition collection, not all. In an era without photocopying, he seems to have found it too time consuming to duplicate the catalog for the AMNH. In fairness, there were thousands of artifacts to document. But without the catalog, the AMNH had a hard time identifying their half of the collection. The curator of the AMNH wrote to Pepper asking for help. They had found the remains of several individuals. The individuals had numbers written on them, but no one knew what they meant. Without context, the HEE collection was quickly becoming scientifically meaningless.[5]

Pepper's time in Pennsylvania was short. In 1910, he was offered a position at a new museum, and he accepted.[6] This museum was founded by George Gustav Heye, the wealthy New York scion Pepper introduced to Putnam in 1904. One archaeologist described Heye's hold on the professional community: "We were all of us, I think drawn towards Heye by the prospect of a new dream museum; hard work demanded, technical skill expected, publication under a great editor . . . assured, financial care for life promised—in days when there were no pension systems for anthropologists."[7] On Wednesday, November 8, 1916, the cornerstone of the "dream museum" was laid at Broadway and 155th Street. By then, Heye had amassed some 400,000 objects and individuals for his Museum of the American Indian, Heye Foundation. As Pepper saw it, with the opening of the museum, Heye "forged his links of hope into a strong chain of reality . . . and open[ed] up a broad field wherein all who are interested in the American Indian can work."[8]

Philadelphia's HEE collection likewise ended up at the Museum of the American Indian.[9] Pepper and Heye had visited numerous museums and studied their cataloging methods before establishing their museum's protocols. And they took care to safeguard the records: "Catalog entries were made on two sets of cards, the individual sets being kept in different buildings, thereby insuring the data against loss by fire."[10] Though standards were improving, much of archaeology remained beholden to the personal attitudes of powerful individuals. Curation standards under Heye seem to have left room for improvement. Archaeologist Samuel Lothrop reported that "no field catalog numbers were entered in the Museum catalog and a great deal of information has thus been lost." Then there was Heye's unwillingness to admit ignorance. Lothrop noted, "Nothing is entered in the catalog as 'provenience unknown.'" He went on to describe a situation where Heye questioned him and a colleague on the provenience of a collection. Neither knew where the artifacts came from. Lothrop explained, "One of us guessed Guatemala, the other Venezuela. I do not remember which Heye chose, but a guess was recorded as fact." Heye also apparently lacked interest in pottery fragments: "Heye had no interest in potsherds.... When the Museum storage was moved to the Bronx, over 70 barrels of sherds were thrown away. Some of these sherds came from stratigraphic cuts which had not been published."[11] Universal curation standards remained a dream for another day. In the meantime, collections suffered.

In New York, Nels Nelson was trying to make sense of it all. Nelson was born in Denmark in 1875 to a poor farming family. He was only seventeen in 1892, the year before the Chicago World's Fair, when an uncle and aunt wrote the family asking for help on their Minnesota farm. Nelson had spent much of his youth bound out to other farms and rarely able to attend school. The chance to see the "New World" was too much to pass up. So, he sailed across the Atlantic to help his aunt and uncle. At age twenty-six, he completed high school, moving on to Stanford the same year. He worked under a paleontologist named John C. Merriam, who used stratigraphic excavation techniques, methods Nelson would use in his own archaeological excavations in the Southwest. As a mature student from a lower economic background, Nelson maintained a job at a bank throughout his undergraduate and graduate studies. In 1912, the AMNH offered him a job and he accepted. He has been described as "quiet and reserved, but with a dry sense of humor . . . universally liked and respected. His curious, inquiring mind was ever eager for new information on almost any subject."[12]

One subject Nelson desperately sought new information on was the provenience of the artifacts and individuals from the Grand Gulch that lay in storage at the AMNH. The museum had materials collected by both McLoyd and C. C. Graham and the Wetherills, but Nelson was missing catalog records and field notes for the Wetherill materials. He knew the general location of their discovery but not more specific information such as the precise alcove the materials came from. That loss of information severely limited his ability to interpret the materials.

Nelson struggled to piece together the recent past, while juggling his other responsibilities. In 1920, Mrs. L. P. Cartier of New York offered Nelson money to launch an expedition in the Southwest. He accepted and used the expedition as an opportunity to see the Grand Gulch for the first time. John Wetherill acted as Nelson's guide, and they identified around one hundred archaeological sites. Despite Nelson's legacy as one of the founders of stratigraphic excavation in archaeology, he did very little excavation in the Grand Gulch. He focused on taking notes and making sketch maps of sites like Turkey Pen Ruin.[13]

Continuing tradition, Nelson made extensive field notes but never published a report on his time in the Grand Gulch. But in 1920, George Pepper finally published his account of the work in Pueblo Bonito. At nearly four hundred pages, Pepper's report describes each room of Pueblo Bonito in exhaustive detail. He enumerated the artifacts observed and collected in each room and drew comparisons to the practices of contemporaneous Indigenous peoples. The report remains a priceless and robust source of information.

The riddle of the Grand Gulch collection may appear to be the product of particular personalities and insufficient records management. To some extent it was. But the Grand Gulch collection was not the only collection with confusing provenience information. Some collections were sold to multiple buyers before ending up in museums with partial, incomplete, complete, or nonexistent catalogs. Other collections followed their discoverer from storage room to storage room. As collections moved around the country, some items became separated from the larger collection. Records got lost. The reasoning behind numbering systems and cataloging strategies became muddled with time. And those who could explain the rhyme or reason died. It was early days, but as museum storage filled with these chaotically cataloged collections, the stage was already set for the ongoing Curation Crisis.

Katherine Sebastian Dring of the Eastern Pequot Tribal Nation offers one perspective on the importance of cultural materials: "These ancient artefacts are rooted in Native American life free from false and contrived interpretations of tribal existence from opponents and the uneducated. These artefacts predate colonialism, oppressive Native

American government policies, inequities of federal recognition decisions and regulations, racism, capitalism, and economic greed."[14] In collecting the nonrenewable evidence of the past, archaeologists took responsibility for preserving the past in perpetuity on behalf of all stakeholders.

In 2018, US federal agencies reported holdings of over 46 million artifacts.[15] That is the count for artifacts under federal auspices only, and some estimates put the number higher. With so much material it should hardly be surprising that storage space is a regular issue across the country. For federal entities, 36 CFR 79—*Curation of Federally-Owned and Administered Archaeological Collections*—outlines curatorial standards. This regulation stipulates that curation facilities meet applicable safety codes, that a fire suppression system is in place, and a pest management plan exists. It also calls for regular inspections of collections and for the manager of the curation facility to meet professional standards, among many other requirements. Nonetheless, many federal agencies continue to store artifacts, ecofacts,* individuals, and documents in facilities that do not meet these standards.

Sometimes this is because of funding. Curation facilities charge intake fees and annual maintenance fees. Other times, agencies may struggle with finding an appropriate repository near them. Many existing repositories fall short of federal requirements, lacking space or staff to properly curate artifacts. The United States Army Corps of Engineers' (USACE) Mandatory Center of Expertise (MCX) for Curation and Management of Archaeological Collections (CMAC) was created to address this issue. Their team works with federal agencies to determine the state of a collection and its needs, and then finds an appropriate curation facility. Part of this workforce hails from the Veterans Curation Program (VCP). The program teaches transferable, marketable skills to military veterans entering the civilian job arena; they help tackle the curation backlog and save deteriorating artifacts.

The USACE's MCX-CMAC mission is a massive undertaking. A 2000 analysis found that 75 percent of federal holdings were stored in

---

* Ecofacts are organic materials unmodified by humans, but common to archaeological sites. Examples include naturally occurring seeds, shells, or stone.

substandard conditions, hastening disintegration of artifacts and records. Saving the collections would require an approximate $20 million investment.[16] Again, this would be just to fix the federal collections, not to save all the other deteriorating collections held by state agencies, universities, or local museums.

Saving collections has become a necessary, though underfunded and under-resourced, priority for archaeologists across the country. Some endangered collections are called orphaned or legacy collections. Commonly these collections have been stored in acidic bags or boxes in substandard buildings. They have often been subjected to water damage and are inadequately labeled. Disintegrating boxes, bags, and objects are common. These issues are not just aesthetic; this deterioration robs artifacts of their information potential and the ability of advanced techniques to properly interrogate valuable evidence. Restoring collections to federal and professional curation standards is a cost- and time-intensive process, as Nels Nelson learned. Unfortunately, most modern archaeologists lack the sponsorship of a prestigious jewelry family; thus, artifacts and individuals rot away every day, taking the secrets of the past with them.

NINETEEN

New Deal,
New Archaeology

Nels Nelson sent word to America's archaeologists that Wetherill and Pepper had exhausted Pueblo Bonito and that the old walls were beginning to wobble.[1] In short, Pueblo Bonito might not stand forever. Nevertheless, frozen in their desert isolation, the mysteries of the great houses continued to pull archaeologists into Chaco Canyon. Neil M. Judd had been one of the student members of the expedition to Rainbow Bridge. From 1921 to 1927, he excavated Pueblo Bonito and Pueblo del Arroyo for the National Geographic Society. Despite the years of hasty, intensive digging, Judd recovered a lot, and his work in Chaco Canyon has been called "the most productive that Chaco archaeology has seen."[2]

Judd's excavations were complemented by Alfred V. Kidder's work at Pecos, where he finally found middens with the stratigraphic layers he had hoped to find with Guernsey in Arizona. At Pecos, Kidder identified several cultural phases lying atop one another. The earliest of these layers were the Basketmakers, whom he further subdivided into three cultural stages. Then came the Pueblo stages. Kidder hosted a meeting where archaeologists compared their findings from other sites and then developed standardized terminology. Rather than the prerogative of the finder or the financial backer, the words used to describe ancient cultures were going to have meaning derived from comparative datasets. However, the agreed-upon terminology retained a bit of the past. The new classifications were Basket Maker I, II, and III, and Pueblo I, II, III,

IV, and V. Archaeologists also began developing uniform pottery typologies and classifications using insights from stratigraphy and seriation.
"The potsherd, by its very nature, became a kind of tab, a statistical unit
highly adapted for counting and manipulation."[3]

Douglass's tree ring studies brought chronological clarity to the
cultural sequences Judd, Kidder, and Nelson were seeing in the earth.[4]
In time, these data would also shed light on how climate impacted life
in Chaco Canyon. Climate was cyclical with long droughts followed
by periods of greater rainfall. In the tenth century, Chaco Canyon
experienced above-average rainfall, coinciding with the great houses'
peak. A severe drought stifled the region from 1130 to 1180, the same
period during which Chaco Canyon was abandoned.[5] Douglass and his
archaeological accomplices had proven that the timber beams of Pueblo
Bonito had value beyond recycled construction materials.

Archaeologists' entire concept of time in America was shifting. In
1908, while surveying flood damage in Folsom, New Mexico, ranch
foreman George McJunkin found fossilized bones. McJunkin was born
enslaved in Texas. After the Civil War, he moved west and worked in the
cattle industry. He tried to get someone interested in the fossils because
he felt they were very old. However, the Colorado Museum of Natural
History did not identify the bones as those of an extinct bison species
until 1926. Subsequent excavations in Folsom recovered spearpoints
at least eight and a half feet below the earth's surface, which became
known as Folsom points and date to around 10,000 or 11,000 years ago.
Archaeologists would later discover an older tool called a Clovis point
that dates to around 12,000 or 13,000 years ago.* Acceptance of these
new dates emerged slowly. Holmes and Hrdlička maintained a strangle-
hold on the antiquity of humans in America. Having successfully dismissed Paleolithic humans through Holmes's rejects and Hrdlička's
skeletal analysis, they maintained that humans had been in America a
relatively short time and refused to give alternative evidence fair consideration.[6] Nonetheless, the Folsom and Clovis points gradually caused

---

* Archaeologists have discovered lithics that appear to predate Clovis points, continuing
to push back the earliest arrival of humans in the United States.

archaeologists to accept a revised chronology that pushed back human arrival in America by several thousand years. Sadly, George McJunkin passed away in 1922 before his finds changed America's chronology.[7]

Archaeology was improving its informative capacity, but not fast enough. Judd gave a speech as the outgoing president of the Anthropological Society of Washington in 1928, saying as much: "Lacking Federal recognition as of national concern, archaeology in the United States has been, and still is being, exploited by selfish or misinformed persons; it is being fettered by local emotions and further handicapped by obsolete conceptions as to the fundamental purpose of original field investigations."[8] He did feel that with stratigraphically based chronology, archaeology "may be said to approach maturity."[9] However, he noted that despite the passage of the Antiquities Act, looting continued and the long-pushed-for law was being poorly enforced. More than ever, pothunters and those who commercialized the past were the archaeologist's enemy. Judd admonished: "Neither strength to wield a shovel nor success in amassing specimens makes an archaeologist. . . . A ruin mutilated by pothunters retains but an incomplete story for the trained observer."[10]

America's archaeologists were harnessing science and data to understand more about the past than ever before, but they were still fighting the same battle against the looter. Legislation on its own had not been sufficient. More was needed to protect the past: more public support, more professionalism, more money. In 1929, the stock market crashed, and the American economy crumbled. Money for archaeology did not seem to be on its way.

By the time Franklin D. Roosevelt took office in 1933, eighteen million people were unemployed. Roosevelt harnessed the federal government to pull the nation from the depths of the Depression. Construction put people back to work, and New Deal programs were established to facilitate construction and restoration workforces including the Federal Emergency Relief Administration (FERA), the Civil Works Administration (CWA), the Civilian Conservation Corps (CCC), and the Works Progress Administration (WPA). The Tennessee Valley Authority Act was also enacted in 1933 allowing for widespread dam construction in the South.

Cumulatively, these work programs helped revive the nation's economy and morale. They also led to widespread disturbance of lands that had previously lain dormant. For archaeologists, spikes in construction efforts are always concerning. Construction raises the probability that archaeological sites will be damaged or destroyed. Pothunters and development were already destroying many historic sites throughout the country. Preservationists had been asking for greater protections, and with John D. Rockefeller Jr.'s financial support they had successfully lobbied for a new law. In 1935 President Roosevelt signed the Historic American Sites Act into law.[11]

The Historic American Sites Act states "that it is a national policy to preserve for public use historic sites, buildings, and objects of national significance for the inspiration and benefit of the people of the United States."[12] When the Antiquities Act was enacted, the National Park Service (NPS) did not exist and responsibility for federally protected archaeological sites fell to the federal government generally. With the new act, responsibility shifted to the NPS. The law created the National Park System Advisory Board, the Historic Sites Survey, and a federal designation—National Historic Site.[13] But this designation was largely honorary and did little to prevent destruction or damage. The act further initiated a collaborative process between private property owners and the federal government and allowed the secretary of the interior to acquire new sites.[14] This was a major shift that expanded the reach of the NPS and the agency's ability to acquire and protect new sites. The strength of these protections would prove questionable in time.

With the New Deal, professionals in universities and museums acquired funds and workers from the FERA, CCC, CWA, and WPA for archaeological investigations. In 1937, the NPS and the Indian Service collaborated to create the Navajo Indian CCC Mobile Unit. Under the supervision of an archaeologist, the unit stabilized archaeological ruins and national monuments throughout the Southwest including Chaco Canyon, Tonto Ruin, Wupatki Ruin, Aztec Ruin, Montezuma Castle, and Gran Quivira.[15]

The national monuments worked on by the Mobile Unit exhibited the stresses of years of climatic events. Accumulated wind and water caused roofs to collapse and walls to separate. Snow and rain caused mortar to seep out; timber beams rotted; and the meld of debris and pools of water subjected the rest of the ruin to heavy moisture and erosion.[16] Pothunters and archaeologists added to the climate's assault, presenting the Mobile Unit with unique challenges. Rather than using blueprints to restore the ruins, the unit relied on "a unique combination of art, archaeology, and a building science in its infancy." They tried to control erosion and patch wall breaks, all the while aware that their modern methods endangered the ancient aesthetic. What resulted was "a compromise between sound building practice and an attempt at authenticity of appearance." As they worked, the Mobile Unit kept records on standardized project forms, documenting and photographing the state of rooms.[17]

Across the country archaeology witnessed additional benefits of the New Deal. The federal government acted as project manager and regulator, while the NPS determined the location of archaeological investigations and the Smithsonian Institution monitored excavation efforts.[18] With the exception of the TVA, projects occurred where the unemployed masses lived. Working with large-scale crews of nonarchaeologists forced professionals to get creative. Premade excavation forms that prompted the digger to answer questions about the site were introduced to excavations. And rather than digging in the area most likely to reveal treasure or bodies, these crews excavated an entire area.[19]

New Deal archaeology presented many challenges. The number of workers always seemed to outstrip the number of trained archaeologists at a site; artifacts and other data were lost after some excavations; and the results of surveys were rarely published.[20] Nonetheless, archaeologists took full advantage of the New Deal programs, with federally funded excavations occurring in a minimum of 381 counties in 36 states.[21]

Through New Deal–backed archaeology, ordinary Americans from all backgrounds collaborated with archaeologists to excavate hundreds of sites. This was the most significant and consistent funding the US government had yet contributed to archaeological investigations. It showed what a relationship between the government and the field of archaeology might look like. There was room for improvement and changes to be made, but New Deal archaeology showed the benefits of organized public engagement with archaeology and that government-backed archaeology worked.

TWENTY

From Potsherds to Process

New Deal archaeology was salvage archaeology. The identification of an archaeological site within the path of a federal road or dam did not mean that the site would be avoided, or the project rerouted. Archaeologists typically had the opportunity to excavate a portion of a site before construction began. Archaeologists preserved many artifacts and associated data, but destruction of hundreds of archaeological sites and historic buildings remained the norm. Salvage was all American archaeology had. During the 1960s the preservation community sought a solution in earnest.

In 1963, the National Trust and Colonial Williamsburg hosted a preservation conference in Virginia's restored colonial capital. There, concerns concentrated on the destruction of sites in the path of interstates and public housing. Afterward, a team traveled to Europe to learn about the laws protecting England's stately homes, France's palaces, and Poland's reconstructed towns.[1] This visit influenced the report published in January 1966, *With Heritage So Rich*. With a foreword by Lady Bird Johnson, the report focused on historic buildings. The first lady wrote of her shock in learning that of 12,000 historic properties recorded by the 1935 Historic Sites Act, nearly half had been destroyed by development.[2]

That same year, the Department of Transportation (DOT) Act was passed. Section 4(f) of this law called for the agency to "protect significant prehistoric and historical sites in the course of DOT funded projects unless there was no alternative to that destruction."[3] In a massive step up, Section 4(f) required agencies to attempt to avoid sites.

Also in 1966, President Lyndon B. Johnson signed the National Historic Preservation Act (NHPA) into law. It was extensive and remains the most significant preservation law in the land. The law made preservation a federal policy and established the federal government as the nation's leader in preservation. To guide these efforts, the NHPA created an independent federal preservation agency, the Advisory Council on Historic Preservation (ACHP). This agency provides preservation guidance to other agencies and advises the executive and legislative branches on the needs of the nation's heritage resources.

The NHPA also charged state historic preservation officers (SHPOs) with creating and managing a State Historic Preservation Program, completing statewide surveys of historic properties, maintaining inventories of historic properties, nominating eligible properties to the NRHP, advising local agencies on historic preservation matters, and initiating public engagement activities, among many other responsibilities.[4] According to the National Conference of SHPOs, in 2022 there were 59 SHPOs representing the 50 states, American Samoa, Guam, the Republic of the Marshall Islands, the Federated States of Micronesia, the Commonwealth of the Northern Mariana Islands, the Republic of Palau, the US Virgin Islands, the Commonwealth of Puerto Rico, and the District of Columbia.[5]

In the 1966 law, tribes were included as consultation partners but not given the same prominence or power as the SHPOs. In 1992, Congress passed amendments to the NHPA that expanded tribal authority. In Section 101(d)(2), the NHPA affords *federally* recognized tribes the right to establish a tribal historic preservation officer (THPO). The THPO can take responsibility for some of the SHPO's responsibilities on tribal lands once approved by NPS. Some tribes had already established their own preservation regulations. For instance, the Navajo Nation passed the Cultural Resources Protection Act in 1988.[6]

As of January 2022, there were 574 federally recognized tribes.[7] Of these, the National Association of Tribal Historic Preservation Officers (NATHPO) reported there were over 200 recognized THPOs.[8] The highest concentrations are in California, Washington, Oklahoma, and New Mexico. The distribution of THPOs represents the geopolitics of removal far more than the archaeological record associated with tribes. For this reason, tribal areas of interest often stretch far beyond tribes' present national borders.

The NHPA also created the Section 106 process for identifying and protecting historic properties. The process is initiated by a federal nexus: a federal agency, federal money, federal land, and so on. Then agencies determine if their actions (i.e., construction, maintenance, land acquisition, etc.) will impact historic properties including archaeological sites, historic buildings, historic cemeteries, or other cultural properties. If there is a potential impact to historic properties, then an area of potential effects (APE) is defined by the relevant stakeholders. The APE is the project area and encompasses the area that may be impacted directly or indirectly by physical, visual, or auditory changes to the landscape.

It is often unclear if archaeological sites will be impacted by a federal agency's undertaking. Excavations near Pueblo Bonito illustrated the dirt's capriciousness in the 1980s. Archaeologists did not expect to find any archaeological materials in the path of a proposed road, but during survey they found wood, daub, and other debris. After consulting the archives, they determined that their finds were likely the remains of one of the Wetherill homes and the family store. By the 1980s, the Wetherills were just another of the canyon's many distant memories. Recording their surprise for posterity, the archaeologists named the site Ohmygod.[9]

To determine if there will be an impact to historic properties within an APE, agencies often need an archaeological survey. Accordingly, the 1960s saw the birth of a new archaeological industry—cultural resources management (CRM). CRM firms take many forms. They vary in size and profitability, but many are private firms that compete for federal projects like any other contractor. Others are branches of university archaeology or anthropology departments that offer students real-world experience. Other times, CRM operates out of larger civil engineering firms. Several Indigenous communities have also started their own CRM firms. In all their variations, CRM now employs most

American archaeologists and accounts for the bulk of archaeological work in the United States. Since the birth of CRM, many have expressed concerns and criticisms over the relationship between CRM archaeology and money. However, inappropriate fiscal relationships can develop in archaeological programs based in universities, government agencies, and private institutions as well.

Many times, during the Section 106 process, archaeologists find nothing. Though not very exciting archaeologically, it is the preferred outcome for everyone. The federal agency can complete its mission without impacting archaeological sites. Of course, the opposite is also true. When sites are found, their eligibility for the National Register of Historic Places (NRHP) must be determined.

The NRHP is another tool created by the NHPA. It is a list of the nation's most significant sites and is overseen by the secretary of the interior and managed by the NPS. Sites in the NRHP represent a variety of periods, places, and historic activities, such as the Woodstock Music Festival Site (New York), the Biltmore Estate (North Carolina), the Paul Revere House (Massachusetts), and Historic Jamestown (Virginia). To be eligible for the list, sites must have significance and integrity.

Significance is established by assessing sites that are at least fifty years old against four criteria (sites less than fifty years old can still be assessed under Criteria Considerations). Criterion A is whether a site is "associated with events that have made a significant contribution to the broad patterns of our history." In Chaco Canyon, as one example, the evidence for population decline suggests that "what came before was very different than what came after."[10] Thus it is reasonable to argue that Pueblo Bonito is significant under Criterion A.

Criterion B focuses on the site's association with a person(s) from the past. It has been argued that Chaco Canyon was likely associated with people with great amounts of regional power, considering the labor force they commanded and their rich burial goods. Even without written names, the great houses may still be significant under Criterion B.[11]

Thematic architecture is the core of Criterion C. The sandstone masonry of Chaco Canyon is a style of architecture seen in few other places. The scale of the great houses in the canyon justifies a determination of significance under Criterion C.[12]

Criterion D is a broad category that requires sites show or have the potential to yield information. This is the criterion under which most archaeological sites are determined eligible. As Chaco Canyon has been excavated for over a century and archaeologists continue to learn more about the Chaco world, the great houses clearly have the potential to yield much more information about the past.[13]

Sites must also have integrity to be eligible for the NRHP. Integrity means that sites can communicate their significance. There are seven different integrity considerations: location, setting, design, materials, workmanship, feeling, and association. Many archaeological sites that have been previously disturbed by construction fail to qualify for NRHP eligibility. Their integrity has been diminished by the loss of one or more of these seven elements.

Missing from these standards of significance and eligibility is any mention of deeper spiritual, ceremonial, or traditional significance. Under the NHPA, these sites fall under the umbrella of Traditional Cultural Properties. They can be difficult to document with dirt and artifacts alone. Archaeologists thus need to work closely with Indigenous peoples to document religious and traditional information respectfully and confidentially, so that these sites too can be protected under the NHPA.[14]

Determining that a site is eligible for listing in the NRHP does not mean that the site will be listed or preserved. Actually, listing a site is another process. A federal agency can decide that a road must be built through a Mississippian mound, or there is just no other place to put that government building except atop that nineteenth-century midden. Archaeologists, SHPOs, THPOs, and the public can fight back, but if an agency has made a "reasonable and good faith" effort to find alternatives and has been unable to do so, the archaeological site will likely be destroyed.

When this happens, agencies must mitigate impacts to historic properties. Shortly after the passage of the NHPA, the New Jersey Department of Transportation received federal dollars to improve several highways and consequently had to complete the Section 106 process. The agency hired a CRM firm that conducted systematic, intensive testing of the APE. They discovered many domestic farm sites associated with the European settlement of the state. One of these sites was Abbott Farm, the former home of Putnam's Paleolithic lithic hunter, Charles Conrad Abbott. To mitigate impacts to Abbott Farm and the other sites, the agency had to pay for data recovery. Data recovery is the most intensive and time-consuming type of modern archaeology. This type of excavation anticipates that the site will be imminently destroyed and thus seeks to tease as much data out of the ground as possible.

In 1996, CRM firm Louis Berger and Associates published results of several years of data recovery at Abbott Farm. The report included details on precontact and postcontact sites across an over 2,000-acre area. At Abbott's home, archaeologists found evidence of thousands of years of occupation stretching continuously from approximately 6000 BCE to European contact.[15] It is not quite glacial, but perhaps Abbott would be comforted that his artifacts were very old and significant to our understanding of the continent's past.

While mitigations like the one involving Abbott Farm show how much can be learned from intensive archaeological investigations, well-founded concerns exist over the frequency of mitigation. Some agencies and industries have become accustomed to the Section 106 process and in a desire to move projects along are all too happy to jump to the end, acknowledge that eligible or listed historic properties will be adversely affected, and write a big check for mitigation. They apply their money Band-Aid, move on, and archaeology disappears. In turn, concerns have been raised over the literal cost of destroying archaeological sites and what the public loses or gains from this trade.

Fundamentally, Section 106 is a process. Often it is difficult, and it is rarely possible to make everyone (or sometimes anyone) happy. Chicago discovered this recently. The Windy City was proposed as the location of several development projects involving the NPS, the Federal Highway Administration (FHWA), and the US Army Corps of Engineers. This project centered around the proposed construction of the Obama Presidential Center and mobility improvements along the South Lakefront. Because of the entities involved, the proponents had to comply with Section 106 of the NHPA, Section 4f of the DOT Act, and the National Environmental Policy Act (NEPA).

The Illinois State Archaeological Survey Prairie Research Institute completed the required archaeological survey. The survey included "visual inspection, geomorphical coring, and hand excavation." Archaeologists recorded new sites during the survey. Some of the sites were associated with the 1893 Chicago World's Fair. All were recommended as not eligible for listing in the NRHP.[16]

The Cultural Landscape Foundation disagreed with these findings. They argued the sites did have the potential to yield additional information and that they were associated with events that have made a significant contribution to the broad patterns of history. Thus, the sites should be eligible under Criteria A and D of the NRHP.[17]

Advice was sought from the ACHP. Under Section 106, the FHWA invited eleven tribes to consultation, two of whom accepted the invitation. Ultimately, it was determined that the project entailed a potential adverse effect to the Jackson Park Historic Landscape District and Midway Plaisance and the Chicago Park Boulevard System Historic District. The FHWA was required to mitigate these adverse effects.[18] However, the proponents were not legally required to avoid destroying any archaeological sites.

Consultation can be tense, the process can be long and convoluted, and mitigation can be expensive. Under the NHPA it remains the nation's policy to identify historic properties before any federal undertaking, determine the impacts that undertaking will have on historic properties, and then make a reasonable and good faith effort to minimize or avoid damage to those sites. Critically, consultation with all stakeholders is an essential part of each step of the Section 106 process.

In the 1880s, when the Wetherills and their associates began collecting from Mesa Verde, archaeology was whatever individuals made it. Today, American archaeology is federally regulated. For good reason, little of past practice is evident in modern fieldwork, but money remains the driving force behind each survey. Today the politics and dollars behind the digs support compliance with federal regulations, instead of filling museum shelves or supporting the hobbies of the wealthy. The result is a new way of preserving America's heritage, but it is far from perfect. Sites continue to be lost. Nomination of sites to the NRHP is not prioritized in most federal budgets. And standards of CRM firms vary. Some firms conduct exemplary excavations and deliver insightful reports. Others run on a motto of *deeper, faster, cheaper*. Dig deeper. Finish faster. Get it all done cheaper. Too often, the pressures of that system are born by underpaid, uninsured temporary skilled laborers. Money continues to make the archaeological world go round.

The 1960s saw one additional change. In 1964, the Smithsonian underwent a reorganization to make way for a new generation of research. The BAE and the Department of Anthropology of the Museum of Natural History were combined into the Smithsonian Office for Anthropological Research. After eighty-five years, the BAE was no more. Its collections, classifications, and ideas would be its legacy.

TWENTY-ONE

The Grand Gulch under Fire

In the fall of 1979, two men slipped through an unmonitored canyon in the Bureau of Land Management's (BLM) Grand Gulch Primitive Area. They entered an alcove with a cliff dwelling, two kivas, and a wattle-and-daub enclosure. Nearly a century before, Richard Wetherill named that enclosure Turkey Pen Ruin.

These two men, Darrell Lyman and Casey Shumway, raided Turkey Pen Ruin. By the end of the year, the BLM would report seven illegal excavations in Turkey Pen Ruin.[1] Lyman and Shumway dug huge pits in the ruin's midden and threw out the less profitable artifacts. When Utah's fall nights became too much, they took a wooden roof beam from the kiva, lit it on fire, and warmed themselves by the glow of destroyed history.[2] BLM rangers spotted the looters and moved to arrest them. They caught Lyman, but Shumway escaped.

The BLM had been watching Turkey Pen. In the 1970s, sites were being damaged by large, destructive equipment and international demand for antiquities. And the looters were soundly beating the archaeologists.

A funny thing happened after the passage of the Antiquities Act. While presidents used it to create national monuments and archaeologists received permits under it, no one used it to prosecute looters. Nor did looting cease.

The first recorded attempt to apply Section 1 of the Antiquities Act occurred in 1974. The case began in 1973, when an Arizona attorney noticed a box of Apache objects in a store window. The attorney asked the owner, Ben Diaz, about the objects' origins. Diaz explained that he recovered the objects from a cave on the San Carlos Indian Reservation. The attorney was concerned enough to pass this information along to law enforcement. Soon, two undercover FBI agents arrived at Diaz's store and asked to see the Apache objects. Diaz showed them the objects, at which point they arrested him.

Apache medicine men crafted the objects in question in 1969–1970. In accordance with Apache tradition, a San Carlos medicine man placed the masks in a medicinal cave following religious ceremonies. Per Apache religious beliefs, the masks were not to leave the cave or be handled by anyone except the medicine man.

Juries found Diaz guilty of violating the Antiquities Act in both magistrate and district court. He had been caught outright and told the FBI agents everything, so that conclusion seems fitting. But Diaz appealed, challenging the constitutionality of the Antiquities Act. Diaz's attorneys attacked the language of Section 1, which protects "any historic or prehistoric ruin or monument, or any object of antiquity."[3] The Antiquities Act did not define any of these terms; therefore, Diaz's attorneys argued he could not have knowingly committed a crime.

The US Court of Appeals, Ninth Circuit agreed:

> One must be able to know, with reasonable certainty, when he has happened on an area forbidden to his pick and shovel and what objects he must leave as he has found them. . . . In our judgment the statute, by use of undefined terms of uncommon usage, is fatally vague in violation of the due process clause of the Constitution. Judgment reversed.[4]

It was not a great start for the use of the Antiquities Act's criminal provisions.

In 1975, Gila National Forest rangers caught two men, Charles and Mike Quarrell, in the act. Located in New Mexico, Gila National Forest was home to the Mimbres culture, which flourished around 1000–1150 CE. During this time, people built pueblo villages and produced black-on-white ceramics with figures painted on the inside of bowls. At trial, the

Quarrells were found guilty of violating the Antiquities Act and sentenced to forty hours of community service and supervised probation of one year.[5] It was something, but not much of a deterrent.

In July 1977, police arrested a Harvard medical student, Scott Camazine, for looting a precontact site on the Zuni Reservation. Camazine's lawyers argued that there was nothing to see because the Ninth Circuit had ruled the Antiquities Act unconstitutionally vague in the Diaz case. The magistrate court concurred, and the Antiquities Act became invalid in New Mexico as well.[6]

The Camazine case was an undeniable blow. But archaeologists, law enforcement, and lawyers kept trying to protect the past.

In 1977, rangers spotted tire tracks near two Mimbres ruins in Gila National Forest. They checked on the sites and found holes, shovels, picks, a screen, and a pottery bowl. The looters also left behind photographs of themselves posing with a human skull and human leg bones. Then, the rangers spotted an abandoned truck nearby. They had it towed just in case. That night, a man showed up with a tragic tale. He claimed that while he was out enjoying a lovely day of legal hunting, thieves stole his truck. He became suspect number one and was shortly joined by his friend, suspect number two. A search of suspect number two's home resulted in the recovery of several Mimbres pottery pieces.

The suspects tried to cite the Ninth Circuit ruling on the Antiquities Act, incriminating photographs notwithstanding. But the US District Court for New Mexico did not share the Ninth's opinion. The judge acknowledged the language was vague but stated the defendants' actions were crystal clear. The Antiquities Act was meant to prevent ruins from flagrant looting. Both men were sentenced to ninety days in jail.[7] Those sentences were the maximum provided by the law and the largest criminal punishments achieved in the act's history at that point. It provided hope that there was still life and penalty in the act.

Then in December 1977, three men were picking and digging their way through a precontact site in Tonto National Forest. Archaeologists and Forest Service officers spotted and arrested them. They had clay pots, bone awls, stone metates (a tool for grinding grain/seed), and human remains. They were on federal land, their crimes were witnessed, and they were in possession of the loot.[8] They filed to have the charges dismissed based on the Ninth Circuit ruling. The district judge for Arizona in the case noted that the only law the men should be charged under was the Antiquities Act, but because of the previous rulings, they could not be prosecuted at all until the Supreme Court sorted everything out. They walked free.[9]

Looting is about the end game: money. A review by the Bureau of Land Management showed that looting increases during times of economic decline, such as the 1890s and 1930s.[10] The 1970s likewise was a period of economic turbulence marked by looting. Throughout the decade of frustrating losses, archaeologists awoke to the fact that they could not rely on the Antiquities Act to solve the problem.

For many, these archaeological resource crimes went beyond property theft. Hopi archaeologist Stewart B. Koyiyumptewa explains, "Taking even one artifact off the landscape is an injustice to the Hopi people, and deprives us of the opportunity to educate younger generations about the importance of these places."[11] Ute Indian Tribe Cultural Rights and Protection Director Betsy Chapoose writes, "When these special places are desecrated, the profound impacts reverberate through all of society."[12] Whether designed to or not, any antilooting legislation would address issues of deeper spiritual and community significance for many communities across the United States.

On February 1, 1979, Arizona congressman Morris Udall introduced the Archaeological Resources Protection Act (ARPA) as the solution to the Antiquities Act's controversial criminal penalties provision. Udall called for the bill's passage, declaring, "To do otherwise would amount to surrender to a pack of vandals of history—and we shall all be the losers." On October 31, 1979, President Jimmy Carter signed the bill into law.[13]

ARPA tried to do more than punish looting. Like the Antiquities Act, the new law mandated that a permit be issued by the federal land manager prior to any excavation or removal of artifacts. It prohibited unlawful excavation as well as trade, purchase, and transportation of antiquities. The new rules seemed like an attempt to close all the loopholes that plagued archaeologists and lawyers throughout the 1970s and prevent anyone from uttering the words "constitutionally vague."

ARPA also increased the penalties for violators. New thresholds were established for first-time offenders—a $10,000 fine and/or a one-year prison sentence.

Joe Watkins also notes that only now "American Indians were given the explicit right to participate in regulating the excavation and removal of archaeological resources on land under the control or ownership of American Indian tribes, organizations, or American Indian individuals."[14]

After his arrest in the Grand Gulch, Darrell Lyman was subject to prosecution under this new law. Lyman pleaded guilty and provided authorities with the identity of his accomplice, Casey Shumway. For his looting and subsequent honesty, Lyman received a fine of $1,500 (half suspended) and two years' probation. The authorities also apprehended Shumway and charged him under ARPA.

Shumway pleaded not guilty and went to trial. During deliberations, the jury focused on where the BLM rangers observed Lyman and Shumway digging—the Turkey Pen Ruin midden. They asked the judge if a midden was an archaeological resource. The judge did not call in an archaeologist to explain that yes, middens are old trash heaps and indeed archaeological resources that contain a wealth of information on diet, health, and resource procurement, among other aspects of life. Instead, he consulted the language of the law. Of the many terms in ARPA, midden was not there. The judge told the jury that a midden was not an archaeological resource. Shumway was found not guilty under ARPA.[15]

The aftermath of the case played out in the editorial pages of the *San Juan Record*. It became clear that there was local antipathy toward archaeologists, who were labeled "glorified pothunters." Archaeologist Winston Hurst wrote, "The citizens of San Juan should be openly grateful to every good archaeologist who has ever worked in the area, for trying to preserve the structure of a site and the context of some very nice artifacts, thus ensuring some of San Juan County's artifacts will always have true meaning and value." Hurst noted that archaeology needed to improve its public engagement initiatives and create more opportunities for the public to be involved in archaeology. Despite these shortcomings, Hurst argued that Shumway's looting of Turkey Pen Ruin "[did] not resemble even the worst archaeology."[16]

Hurst's letter called for collaboration between archaeologists and the public to better understand the past. Shumway was sufficiently insulted to write back. He emphasized that he had been found not guilty (under ARPA, that is; he was convicted of "malicious mischief" under Title 18, USC 1361 for the same actions). He brushed aside criticisms of his destructive actions, writing, "Don't you realize the kind of archaeology you are doing today will be regarded as foolishness fifty years from now?" He praised the bravery and range of pothunters and attacked professional archaeology: "You are pinned down by your profession and forced to hope that answers can be found in those few ruins where you can obtain permits. You hope that your theories and guesses are good ones." He minimized the profitability of looting and argued, "If your desire to know the truth was stronger than your desire to simply earn a living, you, too, would be a pot hunter. . . . Some have an unquenchable desire to learn what you and others like you are unable to provide."[17]

It became clear that laws could not change hearts and minds and that public outreach would be just as vital in the fight against looting. Despite ARPA, looting persisted. A 1987 GAO report acknowledged that federal acreages were so large that staff simply could not monitor every square foot, a fact looters took advantage of. The same report noted that when looters were caught and arrested, they often went free at trial because of "attitudes of prosecutors, judges and juries." There were more Shumways than Hursts in the courtroom. Attorneys informed the GAO that "before presenting specific facts of a looting case they must often first convince the judge and jury that looting is indeed a crime and that the provisions of ARPA should be enforced."[18]

ARPA was amended in 1988 to increase federal land management responsibilities and public engagement and simultaneously decrease looting. Under these amendments, federal land-managing agencies must develop programs for surveying their properties for archaeological sites and then communicate those findings to the public.

Looting continues to be one of the major issues facing the preservation of the past in the United States. In 2016, Congress passed a resolution "condemning the theft, illegal possession or sale, transfer, and export of tribal cultural items" and calling for more prosecutions of looting under ARPA and the Native American Graves Protection and Repatriation Act (NAGPRA). John Fryar, a member at Acoma Pueblo and a retired Bureau of Indian Affairs special agent, notes that while looting slowed in 2020, theft of antiquities is on the rise. Fryar cites increased visitation associated with the establishment of Bears Ears National Monument, increased backcountry hiking as a means of social distancing in the wake of COVID-19, and the emergent use of drones for prospecting.[19] The GAO again assessed the state of looting in the United States and published its findings in 2021. Staffing shortages continued to plague efforts at catching looters, though federal agencies had been able to install surveillance systems and institute stewardship programs, whereby public volunteers learned to monitor sites. From 2009 to 2018, 77 ARPA and NAGPRA violations involving 111 defendants were recommended to courts. Most defendants pleaded guilty, and the jury found the one defendant who went to trial not guilty.[20] At the close of 2022, Congress passed the Safeguard Tribal Objects of Patrimony (STOP) Act, prohibiting the export of illegally acquired Native American cultural items and archaeological resources. The STOP Act also increased the maximum sentence for those convicted of selling, buying, or transporting illegally obtained human remains or cultural resources from five years to ten years.

Frighteningly, over a century after getting political and legal support to combat looting, American archaeology now finds itself on an ideological offensive. Put simply, no one is special. No one is above the law. Regardless of race, creed, social status, or family history, looting is a crime. Looters are criminals. Cultural resources are nonrenewable, and the past should be protected under the full force of the law. But clearly, we all have to believe that for the past to have a chance.

TWENTY-TWO

People without Names

After the disappointing verdict at Turkey Pen Ruin, archaeologists worked to repair the site. Subsequent excavation and analysis demonstrated the importance of the infamous midden.

Archaeologists cut a single test unit into the midden. They divided the test unit into three rectangular columns measuring 50 x 50 centimeters each. The two outside columns were exposed one layer at a time in careful increments. Archaeologists removed the soil by stratigraphic layer and screened each layer separately, collecting distinct stratigraphic deposits of material. The center column was removed intact, to be preserved and evaluated later.[1] This process was undoubtedly slow, tedious, challenging, and worth it.

As they screened, archaeologists recovered plant remains, basket fragments, feathers, faunal remains, human hair, and coprolites (or fossilized feces). Of the thirty coprolites, twenty-eight were human and two were turkey. Analysis of the pollen and macrofossils in the coprolites identified maize, piñon hulls, chenopod leaves, chenopod or amaranth seeds, and Indian rice grass seeds. Radiocarbon analysis dated the remains to ca. 50 BCE–200 CE, while the coprolite studies showed a community dependent on maize cultivation.[2]

Subsequent study of the hair strands via single amino acid stable carbon analysis suggested that the people of Turkey Pen Ruin subsisted on a diet low in animal protein. Combined with analysis of the artifacts associated with turkeys, archaeologists now believe that turkeys were domesticated for their feathers, rather than for food.[3] Additional assessment of the coprolites included analyses of human mitochondrial haplotypes, animal genetic material, and the ancient DNA of corncobs.[4]

Coprolites are not pretty bits of antiquity that fit nicely on the mantel beside a Mimbres pot or a Clovis point. As such, they and other information-rich bits of food and ceramic waste were discarded carelessly by looters throughout time. That is one of the many issues with looting. Looters do not care about data or learning. They care about beautiful things that can make them money. Sites can take only so much destruction before they are exhausted of knowledge.

As evidenced by the research at Turkey Pen Ruin, archaeologists have harnessed science to interrogate chemical, biological, and physical aspects of material culture to better understand the past. The chemical analyses of the coprolites from Turkey Pen Ruin helped archaeologists understand diet and turkey domestication in the Grand Gulch. Likewise, scientific techniques have been used to better understand individuals discovered there.

The Hyde Exploring Expedition (HEE) took inspiration from the individuals they disinterred as they interpreted the past. Bodies hold a wealth of information, the most basic of which is demographic and health. Individuals removed from Chaco Canyon by the HEE and other visitors have been analyzed to determine the age and sex of individuals, observed congenital and developmental disorders, dental conditions, arthritis and trauma, hematological conditions, and unique disorders. Skeletal analysis showed dental pathologies consistent with consumption of high amounts of carbohydrates and nutritional stress. The people buried in turquoise in Rooms 33 and 53 of Pueblo Bonito appeared to have suffered from osteoarthritis, and their skulls showed signs of porotic hyperostosis* and cribra orbitalia,[†] both potentially caused by anemia.[5]

A century after Wetherill uncovered ninety or so people from Cave 7

---

* Porotic hyperstosis appears as small perforations on the surface of cranial bones and serves as an indicator of health and nutrition.

† Cribra orbitalia manifests as porous lesions on the cranium.

and Talbot Hyde named them the Basket Makers, archaeologists pulled them out of storage at the AMNH and gave them a second look. Sixty-one burials were assessed. Archaeologists analyzed the bones and determined that the group included forty males, fifteen females, and six people of uncertain sex. The HEE reported that the group had fallen victim to a massacre, and on roughly half of the bodies, archaeologists found osteological evidence of violence. Perimortem damage was concentrated on male individuals except for a female body with a dart fixed in a vertebra.[6] However, questions remain about the fates of these people. Increasingly, analysis points to multiple phases of violence and interment, rather than a single mass burial.

A follow-up study by different archaeologists extracted collagen from ninety-eight bones. The collagen was purified and combusted, converted to graphite, and measured. The measurements helped establish radiocarbon years. The hope was that this data would help establish radiometric dates "key for chronological ordering of the isotope values," which could be used to determine the dates and scale of maize cultivation.[7]

In 2017, archaeogenomic evidence from individuals disinterred from Pueblo Bonito's Room 33 was published. Accelerator mass spectrometry and radiocarbon dating were used to try to establish a genetic lineage of Pueblo Bonito's "elite." By analyzing the nuclear genome of several individuals interred in Room 33, researchers showed that nine of them shared identical mitochondrial genomes and suggested that a matrilineal dynasty ruled Chaco Canyon.[8] Response to the publication of these results was swift and harsh and had little to do with the science or the results of the study.

Of the people they disinterred, Al Wetherill once wrote, "They were not really mummies, but just dried up remains of people without a name."[9] Al's description was a common, clinical view of the skeletal remains encountered during excavations. But for others it was cold and disrespectful. For many the bodies that emerged from the earth were not *remains* or *artifacts* or *materials*. They were people. Maybe their first and last names were not written down, much less their group identity or allegiance. But they were still people. And especially for those who claim descent from the individuals disinterred, the way these people are treated still matters.

A group of concerned professionals outlined three aspects of the 2017 archaeogenomic study that they found problematic. The chief complaints were that tribes were not consulted during design of the study, "culturally insensitive" terms were used, and the study did not consider its impact on "marginalized groups." It was argued that tribal histories on matrilineal relations would have added to the archaeogenomic analysis and/or made it possible to bypass destructive genetic analysis. The extraction and combustion of collagen is considered by some Indigenous people to be harmful to their ancestors.

Culturally insensitive language included terms that some felt reduced the individuals' bones to objects. For example, "terminology like 'cranium 14' and 'burial 14.' These ancestors should be treated respectfully and referred to as individuals, rather than as disaggregated body parts and disinterred objects," argued concerned professionals.

As for long-term impacts, it was argued that mistrust of scientists could prevent Indigenous people from pursuing careers as scientists.[10] In many Indigenous communities there is a great deal of unease surrounding genetic analysis. Some feel that studies of ancestral and modern genetics are reducing people to "mere repositories of DNA" and that scientists in search of genetic data are laying claim to resources that are not theirs in a repeat of the colonization of the United States.[11] The distrust some Indigenous peoples have toward scientists has deep roots.

It should be noted that the 2017 archaeogenomic study followed the law. Researchers submitted their study proposal to the AMNH. The AMNH Review Committee assessed it. The individuals disinterred from Room 33 were categorized as "culturally unidentifiable," meaning that based on current knowledge scientists could not associate the individuals with a specific Indigenous tribe. It seems that because of the unaffiliated status, no tribal consultation was deemed necessary. The AMNH approved the research proposal and provided skeletal samples from the individuals interred in Room 33.[12] But for some, compliance with the law was not enough. They argued that it was unethical to conduct research on ancestral individuals without consulting with tribes.[13]

This intersection between scientific analysis and Indigenous beliefs has spurred decades of debate. Some argue that the two cannot be reconciled. In a 1998 opinion piece in the *Society for American Archaeology*, the pro-science side of the polarization was articulated:

> No one disputes that Indians have suffered mightily at the hands of the European colonists who have come to dominate U.S. society. No one is claiming that scientists have always acted responsibly with respect to human skeletal material under their curation. . . . I am saying, however, that the loss of prehistoric skeletal material to science is incalculable, and that that consideration takes precedence, or should take precedence, over the religious concerns of Native Americans. The worldviews of science and religion are fundamentally incommensurate and cannot be reconciled.[14]

In 2021, the debate continued. At the meeting of the Society for American Archaeology (SAA), an archaeologist and an attorney delivered a presentation called "Has Creationism Crept Back into Archaeology?" exploring the power the Native American Graves Protection and Repatriation Act (NAGPRA) gives Indigenous communities over studies of human remains. Some scholars felt that the SAA had failed to consider how such a presentation could cause harm. They protested on social media, deploying the hashtag #IAmNotTheSAA on Twitter. Some suggested leaving the organization and starting a new archaeological society.[15]

Section 7 of NAGPRA states:

> If the lineal descendant, Indian tribe, or Native Hawaiian organization requests the return of culturally affiliated Native American cultural items, the Federal agency or museum shall expeditiously return such items, unless such items are indispensable for completion of a specific scientific study, the outcome of which would be a major benefit to the United States. Such items shall be returned by

no later than 90 days after the date on which the scientific study is completed.[16]

A congressional committee report in relation to the creation of NAGPRA acknowledged the importance of science and called for scientists to find "mutually agreeable situations" with Native Americans and Native Hawaiian organizations.[17]

Because of these expressions in the record, some argue that NAGPRA does not prohibit science. There is no written prohibition against scientific analysis of human remains in the law. However, it is fair to acknowledge how science is limited by repatriation. When new technology and methods emerge in the future, the repatriated individuals will not be available for comparative analysis or reevaluation. For those who wish for these individuals to be left in peace, this is an ideal outcome that prevents the continued treatment of people as specimens. For those interested in answering questions about life in the past that may only be answered through analysis of human remains, repatriation can represent lost opportunities for understanding.

At the heart of these disagreements lie different conceptions of the past. For many archaeologists, the past is a period represented by fragments of documents, sherds of pottery, stone monuments, and earthen mounds. The past is something that no longer exists but that professionals can piece together through science and theory. Because the past influences the present and the future, this is a worthy endeavor that benefits all of humanity.

Archaeologist T. J. Ferguson writes, "Many Native Americans perceive time differently. For Native Americans, the past can and does exist in the present, and it can therefore be known through contemporary oral traditions, rituals, and spiritual activities."[18] The Hopi Tribe's view of the relationship between the past and archaeology offers further insight: "Hopis do not require archaeological theories to comprehend their past because they have independent and highly-valued traditional sources of knowledge that are the legacy of their ancestors . . . essential information about the past is found in esoteric cultural knowledge; scientific views of the past are valuable but secondary."[19]

While placing a higher priority on traditional sources of knowledge, many Indigenous peoples continue to recognize the value of science and collaborative research in protecting the past. Former director of the Hopi Cultural Preservation Office Leigh J. Kuwanwisiwma writes of collaborative investigations of corn DNA, dental morphology, and diet: "Under NAGPRA, anything that we can produce to fight for ancestral history is important—anything that will support NAGPRA's ten lines of evidence, ranging from biology to kinship to oral tradition, that are used to establish cultural affiliation between the tribe and claimed cultural items or human remains."[20] Thus, many Indigenous communities remain open to discussions of the ways scientific analysis can illuminate the past.

Through America's complicated history of archaeology, colonialism, and Indigenous civil rights movements, a field of practice called Indigenous archaeologies has emerged. Indigenous archaeologist Sonya Atalay describes Indigenous archaeologies as community-oriented, using an oft repeated phrase "with, for, and by" Indigenous peoples and communities.[21] This prepositional prioritization concerns some archaeologists. *For* is the preposition that seems to cause the most concern. Deborah H. Williams and Gerhard P. Shipley write that some use archaeology for Indigenous peoples to "limit scientists to research and results that serve and benefit Indigenous peoples' social and political interests . . . suppressing undesirable research or results, manipulating scientists or the scientific process, and avoiding research into certain subjects, all of which are presented as morally required efforts toward 'the good' of decolonization."[22] Others argue that Indigenous archaeologies are better understood as "Indigenous and non-Indigenous people, and Indigenous and non-Indigenous archaeologists according each other equal respect in our interests, rights, and responsibilities."[23]

Despite continued and much-needed debates, many archaeologists and Indigenous communities have found ways to collaborate and have tried to forge a more cautious and empathetic field. For instance, before testing the cylinder jars from Pueblo Bonito's Room 33, researchers submitted multiple versions of the research proposal to the Chaco Canyon National Historic Park, the Tribal Consultation Committee (a body of representatives from twenty-two tribes), and senior archaeologists with regional experience. Only after revising the proposal based on the comments of these entities was funding requested and an excavation permit issued.[24] This description of the research proposal review process has the potential to oversimplify what is a diplomatically fragile and time-consuming process. But advocates argue that the extra effort is worth it and promises a "stronger, more informed science and the equitable distribution of research benefits for all."[25]

After collaborating with Pueblo peoples during a National Science Foundation–funded effort to develop new methods of studying past diet and environments, researchers reported that

> establishing dialogues with Pueblo peoples has not constrained opportunities for practicing archaeological research, but has had an important outcome of clarifying the potential harmful impacts of how research might be communicated and contextualized. A goal should be to achieve balance among empowering archaeological research, welcoming conversations with local people, and reducing the potential for unintended harm.[26]

In 1896, the HEE began its first season in Pueblo Bonito. Pepper and Richard used Diné labor to unearth the bodies of individuals. They earned their livings and their reputations from these endeavors. Navajo workers received paltry pay, and some men like Juan faced nightmares because of the dead who were disturbed. The gains of the HEE, like most of nineteenth- and twentieth-century archaeology, were largely one-sided.

The relationship between archaeologists and Indigenous communities continues to evolve. There are still bumps on both sides of the road and disagreements over conduct and communication in scientific studies. Evolution is not strictly progressive. A lot of positive collaborations have occurred between archaeologists and Indigenous communities. Negotiations between science and religion will continue to present a delicate tightrope walk for all involved. And for some, there remains only one way to truly rectify historical injustices and put the past to rest.

TWENTY-THREE

Repatriation

Numbers vary, but it is estimated that US museums, universities, and federal agencies have accumulated between 200,000 and 600,000 remains of Indigenous individuals. For scale, Birmingham, Alabama, has a population of around 200,000.

As scientists tried to learn more about human anatomy, the mind, race, and the evolution of humankind, they turned to the body for answers. They relied on grave robbers, who preyed on the burials of vulnerable populations: the poor, the enslaved, and the incarcerated. Indigenous bodies were snatched from communities decimated by epidemics, battlefields, massacres, cemeteries, and ancient mounds and towns. Often, state and federal entities paid collectors for skulls. The predatory and degrading means of acquiring Indigenous bodies was never a secret; their collection and sale were common practice.

Archaeology contributed significantly to the exhumation of Indigenous peoples and the curation of their bodies in museums and laboratories across the nation and the world. The Wetherills, before and during the Hyde Exploring Expedition, sold skulls and bodies across the nation and world. They separated skulls from bodies. Skulls of disinterred individuals were used to scare Indigenous laborers. They labeled individuals with ink. Body parts were scattered across sacred burial chambers. Trash was thrown around the sacred chambers as well. After the expedition, individuals were put on display, moved from museum to museum, and studied to better understand who they were and the world they lived in.

All this archaeological work violated Indigenous beliefs about re-spectful treatment of the dead and made the archaeologist and anthro-pologist an enemy to many Indigenous communities. One director of the Navajo Nation Archaeology Department wrote that archaeologists gained a reputation for being "insensitive and arrogant, and not partic-ularly sensitive to traditional points of view."[1] Apache tribal member and anthropology professor Nicholas C. Laluk writes that beyond the desecration of ancestral individuals, these actions impact modern life through "the inability to keep the world in balance by having ancestors taken from their homelands and made unable to return."[2]

The middle of the twentieth century saw Indigenous Americans or-ganize human rights movements across the country. At Alcatraz and beyond, Indigenous communities reminded Americans that they ex-isted and demanded respect for their culture, lands, treaty rights, and ancestors.

In the 1960s, a couple of archaeologists returned the remains of ex-cavated individuals to descendant communities. They were not in the majority, and the practice did not catch on. Rather, archaeologists dug in and discord followed. In the summer of 1971, a field school opened at a site dating to approximately 1500 CE. The students encountered buried individuals, recorded them, and classified them as artifacts. Members of the American Indian Movement (AIM) arrived one June night, confiscated the shovels, reburied the individuals, burned all records of the excavation, and demanded all digging cease. They did offer to compensate the students for lost property, but "they did not believe their ancestors had buried their dead for the express purpose of providing summer adventures."[3] That sentiment is probably true for every bog body and sarcophagus in every museum in the world. The AIM's position is understandable. It would also be reasonable for the students and archaeologists at that dig to be upset at the disruption to their work and the destruction of their records.

The culture clashes between archaeologists and Indigenous Amer-icans continued throughout the 1970s. In 1971, Running Moccasin or Maria Pearson, a traditional Yankton Sioux activist, learned of an Iowa road construction project in which twenty-six White burials and one

Indigenous American burial were encountered. All White bodies were reburied at a local cemetery. The body of the Indigenous girl was taken to the state archaeologist's office for study. For Running Moccasin, the race-based treatment of human remains was unacceptable. She demanded respectful treatment and reburial of the Indigenous girl. Iowa and Running Moccasin came to an agreement. In September 1971, the girl's body was reinterred at the cemetery where the other White bodies were interred. The continued view of Indigenous corpses as specimens rather than people increasingly arose as a point of contention between archaeologists and Indigenous communities. Running Moccasin's protest showed what could be done, and she advocated for additional protections for the dead.[4] During this same period, many Indigenous communities created their own heritage programs and formally advocated for their ancestors and their sacred places.[5]

Native Hawaiians shared similar concerns over the treatment of their ancestors' remains. In 1987, Native Hawaiian worries surfaced prominently at Honokahua Bay on the island of Maui. During construction of a 13.6-acre luxury resort, archaeologists excavated 870 burials in just one acre of the project area. A concerned Hawaiian legal student, Edward Halealoha Ayau, started a group called Hui Mālama. Hui Mālama orchestrated twenty-four-hour vigils at the Hawaii state capitol. Turnout was high and large groups of Native Hawaiians prayed, chanted, and beat drums outside state officials' offices. Their protests were successful. The Hawaiian government paid the landowner $5.5 million to preserve the burial location and allocated $500,000 for the reburial of the unearthed Hawaiians.[6] Native Hawaiians had been successful in reburying the dead, but there were no guarantees for next time.

While significant, these repatriation victories were just a drop in the ocean. As with nineteenth-century antilooting advocates, supporters of the repatriation movement needed legal support. As noted, a handful of archaeologists did move toward repatriation, but not in droves. Then in 1989, a few hundred people met in Vermillion, South Dakota, for the World Archaeological Congress' inaugural Inter-Congress on "Archaeological Ethics and the Treatment of the Dead." More than twenty countries and twenty-seven tribal nations attended. The event culminated with the Vermillion Accord, six tenets of professional conduct that called for respect for mortal remains, the wishes of the dead, the wishes of communities and descendants, and the scientific research value of the dead.

Conference participants traveled to Wounded Knee, where US soldiers massacred Sioux Indians in 1890. They went to rebury individuals unearthed during construction near Tampa, Florida, and then housed in standard curation boxes at the University of South Dakota for three years. Indigenous Americans and archaeologists worked together to dig a grave, while a spiritual leader from the Oglala Sioux prayed. American Indians Against Desecration helped organize the reburial event, and their founder, Jan Bear Shield, declared, "We're making sure we bury these people in a place that will never be touched by archaeologists. That is why we picked Wounded Knee. As long as there is an Indian alive, they will never be touched."[7]

The Vermillion Accord was a code of ethics. It was noble and noteworthy. The accord was also fairly balanced toward the interests of the dead, descendants, and scientists alike. But like so many efforts in archaeology and preservation, the Vermillion Accord was all gum, no teeth. The only means of accountability was arbitration by the World Archaeological Congress. Legislative action was still lacking.

In 1989 Senator Daniel Inouye of Hawaii and Representative Ben Nighthorse Campbell of Colorado introduced the National Museum of American Indian Act (NMAIA). The Panel for a National Dialogue on Museum/Native American Relations was created at the same time.[8] The NMAIA outlined a process for "Inventory, Identification, and return of Indian Human Remains and Indian Funerary Objects in the Possession of the Smithsonian Institution."[9] In terms of human rights, sovereignty, and representation, the NMAIA promised a lot, but only for collections under the Smithsonian umbrella. Across the country, museums and universities sought to maintain osteological collections.

Many museums pulled bodies from museum displays long before the 1990s. Many, but not all. Out of sight, out of mind did not work for Indigenous communities. For many Indigenous peoples it was more important to remedy the injustices and disrespect of the past than to scrutinize individuals for insights into the past. Certainly, most archaeologists intended to research deferentially, but respect is in the eye of the beholder. Many scholars maintained their ties to these bodies lay in their commitment to public education, but for Indigenous communities it appeared that passing by shelves and cases full of bodies had inured researchers to the atrocities surrounding them every day.

Most, if not all, archaeologists can acknowledge that the ways human remains came to museums and laboratories were immoral. Most, if not all, Indigenous Americans would agree. There is common ground. The discord around repatriation highlights the different interpretations of the meanings of that immorality. For some archaeologists, it is enough to acknowledge the inhumanity of the past, while gaining knowledge from its profits. For many Indigenous Americans, the only way forward is to return ancestors to a peaceful resting place where they can be people, not specimens. The opposing consequences reflect the differences in Western culture, religion, scientific authority, and human rights. In two acts, Congress tried to solve it all.

The NMAIA also gave Indigenous communities a means of creating their own public narrative. By 1989, George Heye's collection contained some 800,000 objects and was the largest collection amassed. His own museum had struggled to survive for decades. Cheyenne and Hodulgee Muscogee poet, author, and human rights activist Suzan Shown Harjo remembers visiting the Heye Museum in the 1960s:

> There were shrunken heads on display, there was an Indian mummy on display—a woman, there were burial clothes on display, there were sacred objects—live false face masks with medicine on display, there were pouches with baby chords in them that were on display. It was a terrible place, and filled with things that should not have been there, that had been stolen from Indian people, either from them when they were living or from them when they were dead. . . . We saw something that later would stay with me for decades as a recurring dream. And that was a Cheyenne girl's dress, with a bullet hole where her belly had been, and rust patterns surround that bullet hole. So there was the dried blood and the buckskin dress, and a dead baby somewhere, a dead Cheyenne baby, so we immediately left that place.[10]

Harjo joined other advocates in a decades-long fight for Indigenous religious rights and repatriation. The passage of the NMAIA offered a solution. The Heye collection, including the items obtained by Pepper, were absorbed as the foundation of the new National Museum of the American Indian (NMAI), which opened in 2004.[11]

The rest of the nation's collections remained unregulated until November 23, 1990, when President George H. W. Bush signed the Native American Graves Protection and Repatriation Act (NAGPRA). The law was the result of years of lobbying efforts by Indigenous Americans that focused on the treatment of individual bodies and sacred objects as a human rights issue. As the name suggests, NAGPRA focused on two issues: protecting known Indigenous burials and repatriating remains and objects held in museums, institutions, and agencies. The law also defines a hierarchy of ownership that should be followed in repatriating remains and objects. Crucially, NAGPRA applies to federal agencies, federal collections, federally funded museums, agencies, institutions, and discoveries on federal and tribal lands. Some states have adopted local regulations that are comparable to NAGPRA. Some states have minimal protections of human remains. By contrast, Maine has very extensive human remains protections that are not based on concepts of race or ethnicity.[12]

NAGPRA is fundamentally a human rights, property act. Senator Daniel Inouye made that clear when he and Senator John McCain brought the bill forward:

> When human remains are displayed in museums or historical societies, it is never the bones of white soldiers or the first European settlers that came to this continent that are lying in glass cases, it is Indian remains. The message that this sends to the rest of the world is that Indians are culturally and physically different from and inferior to non-Indians. This is racism. In light of the important role that death and burial rites play in native American cultures, it is all the more offensive that the civil rights of America's first citizens have been so flagrantly violated for the past century. Mr. President, the bill before us today is not about the validity of museums or the value of scientific inquiry. Rather, it is about human rights.[13]

That NAGPRA is human rights–centric is not a bad thing, but it is a different beast than an archaeologically centered act.

Before repatriation can start, Indigenous communities need to know where ancient individuals are. Federal agencies are required to inventory their collections and publish a Notice of Inventory Completion that lets tribes know what human remains and funerary objects reside within their collections. Chaco Culture National Historical Park (CCNHP) completed and published its Notice of Inventory Completion in March 1999. The notice listed 282 individuals and 725 funerary objects.[14]

Next, CCNHP had to figure out to whom to repatriate individuals. NAGPRA gives priority to lineal descendants, people with direct, uninterrupted lines of ancestry to the individual.[15] In most cases, it is very difficult to trace direct descent from disinterred individuals to present Indigenous communities, aversions to DNA analysis aside. Even when lineal descent is known, repatriation may not be straightforward. For instance, just five years after he went on display at the St. Louis' World Fair, Geronimo died of pneumonia at Fort Sill, Oklahoma. He was still a prisoner of war. He was buried in the Fort Sill Apache Prisoner of War Cemetery. At least two grandsons were determined to be lineal descendants of Geronimo, and they disagreed on what should be done with his body. One argued for repatriation to New Mexico. The other saw value in the protection Fort Sill offers.[16]

NAGPRA offers repatriation via cultural affiliation. Cultural affiliation means that descendant communities can demonstrate a collective identity through time with groups of known people in the past. CCNHP first consulted with tribes regarding the individuals listed in the inventory in June 1990, five months before NAGPRA was signed. At the first meeting, representatives of the Pueblos of Acoma, Zia, and Zuni, the Hopi Tribe, and the Navajo Nation stated that the individuals should be reburied, but none of the representatives requested repatriation. However, over the next eight years, the Hopi claimed cultural affiliation in 1994; the Navajo in 1995; and the Pueblos of Acoma, Zia, and Zuni in 1998. Twenty-five tribes ultimately claimed cultural affiliation with the individuals disinterred from Chaco Canyon. Then the Pueblos of Acoma, Zia, Zuni, and the Hopi all requested repatriation.[17]

Under NAGPRA, decisions are made based on a "preponderance" or 51 percent of the evidence. The CCNHP considered the historic record, correspondence with tribes, minutes from tribal consultations, and cultural affiliation studies from Aztec Ruins National Monument and Mesa Verde National Park. From these resources, CCNHP decided that twenty of the tribes were culturally affiliated with the individuals from Chaco Canyon. Although the Hopi and Zuni were among them, they filed a complaint with the NAGPRA Review Committee because of "procedural inconsistencies." Both tribes also took issue with the CCNHP's decision that the Diné were culturally affiliated with the ancestors of Chaco Canyon.[18]

As mentioned, historians believe the Navajo migrated from the north as early as the fourteenth century, while Diné scholars propose an origin history that intersects and fuses with the histories of other Pueblo peoples. One archaeologist testified before the NAGPRA Review Committee that archaeological evidence of the Diné does not appear in the Chaco region until the sixteenth century, well after the construction and abandonment of Chaco Canyon. Others argued that molecular genetic studies of mtDNA showed a historic relationship between the present-day Diné and Pueblo groups like the Hopi and Zuni.[19]

The individuals disinterred from Chaco Canyon were finally reburied in 2006. It took years for the CCNHP to come to a decision on cultural affiliation that still left many upset. This outcome is not unusual. Federal agencies are faced with unraveling a century-old human rights violation with very little reliable evidence and very many concerned and passionate communities. The odds are not in the agency's favor. It took centuries of decisions and actions to create these circumstances. It should be expected that repatriating individuals will be a fraught process.

In 2016, the Hopi Cultural Preservation Office reached out to the National Museum of Finland regarding the collection Gustaf Nordenskiöld took from Mesa Verde. NAGPRA does not apply to foreign museums, many of which object to the notion of repatriation. But the National Museum of Finland inventoried Gustaf's collection and reported that there were twenty individuals and twenty-eight funerary items in the 614-item collection.

In 2018, Finland notified the United States that it would consider repatriating the individuals and funerary items. The Hopi, Acoma, Zia, and Zuni were selected by a tribal committee to manage the effort. Without NAGPRA, the tribes and Finland had to enter into a separate agreement. This took years to complete, but in September 2020, the ancestors of Mesa Verde arrived in Durango, Colorado. They were later reinterred in Mesa Verde National Park by their descendants. The tribes praised the Finnish government for their willingness to engage in repatriation and expressed their hopes that other museums across Europe would follow suit.[20]

Although repatriation is often the desired outcome for Indigenous communities, the process can be daunting for those involved. Leigh J. Kuwanwisiwma explained the weight of repatriating another group of individuals from Mesa Verde:

> there [were] remains of 1,500 ancestors. The cultural advisors and I have seen the spreadsheet of data, but when we opened the boxes and the remains were handed to us, we saw the cradle boarding—the flat backs of the skulls that had been shaped by continuously placing the children's soft heads against the hard wood of a cradle board. We had to ask who they were. I don't dwell on it, but when I talk about it now, it comes back and I visualize it again. So we cleansed ourselves. . . . There is a personal reaction, an anger that comes with the reburial process. We felt this anger and we tried to balance it with what the Hopi Tribe and the Hopi Cultural Preservation Office have decided to do, which is to rebury these people . . . and then you try to balance that emotion by personally accepting that the tribe's decision was the best thing that could be done.[21]

There will probably never be a day when human remains are not in American universities, museums, or federal agencies. Part of that is because of unaffiliated remains (individuals that cannot be confidently tied to a descendant community) and the slow and expensive nature of repatriation. One estimate calculates the price for the inventory, consultation, repatriation, and reburial to be approximately $581 per individual.[22] The federal government does provide NAGPRA grants to help with the cost. However, there are 574 federally recognized tribes and hundreds of thousands of individuals and funerary objects.

Additionally, archaeologists continue to find human remains. During the project that discovered cacao residue on the cylinder jars from Room 28 at Pueblo Bonito, archaeologists found several toe bones in a tin can. The body parts seem to have been discovered and discarded during the excavations in the 1890s. It could have been done by any member of the Hyde Exploring Expedition or the Moorehead group. Today, a finding of human remains like this is called an inadvertent discovery. The archaeologists had established a protocol in the event of inadvertent discoveries that was approved by the CCNHP and relevant tribes. Thus, they stopped digging and scheduled consultation with the tribes. The project was only permitted for thirty days, and the inadvertent discovery took seven days of excavation away. The tribes agreed that excavations could resume, but reburial of the human remains became a priority.[23]

For all its flaws, NAGPRA has resulted in the repatriation of thousands of individuals and funerary objects. Other groups look to NAGPRA as precedent for protections. For instance, in 2022 Congress passed the African-American Burial Grounds Network Act. However, after over three decades of repatriations, estimates suggest that over 100,000 Indigenous individuals remain in institutions with no path home.[24] Indigenous communities continue to call for improvements to the law. In 2022, proposed changes to NAGPRA were posted in the Federal Register seeking to "describe the processes in accessible language with clear timelines and terms, reduce ambiguity, and improve efficiency in meeting requirements. . . . The changes emphasize consultation in every step and defer to the customs, traditions, and Native American traditional knowledge of lineal descendants, Indian Tribes, and Native Hawaiian Organizations."[25]

Legally, NAGPRA is about property; but literally, it's about people. NAGPRA shows that America can openly and honestly acknowledge actions acceptable in the past, but reprehensible in the present, redress historic injustices, and collaborate with offended communities to build bridges. NAGPRA makes clear that this is a difficult, messy, and uncomfortable process that requires continuous efforts beyond votes in Congress, language censorship, hashtags, or strikes of the executive pen. Making peace with the past is not easy, and there is no reason it should be, but the process of repatriation offers many opportunities for reconciliation.

TWENTY-FOUR

The Past

With repatriation the law of the land, it may seem that the exploration of the past has come full circle. What has been dug, has been undug. But the saga of American archaeology makes clear that the past is never really the past. Human beings, without any control of the present or future, fixate on the tangible remnants of the past. American archaeology remains the high-stakes endeavor Richard Wetherill lost it all on. How and if the past should be protected and preserved continues to be the subject of debate and legislation, as evidenced by four recent heritage disputes.

In December 2017, the White House issued Executive Order (EO) 13792, "Review of Designations under the Antiquities Act." The EO sought to review national monument designations since 1996 with a particular view to reducing Bears Ears National Monument, which President Obama had designated in December 2016. Utah's 1.35-million-acre monument includes thousands of years of history, ancestral ties, and sacred spaces. The original monument boundary held the first recorded Clovis site in the northern Colorado Plateau.[1] The Dark Canyon complex within the monument contains other tool assemblages unique in their diversity and quantity that date to the Archaic period. Families lived and farmed on mesa tops in the monument by at least the Basketmaker II period (ca. 200 CE–500 CE) through the thirteenth century CE. The Grand Gulch explored by Wetherill and the HEE is also there.

In the mid-2010s, only a very small percentage of the original monument's area had been surveyed to modern archaeological standards.

From those surveys, thousands of archaeological and cultural sites had been recorded within the Bears Ears region.[2] The Antiquities Act exists to protect the nation's most scientifically, culturally, and historically unique resources. Consequently, preservationists have long advocated for the protection of the Bears Ears area. Edgar Lee Hewett called for the protection of the region two years before the enactment of the Antiquities Act of 1906. Over a century after Hewett's call to action, the Ute Mountain Ute Tribe, the Navajo Nation, the Ute Indian Tribe of the Uintah Ouray, the Hopi Tribe, and the Zuni Tribe in collaboration with SHPOs, preservation organizations, archaeological associations, and the public successfully lobbied the White House for the creation of Bears Ears National Monument. This was the first time sovereign tribal nations came together to advocate for protection under the Antiquities Act.[3] Though it should be noted that not all Indigenous people agree with the designation. For example, Rebecca Benally, a Navajo woman and former San Juan County commissioner, argued against monument designation because of concerns about economic development and increased federalism.[4]

The designation was immediately and loudly opposed by others, too. Disagreement with executive withdrawal of large tracts of land has elicited backlash in the past. When President Franklin D. Roosevelt designated Jackson Hole a national monument, he was accused of pulling a Pearl Harbor. Executive powers under the Antiquities Act were then curtailed, when the law was amended to require congressional approval of future monuments in Wyoming. Just before he signed ARPA, President Jimmy Carter designated 56 million acres as a national monument in Alaska. The size drew scrutiny because as one legal reviewer wrote, "In one day, President Carter withdrew over four and a half times as much public land as the total land withdrawn under the Antiquities Act by all prior Presidents in seventy-two years."[5] Some Alaskans responded by burning Carter in effigy. In 1980, President Carter signed the Alaska National Interest Lands Conservation Act, which among other things required that Congress approve any future monument designations of more than 5,000 acres in Alaska.[6]

Controversy is not new to the Antiquities Act, but the actions of the Trump administration were unparalleled. Eighty-five percent of Bears

Ears National Monument was pulled from protection. A conglomerate of the concerned came together to sue the Trump administration including the National Trust for Historic Preservation, the Utah Diné Bikéya, Patagonia Works, Friends of Cedar Mesa, Archaeology Southwest, Conservation Lands Foundation, Access Fund, and the Society for Vertebrate Paleontology. American citizens sent over 3 million public comments to the Trump administration, 98 percent of which called for the reestablishment of the original monument boundaries.[7] Critics of the dismemberment of Bears Ears National Monument argued that the Antiquities Act does not give the president the authority to reduce or destroy national monuments; only Congress has that authority. The Antiquities Act is only four paragraphs of twentieth-century protections. It does not explicitly say that the president can or cannot destroy or reduce monuments. Presidents have altered national monuments in the past without congressional approval. However, no president has ever reduced national monuments to the extent that President Trump reduced Bears Ears National Monument.

In February 2020, the Bureau of Land Management announced that it would open previous portions of the monument to energy developers and ranchers. There are large quantities of coal and oil within the boundary of Bears Ears National Monument. For many, the value of these resources is more important than the preservation of nonrenewable cultural resources.

In his first week in office, President Biden took steps to reverse the downsizing of Bears Ears through an executive order. In 2021, Bears Ears National Monument was restored to its 2016 acreage. The antiquity of the Grand Gulch is once again protected. But what an executive order giveth, it can taketh away. In August 2022, Utah's attorney general sued to block the national monument designation of Bears Ears and Grand Staircase–Escalante National Monuments, arguing that the monuments would increase tourism without providing the tools for increased security, thereby jeopardizing the region's cultural resources. The tussle continues.

In 2018, House Bill 2498 was introduced in Arizona. HB 2498 declared that any member of the public who took a forty-hour archaeology training course would be qualified to conduct archaeological surveys and write archaeological reports assessing potential impacts of federal actions on cultural resources. The bill was introduced by representative and cattle rancher David Cook. Cook stated the need for HB 2498: "What's going on, in my opinion, is government corruption at its best. Government agencies are being held hostage to mandate giving work to these archaeologists. This mechanism that's going on inside government is doing nothing but driving funding towards the individuals that do this type of work."[8]

There are many reasons archaeologists may be asked to conduct surveys on agricultural properties. The Department of Agriculture's Natural Resources Conservation Service (NRCS) provides technical assistance to private landowners. Many of these undertakings involve ground disturbance. The NRCS is a federal agency; therefore, its actions are subject to compliance with the National Historic Preservation Act and the Section 106 process.

Many ranchers in Arizona felt archaeological surveys were taking too long. That may at times be a fair criticism of any archaeological survey. This could be rectified by providing local archaeologists additional staff or other resources in many cases, while also acknowledging the nation's history of hasty archaeology and the subsequent damage that followed. The NHPA offers other resolutions through memoranda of agreement and programmatic agreements. In October 2017, the State Historic Preservation Office (SHPO) signed a Prototype Programmatic Agreement with the NRCS for projects on Arizona state land. The agreement allowed the SHPO and NRCS to streamline archaeological surveys on state lands as desired by local ranchers, while ensuring that cultural resources would not be adversely affected by agricultural work. Yet HB 2498 was introduced on the pretext that archaeological surveys were too time consuming, and this bill was the only solution.

The Pascua Yaqui Tribe, the Tohono O'odham Nation, the Gila River Indian Community, the Salt River Pima Maricopa Indian Community, the Cocopah Indian Tribe, the Arizona SHPO, and the Arizona Archaeological Council all opposed the bill. Nevertheless, HB 2498 passed the Arizona House and then the Senate. At Governor Doug Ducey's desk, the bill died. The veto of HB 2498 allowed for a sigh of relief, but there was not much to celebrate. The House and Senate had agreed to let anyone excavate Arizona's archaeological sites with little evidence that the existing system or the Programmatic Agreement were ineffectual. States tend to copy each other, whether their ideas are good or bad. If HB 2498 had been signed into law, it is likely that other states would have followed Arizona's lead. There is no assurance that other states or territories will not try something similar in the future.

In 2019, the National Park Service proposed substantial rule changes to the National Register of Historic Places without consulting the public, tribal, Native Alaskan, Native Hawaiian, federal, or state entities.

The National Park Service (NPS) manages the NRHP, and the keeper of the NRHP is a NPS employee. The proposed rule changes were multifaceted but focused on who could nominate historic buildings and archaeological sites to the NRHP. In March 2019, the NPS proposed that only federal preservation officers should be able to nominate cultural resources on federal properties for listing in the NRHP. The rule change also allowed federal preservation officers to block nominations of historic properties by other entities. Per Section 110 of the NHPA, federal agencies must survey federal land holdings for cultural resources. The public, tribes, Native Hawaiian organizations, and SHPOs can also nominate historic properties on federal land for inclusion in the NRHP.

Descendants of landowners subjected to eminent domain on current federal lands could have interests in the protection of cultural resources associated with their dispossessed families. Similarly, many Native American tribes may have close ties and interests in the protection and preservation of archaeological sites or Traditional Cultural Properties on federal lands. In Hawaii, the US military alone occupies 21 percent of the island of Oahu. Native Hawaiian organizations probably have interests in a lot of that federal property. The NHPA's recourse for protection and preservation of sites, if federal agencies are not complying with Section 110 of the NHPA, is thus critical to many groups.[9]

The NPS issued the notice of these proposed rule changes under the guise of complying with amendments to the NHPA passed in the National Parks Centennial Act of 2016. The amendments made minor changes to the law that most practitioners did not notice. The 2016 amendments sought to include key preservation players in major preservation decisions and make those decisions more transparent. NPS's rule change took the amendments in the opposite direction by isolating preservation authority to federal entities.

If you scratch the surface, as archaeologists are prone to do, there may be a bit more to the NPS's rule change. In March 2016, the Chi'chil Bildagoteel Historic District was listed in the NRHP. The San Carlos Apache Tribe, NPS, and the National Forest Service collaborated to submit the district for listing in the NRHP. The district is the ancestral home of several tribes and continues to be used by the San Carlos Apache Tribe for religious purposes. Members of the tribe pray, collect medicinal plants, and honor the dead there.[10]

The district goes by another name as well, Oak Flat. Two years before Oak Flat was made a historic district, Congress added an amendment to the defense funding bill that would transfer 2,400 acres of federal land in Arizona to a private company, Resolution Copper, in exchange for 5,000 acres of land in southeastern Arizona. Included in the 2,400 acres of federal land was Oak Flat. The sacred ceremonial land and its surrounding areas had been identified as copper rich and were being offered to the highest bidder.[11]

Land transfers are federal actions and subject to compliance with Section 106 of the NHPA. Once a historic building or archaeological site is removed from federal or tribal auspices, the mandate to comply with the NHPA largely evaporates. An eligible site on private land is not entitled to the NHPA's federal protections. Listed sites are typically protected under state laws, but unless the Feds fund actions on private land, the eligibility status of a site is insufficient to protect it from private destruction or damage. While land transfers between the federal government and private individuals are perfectly understandable, the preservation community maintains legitimate concerns about the fate of privatized cultural resources.

The extent of proposed development at Oak Flat raised a lot of concerns for archaeological sites. According to the environmental impact statement on the land transfer, "the mine proposal would create one of the largest copper mines in the United States, with an estimated surface disturbance of 6,951 acres. It also would be one of the deepest mines in the United States, with mine workings extending 7,000 feet beneath the surface." That is a lot of potential to encounter archaeological sites. Previous surveys had already identified 644 archaeological sites in the project area, including 506 that were recommended or determined eligible for listing in the NRHP.[12] The project sits in an archaeologically dense area with an extensive history, on land sacred to many communities. It is not that archaeologists or the preservation community are against development. However, protection and preservation of nonrenewable cultural resources naturally conflicts with development at times.

The National Trust for Historic Preservation issued a statement warning about the impending damage to hundreds of archaeological sites and the desecration of a sacred place of worship.[13] In Congress, some opposed the designation of Chi'chil Bildagoteel Historic District. Representative Paul Gosar argued, "Oak Flat has never been a sacred site, as confirmed by the local tribe's own former historian. Yet, Obama's minions are hell-bent on sabotaging an important mining effort by listing a small, public campground 20 miles away from the nearest tribe's reservation as a historic site."[14] The fact that a ceremonial ground is several miles away from a reservation reflects the nature of the reservation system and its lack of concern for peoples' ties to their homes, traditions, or land. This regrettable program of land acquisition is a darker chapter of America's history where motivations for resources and wealth trumped all other considerations.

There are clearly reasons some would like to isolate control of nominations of sites to the NRHP. There might have been less outcry regarding the Oak Flat land transfer if the Chi'chil Bildagoteel Historic District did not exist. The case of Oak Flat also shows that those who do not own the land may have a justifiable interest in the protection of the land's resources. The proposed changes to the NRHP were exclusionary in their nature and hold the potential to destroy valuable sites, data, and stories that the public has yet to enjoy. The National Association of Tribal Historic Preservation Officers (NATHPO) also noted that the rule change sought to transfer preservation from the public: "The proposed rule takes several steps to create a federal pocket veto, introducing an opportunity for political motivations or interests contrary to historic preservation to control the National Register process, originally intended to protect public interests."[15]

In 2020, the White House limited public review of development projects under the National Environmental Policy Act (NEPA). NEPA was born as the 1960s ended. The decade witnessed a growth in public awareness of human impacts on the environment. Rachel Carson introduced the public to the chemical industry's detrimental effects on the natural environment and highlighted the dangers of pesticides in *Silent Spring*. In January 1969, an offshore oil rig cracked the ocean floor and millions of gallons of oil spread uncontrollably. Wildlife perished in droves on camera and off, and beaches were engulfed by crude oil.

Accidents of this magnitude were hard on the eyes as they tarnished beautiful landscapes and left dead animals on the shores. They also hurt the economy, killing jobs and much needed tourism. Following public calls to action, President Nixon signed Executive Order 11472 in 1969 establishing the Environmental Quality Council and the Citizens Advisory Committee on Environmental Quality. By the end of the year, he also signed NEPA into law as a means of ushering in a new era of environmental protections. President Nixon stated, "The 1970's absolutely must be the years when America pays its debt to the past by reclaiming the purity of its air, its waters, and our living environment. It is literally now or never."[16]

NEPA requires federal agencies to determine what impact their actions will have on the environment. Agencies are instructed to take an interdisciplinary approach and consider impacts to threatened and endangered species, water, air, and cultural resources. NEPA has several levels of analysis, and review can take anywhere from ninety days to many years. Some agencies and industries alike have become frustrated with these requirements.

The summer of 2020 saw the result of this frustration when the CEQ finalized its changes to NEPA. The new NEPA excludes many classes of federal actions from review including projects that receive "minimal federal funding." Previously any federal funding, manpower, action, or property was enough to trigger NEPA. Under the guise of streamlining review for new jobs and economic development, the new NEPA reduces the public's ability to comment on the impacts of federal projects. Public comment is an important right for all Americans on projects that transform their homes and neighborhoods. For the Oak Flat copper mine development, a ninety-day comment period was held initially. Government staff and contractors held six public meetings throughout the fall of 2019. NEPA documentation is highly technical and can span hundreds of pages of dense text, maps, and charts. Members of the public likely have a lot of questions about the jargon therein. Further limiting the comment period is a step against the public's interests.

There may be an underlying reason for limiting the comment period. Public comments exist as part of federal agencies' administrative record. Federal agencies must consider the administrative record including public comments prior to any rule change. When federal agencies or the executive office end up in court, the trial judge reviews the administrative record and whether the agency heeded the public's comments. Limiting the amount of time for comment or the types of projects the public can comment on prevents contrary opinions from finding their way to a judge's desk and allows development to carry on without the pesky influence of meddlesome citizens.

To the new NEPA's very limited credit, the new language of the law included tribes as stakeholders for the first time. Other than that inclusive measure, the changes were as President Trump promised, "something very dramatic."[17] The new NEPA required fewer reviews, fewer alternatives, and less public consultation or consideration. The new regulations became effective September 14, 2020. The Biden administration began a process of reversing these changes to NEPA upon taking office, but the previous requirements of NEPA were not fully restored. The debt President Nixon referenced in 1969 is growing.

Just as in the 1890s, America continues to debate how much land the federal government should withdraw to protect antiquities, who should excavate archaeological sites, which should take precedence, cultural resources or economic resources, and what the public's role in the preservation of the past should be.

Years of advocacy and efforts by hundreds of little-known enthusiasts, politicians, and archaeologists resulted in the passage of several laws intended to preserve the nation's heritage. These laws are as flawed as the people who advocated for, wrote, and voted on them. Yet they have salvaged and protected thousands of sites that we continue to learn from today. American archaeology remains on shaky ground, and alternative interests will continue to pose challenges. The NHPA called for the nation to pursue harmony with the past, present, and future. That pursuit is a messy business, but the goal is attainable and necessary. As Theodore Roosevelt put it, "We have fallen heirs to the most glorious heritage a people ever received, and each one must do his part if we wish to show that the nation is worthy of its good fortune."[18]

Epilogue

In August 1946, Al Wetherill visited Mesa Verde National Park. He was in his mid-eighties. He stood unassumingly, one with the crowd of tourists listening to the NPS ranger. It had been over half a century since his brother and brother-in-law climbed into Cliff Palace. Now such an adventure was considered trespassing, a federal offense no less. He listened quietly as the ranger described how the discovery of Cliff Palace ushered in an era of careless looting and exploitation by the Wetherill family.

Al was heartbroken. After Richard's death, Al carried on much as the family always had, taking any job necessary to keep his family fed. He worked at a post office, a trading post, and a railroad.[1] John continued trading and guiding scientists, and Clayt carried on guiding parties throughout the Southwest, too. Win also dabbled in trading, guiding, and farming. Life in the Southwest was still life in the Southwest for the Wetherill brothers, despite the changes wrought by the twentieth century.

By 1946, as the ranger enumerated the Wetherill family's sins against American archaeology, Al stood alone. The family matriarch, Marian, had passed away in 1923. John, Clayt, Win, and Anna had all passed away, too. Al said nothing to the ranger. He had heard the rumors about his own family before. He had never considered them vandals or profiteers. Richard, Al, John, Clayt, and Win thought they had been good stewards of the past and allies to America's archaeological corps. As the "last of six," Al could only hope "the powers-that-be will think of us kindly."² Al's address book contained a short poem called "Growing Old." It reads:

A little more tired at close of day
A little less anxious to have our way
A little less ready to scold and blame
A little more care for a brother's name
And so we are nearing the journey's end
Where time and eternity meet and blend
A little more love for friends of youth
A little less zeal for "accepted" truth
A little more charity in our views
A little less thirst for the daily news
And so we are folding our tents away
And passing in silence at close of day
The book is closed and the prayers are said
And we are a part of the countless dead.³

Al did write to the NPS to have the Wetherills' role in the discovery and excavation of Mesa Verde recast. It must have been a heavy burden to defend the family name as a lone, retired cowboy, when he had lived so much of his life in the saddle surrounded by his brothers. Four years later, Al's wife Mary called their daughter to her side and confirmed the news: "Richard came for Al. They rode off together toward the La Platas and when they went over the ridge, Al turned and waved his hat to me."⁴ Al was no longer alone.

George Pepper passed away at age fifty-one after a brief illness. He had devoted much of his life to Heye's Museum of the American Indian. He also cofounded the American Anthropological Association and died a fellow of the American Association for the Advancement of Science and the American Ethnological Society of New York. It has been said that his work as an archaeologist "exhibited punctilious care and ability, and his notes were always models of detail and completeness."⁵ His early death cut short a burgeoning career and left his archaeological legacy unclear.

Talbot Hyde retired from Babbitt Soap Company in 1912. He dedicated much of his later years to museums and the Boy Scouts, frequently sporting a scout uniform. He devoted himself to teaching scouts about nature and Indigenous Americans and curbing the behavior of "wild and incorrigible boys." "Regardless of type or temperament, they were all potter's clay in the hands of 'Uncle Bennie.'"[6] Talbot died in a car accident in 1933, aged sixty or sixty-one. *The Historical Encyclopedia of New Mexico* noted, "His passing marked the close of the career of one of the most beloved and outstanding citizens of the Capital City."[7] The Hyde family donated 350 acres to create the Hyde Memorial State Park in Santa Fe County, New Mexico. In 2021, it was listed in the NRHP.

Fred Hyde lived until 1944, but, though more numerous than his brother's, his days remain obscure. He spent his youth wandering the world, showing up unannounced, and indulging his curiosities. He seems to have left this world much the way he lived it, popping out unannounced without fanfare, but a bit of mystery.

While the Wetherill name became synonymous with looting in many circles, Mamie Wetherill's reputation fared much worse. Widowed at thirty-three, Mamie "was a gypsy the rest of [her] life."[8] Her personal life drew speculation from many, to her apparent annoyance. Historians took an interest in Richard in Mamie's twilight years, and they turned to her for answers about the archaeology and antiquities industry of the Southwest. Mamie gave interviews and wrote articles. This was important work to her, as she explained:

> I want to live long enough to see the world give Mr. Wetherill credit for what he did. I don't care about myself, I just want someone to get it down about what he did and the sort of person he was. I will tell you this: if we could put the time back and I was a girl again there is no man I would want to marry but Mr. Wetherill.
>
> I wanted to learn all about the Indians. I came pretty close to doing it. I lived among them most of my life, and the more I learn about them the more I know that I don't know all about them. I've learned they're my superiors.[9]

Inconsistencies and untruths quickly became apparent in Mamie's stories. She claimed to have been kidnapped, to have met Geronimo, and to have been adopted by the Diné. These and other claims have been interpreted as exaggerations by kind reviewers and outrageous lies by less tolerant ones. One historian concluded, "I do not need to tell you that Mrs. Wetherill had a vivid imagination and it is difficult to separate fact from fiction in writing her life, but she was a great lady and we were privileged to have known her."[10] Despite her imperfect record of the past, Mamie was one of the few core members of the Hyde Exploring Expedition to record her version of life at Pueblo Bonito. History is in debt to her for many of the quotidian aspects of the expedition. So, warts and all, Mamie had the last word on the Pueblo Bonito years. She died age seventy-seven in 1954 and was buried next to Richard in Chaco Canyon.

Nothing about the past is simple. The Hyde Exploring Expedition is no exception. The HEE was an archaeological expedition of its time and only just. The nineteenth century and before saw years of digging dangerously. People invaded precious sites from antiquity and grabbed as much as they could carry. There was nothing scientific about their endeavors. Often they had monetary incentives. These were days of amassing wonderful things.

These "excavations" left behind a chaotic jumble of things that had lost their meaning and ability to communicate their importance. The late nineteenth century saw archaeologists in museums, government agencies, and universities begin to push the strange practice of digging through other peoples' trash away from commercialism and collection. They wanted to make a scientific field that could answer questions about America's past through data and theory. And they did. Regulation and professionalization emerged as the cure-all. Through personal and professional partnerships, compromises, and slights they built a field of inquiry as imperfect as themselves.

The archaeology that followed the HEE was both familiar and different. As new expectations, new regulations, new scientific techniques, and new theories emerged, American archaeology evolved. But change never completely erased the past. American archaeology remains flawed and has plenty of room for improvement. The archaeology of today carries traces of the archaeology of 1893 and 1906. It always will. Still, every day the field expands our knowledge of the past and helps us better understand who we are.

Indigenous scholars perceive archaeological progress variably. Joe Watkins writes:

> To their credit, however, more and more archaeologists are trying to accommodate indigenous values. This is being done in a variety of ways, including focusing on the identification and study of archaeological sites using nondestructive survey techniques; excavating only those sites that are threatened by land development, vandalism, or some other form of destruction; providing training to native students in an archaeological field school situation; and involving native communities in excavations of cultural sites.[11]

Davina Two Bears expands on the changes in American archaeology, writing: "In fact, it is no longer accurate to frame discussion as between 'Indians and archaeologists,' because in this day and age many Indians are professional archaeologists, and our numbers are steadily increasing."[12] Still, Paulette Steeves concludes, "it has been my experience that overall very little in the field of American archaeology and CRM has changed."[13] The hard work of improving a dynamic and ever challenged field continues.

The HEE's methods were really no better or worse than most of nineteenth-century archaeology. Professional archaeologists sold artifacts and bodies just like the HEE. Did they sell artifacts and individuals to the same extent? It is arguable that the HEE was a much more lucrative enterprise with longer tentacles, which in the end caused its demise.

Money and its awkward and unwanted influences and obligations is an uncomfortable subject for many scientific disciplines. And yet, Charles Conrad Abbott's words remain as true then as now: "Money makes science, as well as the man go." Money has always dictated how American archaeology functions. It likely always will. A 2022 forecast of the CRM industry suggests that millions of dollars will be pumped into the sector, but the industry will face a shortage of qualified archaeologists to meet increased demand. Calls for changes to the archaeology academy and curriculum have followed the forecasts generated by the dollar.[14]

Since the nineteenth century, American archaeology has achieved international renown. Twenty-four sites in the United States have been added to the UNESCO World Heritage List, including Mesa Verde National Park and Chaco Culture (encompassing Chaco Canyon, the Aztec Ruins, and smaller BLM properties). The United States stopped paying UNESCO dues in 2011, limiting the nation's ability to list future sites, such as the Serpent Mound, which has been on the tentative list since 2008. There is much to be learned from the ways money influenced archaeology in the Grand Gulch, Mesa Verde, and Chaco Canyon. We are fortunate to have the opportunity to learn from the HEE's imperfections. Ideally, their mistakes will make for more than judgment-filled anecdotes and instead foster mature reflection as the digging and spending continues.

As we remember the HEE, it is important to acknowledge the biases and mistakes of the expedition, while also recognizing that no one group has ever preserved, protected, or destroyed the past. The past is a universal, nonrenewable resource for which all are responsible.

It never belonged to the looters.

It never belonged to the wealthy.

It never belonged to the archaeologists.

The past belongs to everyone, but it can be bought, controlled, and leveraged by anyone. Thus, the wonderful mess.

Acknowledgments

I am grateful to many people for contributing time and assistance to this project. Research for this book was completed during the height of the COVID-19 pandemic. Despite closures and less than ideal working conditions, numerous research institutions made access to their invaluable records safe and feasible. I am particularly appreciative of the help received from Tracy L. Murphy at the Bureau of Land Management's Canyons of the Ancients Visitor Center and Museum; Kristen Mable at the American Museum of Natural History; Marie Wasnock at the Peabody Museum of Archaeology and Ethnology; Dr. Nathan Sowry at the National Museum of the American Indian; Ida A. Schooler and Diego Hernandez at the Latin American Library, Tulane University; Betsey Wellend at the University of Utah's J. Willard Marriott Library; Katherine Crowe and Daisy Njoku at the National Anthropological Archives; and Sarah E. Payne and Lyle Balenquah of the Crow Canyon Archaeological Center. Research for this book would not have been possible without public libraries across the country and the indispensable Interlibrary Loan service.

I would also like to thank my agent, Amy Bishop at Dystel, Goderich, and Bourret, for her patience and support along the way. From the start, this project benefited from the feedback and comments of blind reviewers; thus, I would like to extend my appreciation to these anonymous scholars as well. I would also like to thank the team at the University of Chicago Press and editor Timothy Mennel for their thorough review, comment, and guidance throughout this process.

Notes

Prologue

1   J. Reyman, "The History of Archaeology and the Archaeological History of Chaco Canyon, New Mexico," in *Tracing Archaeology's Past: The Historiography of Archaeology*, 45.

2   Reyman, "The History of Archaeology and the Archaeological History of Chaco Canyon, New Mexico," 45.

Chapter 1

1   Headline Story of the Wetherill Family, *Mancos Times-Tribune*, Mancos, Colorado, June 19, 1980, 2004.84.D.81.0, Canyons of the Ancients National Monument, US Department of the Interior, Dolores, Colorado.

2   K. Gabriel, *Marietta Wetherill: Life with the Navajos in Chaco Canyon*, 42.

3   F. Blackburn, *The Wetherills: Friends of Mesa Verde*, 97.

4   R. Wetherill, letter to Marcia Billings, undated, in *Richard Wetherill: Anasazi. Pioneer Explorer of Southwestern Ruins*, 348.

5   F. McNitt, *Richard Wetherill: Anasazi. Pioneer Explorer of Southwestern Ruins*, 23–24.

6   C. Mason, "The Story of the Discovery and Early Exploration of the Cliff Houses at the Mesa Verde," in *Richard Wetherill: Anasazi. Pioneer Explorer of Southwestern Ruins*, 324.

7   J. Robertson, *The Magnificent Mountain Women: Adventures in the Colorado Rockies*, 61–68.

8   J. Robertson, *The Magnificent Mountain Women: Adventures in the Colorado Rockies*, 62.

9   "Cliff Dwellers' Homes," *Lenora News*, November 14, 1901, 5.

10   S. Jones, *Being and Becoming Ute: The Story of an American Indian People*, 117.

11   Jones, *Being and Becoming Ute: The Story of an American Indian People*, 190–95.

12 "Grand Valley!" *Grand Junction News*, December 2, 1882, 1.

13 V. McClurg, "Colorado," in *Evenings with Colorado Poets: A Compilation of Selections from Colorado Poets and Verse-writers*, 12.

14 C. Pratt, *The Quaker Doctrine of the Inward Light Vindicated with Some Criticism of Thomas Kimber's Review of an Essay by Augustine Jones, upon the Principles, Methods, and History of the Society of Friends*.

15 McNitt, *Richard Wetherill: Anasazi. Pioneer Explorer of Southwestern Ruins*, 24.

16 Mason, "The Story of the Discovery and Early Exploration of the Cliff Houses at the Mesa Verde," 324.

17 Blackburn, *The Wetherills: Friends of Mesa Verde*, 37.

18 A. Harris et al., *Geology of National Parks*.

19 J. Fewkes, *Antiquities of the Mesa Verde National Park, Cliff Palace*.

20 Harris et al., *Geology of National Parks*.

21 S. Koyiyumptewa, "A Hopi Perspective on Archaeological Resource Crime: Safeguarding Ancestral Footprints," 27.

22 Mason, "The Story of the Discovery and Early Exploration of the Cliff Houses at the Mesa Verde," 326–28.

23 A. Wetherill, Al Wetherill's Journal Tan and Wine Ledger Book, AWD #1, 2000.19.D.253.O, Bureau of Land Management, Canyons of the Ancients National Monument, Department of the Interior, 200.

24 Mason, "The Story of the Discovery and Early Exploration of the Cliff Houses at the Mesa Verde," 324.

25 A. Phillips, "Archaeological Expeditions into Southeastern Utah and Southwestern Colorado between 1888–1898 and the Dispersal of the Collections," 103–20.

26 B. Wetherill, *The Wetherills of the Mesa Verde: Autobiography of Benjamin Alfred Wetherill*, 111.

Chapter 2

1 G. Nordenskiöld to his Father, June 24, 1891, *Letters of Gustaf Nordenskiöld*, 26.

2 Nordenskiöld to his Mother, March 2, 1891, *Letters of Gustaf Nordenskiöld*, 15.

3 Nordenskiöld to his Mother, May 15, 1891, *Letters of Gustaf Nordenskiöld*, 16.

4 Nordenskiöld to his Mother, May 30, 1891, *Letters of Gustaf Nordenskiöld*, 19.

5 Nordenskiöld to his Mother, June 10, 1891, *Letters of Gustaf Nordenskiöld*, 24.

6 Nordenskiöld to his Father, June 2, 1891, *Letters of Gustaf Nordenskiöld*, 20.

7 G. Nordenskiöld, *The Cliff Dwellers of the Mesa Verde*, 1.

8 Nordenskiöld, *The Cliff Dwellers of the Mesa Verde*, 3.

9 Jones, *Being and Becoming Ute: The Story of an American Indian People*, 8–11.

10 Jones, *Being and Becoming Ute: The Story of an American Indian People*, 13.

11 Jones, *Being and Becoming Ute: The Story of an American Indian People*, 34.

12 Jones, *Being and Becoming Ute: The Story of an American Indian People*, 57–67.

13 Jones, *Being and Becoming Ute: The Story of an American Indian People*, 124.

14 Jones, *Being and Becoming Ute: The Story of an American Indian People*, 129–35.

15 Jones, *Being and Becoming Ute: The Story of an American Indian People*, 183–85.

16 R. Dunbar-Ortiz, *An Indigenous Peoples' History of the United States*, 157–61.

17 F. Chapin, *The Land of the Cliff-dwellers*, 101.

18 Chapin, *The Land of the Cliff-dwellers*, 101.

19 Wetherill, *The Wetherills of the Mesa Verde: Autobiography of Benjamin Alfred Wetherill*, 215.

20 Blackburn, *The Wetherills: Friends of Mesa Verde*, 24.

21 F. Gillmor and L. Wetherill, *Traders to the Navajos*, 4.

22 Gillmor and Wetherill, *Traders to the Navajos*, 9.

23 Blackburn, *The Wetherills: Friends of Mesa Verde*, 98.

24 McNitt, *Richard Wetherill: Anasazi. Pioneer Explorer of Southwestern Ruins*, 17.

25 R. Wetherill II, oral history interview conducted by R. N. Sandlin, December 1–4, 1977, http://wetherillfamily.com/.

26 Wetherill, *The Wetherills of the Mesa Verde: Autobiography of Benjamin Alfred Wetherill*, 62.

27 Jones, *Being and Becoming Ute: The Story of an American Indian People*, 134.

28 Gillmor and Wetherill, *Traders to the Navajos*, 19.

29 Nordenskiöld, *The Cliff Dwellers of the Mesa Verde*, 59.

30 Nordenskiöld to his Father, July 2, 1891, *Letters of Gustaf Nordenskiöld*, 29.

31 Nordenskiöld to his Mother, July 31, 1891, *Letters of Gustaf Nordenskiöld*, 42.

32 Nordenskiöld to his Father, June 10, 1891, *Letters of Gustaf Nordenskiöld*, 23.

33 Nordenskiöld to his Father, November 1, 1891, *Letters of Gustaf Nordenskiöld*, 42.

34 Wetherill, *The Wetherills of the Mesa Verde: Autobiography of Benjamin Alfred Wetherill*, 215.

35 Nordenskiöld, *The Cliff Dwellers of the Mesa Verde*, 14.

36 Blackburn, *The Wetherills: Friends of Mesa Verde*, 67.

37 McNitt, *Richard Wetherill: Anasazi. Pioneer Explorer of Southwestern Ruins*, 37.

38 Nordenskiöld, *The Cliff Dwellers of the Mesa Verde*, 19.

39 Nordenskiöld, *The Cliff Dwellers of the Mesa Verde*, 19.

40 Nordenskiöld, *The Cliff Dwellers of the Mesa Verde*, 21.

41 Blackburn, *The Wetherills: Friends of Mesa Verde*, 109.

42 Wetherill, *The Wetherills of the Mesa Verde: Autobiography of Benjamin Alfred Wetherill*, 119.

43 Nordenskiöld to his Mother, July 31, 1891, *Letters of Gustaf Nordenskiöld*, 42.

44 Wetherill, *The Wetherills of the Mesa Verde: Autobiography of Benjamin Alfred Wetherill*, 217.

45 Nordenskiöld to his Mother, July 31, 1891, *Letters of Gustaf Nordenskiöld*, 42.

46 Nordenskiöld, *The Cliff Dwellers of the Mesa Verde*, 21.
47 Wetherill, *The Wetherills of the Mesa Verde: Autobiography of Benjamin Alfred Wetherill*, 216.
48 Nordenskiöld to his Father, June 10, 1891, *Letters of Gustaf Nordenskiöld*, 23.
49 Nordenskiöld, *The Cliff Dwellers of the Mesa Verde*, 55.
50 Nordenskiöld to his Father, August 18, 1891, *Letters of Gustaf Nordenskiöld*, 45.
51 Nordenskiöld to his Father, August 23, 1891, *Letters of Gustaf Nordenskiöld*, 46.
52 R. Riley and J. Welch, "An Apache Perspective on Archaeological Resource Crime: Everything Is a Sacred, Living Entity," 23–25.
53 Nordenskiöld to his Father, August 23, 1891, *Letters of Gustaf Nordenskiöld*, 46.
54 A. Gulliford, *Preserving Western History*, 131.
55 Gulliford, *Preserving Western History*, 52.
56 "The Latest," *Parker Pilot*, September 18, 1891.
57 Nordenskiöld to his Father, September 17, 1891, *Letters of Gustaf Nordenskiöld*, 53.
58 "An Antiquarian in Trouble," *Muscatine News-Tribune*, September 20, 1891, 10.
59 "A Noted Baron Arrested," *Colorado Daily Chieftain*, September 19, 1891.
60 *Letters of Gustaf Nordenskiöld*, 12.
61 Nordenskiöld to his Father, September 19, 1891, *Letters of Gustaf Nordenskiöld*, 53.
62 A. Bandelier, "Report on the Ruins of the Pueblo of Pecos," 42, 63.
63 S. Koenig and H. Koenig, *Acculturation in the Navajo Eden: New Mexico, 1550–1750*.
64 Blackburn, *The Wetherills: Friends of Mesa Verde*, 51.

Chapter 3

1 W. Hough, "William Henry Holmes," *American Anthropologist*, 752–64.
2 R. Woodbury and N. Woodbury, "The Rise and Fall of the Bureau of American Ethnology," *Journal of the Southwest*, 284.
3 Woodbury and Woodbury, "The Rise and Fall of the Bureau of American Ethnology," 285–86.
4 W. Holmes, "A Quarry Workshop of the Flaked-Stone Implement Makers in the District of Columbia," *American Anthropologist*, 1–26.
5 *Miscellaneous Documents of the House of Representatives for the Second Session of the Fifty-Second Congress, 1892–1893*, 484.
6 F. Cushing, "Monthly Report of Mr. Frank Hamilton Cushing," 212–31.
7 A. Chamberlain, "In Memoriam: Frank Hamilton Cushing," *Journal of American Folklore*, 129–34.
8 T. Wilson, "Archaeology and Anthropology," *American Naturalist*, 271–75.
9 R. Lee, "The Antiquities Act of 1906," *Journal of the Southwest. A Special Issue: The Antiquities Act of 1906*, 208–9.

10 D. Miller, *Matilda Coxe Stevenson: Pioneering Anthropologist*, 43–44.

11 Miller, *Matilda Coxe Stevenson: Pioneering Anthropologist*, 36, 43–44, 52, 89, 102.

12 Cushing, "Excerpts from the Diary of Frank Hamilton Cushing at the World's Fair," 166.

13 D. Meltzer, "In the Heat of Controversy: C. C. Abbott, the American Paleolithic, and the University Museum, 1889–1893," 48–87.

14 Meltzer, "In the Heat of Controversy: C. C. Abbott, the American Paleolithic, and the University Museum, 1889–1893," 62.

15 H. Chester, "Frances Eliza Babbitt and the Growth of Professionalism of Women in Archaeology," 167.

16 D. Meltzer, "When Destiny Takes a Turn for the Worse: William Henry Holmes and, Incidentally, Franz Boas in Chicago, 1892–97," 224.

17 C. Abbott to F. Putnam, June 21, 1889, Peabody Museum of Archaeology and Ethnology at Harvard University, 999–24, Frederic Ward Putnam papers, Box 3, Folder 15.

18 C. Hinsley, "Anthropology as Education and Entertainment: Frederic Ward Putnam at the World's Fair," 3.

19 A. Kroeber, "Frederic Ward Putnam," *American Anthropologist*, 712–18.

20 C. Peabody, "Frederic Ward Putnam," *Journal of American Folklore*, 304.

21 D. Browman and S. Williams, *Anthropology at Harvard: A Biographical History, 1790–1940*, 266; C. Colwell-Chanthaphonh, *Inheriting the Past: The Making of Arthur C. Parker and Indigenous Archaeology*.

22 Peabody, "Frederic Ward Putnam," 302–6.

23 C. Hinsley, "Anthropology as Education and Entertainment: Frederic Ward Putnam at the World's Fair," 24.

24 F. Cole, "In Memoriam Franz Boas," *American Journal of Sociology*, 603.

25 W. Moorehead, "The Ancient Man: The Anthropological Exhibit at the World's Fair. It Will Open Next Month. The Work Which Has Been Done by Professor Putnam," 370.

26 F. Putnam, "Draft of Speech to the Committee on Liberal Arts," 16. Cited in Curtis Hinsley, "Anthropology as Education and Entertainment: Frederic Ward Putnam at the World's Fair."

27 I. Wells et al., *The Reason Why the Colored American Is Not in the World's Columbian Exposition*.

28 Hinsley, "Anthropology as Education and Entertainment: Frederic Ward Putnam at the World's Fair," 25–26.

29 "It Is Now History," *Daily Independent*, November 6, 1893, 1.

30 D. Beck, *Unfair Labor? American Indians and the 1893 World's Columbian Exposition in Chicago*.

31 Hinsley, "Anthropology as Education and Entertainment: Frederic Ward Putnam at the World's Fair," 41–42.

32 Hinsley, "Anthropology as Education and Entertainment: Frederic Ward Putnam at the World's Fair," 47.

33 C. Hinsley and D. Wilcox, "Introduction: The Chicago Fair and American Anthropology in 1893," xv.

34 F. Boas, "Ethnology at the Exposition," 79.

35 F. Putnam, "The Serpent Mound of Ohio," *Century Illustrated Monthly Magazine.*

36 Putnam, *The Serpent Mound of Adams County, Ohio, and Its Preservation by the Peabody Museum of American Archaeology and Ethnology.*

37 Moorehead, "The Ancient Man: The Anthropological Exhibit at the World's Fair. It Will Open Next Month. The Work Which Has Been Done by Professor Putnam," 371.

38 Nordenskiöld, *The Cliff Dwellers of the Mesa Verde.*

39 R. Rohner, *Franz Boas: Ethnographer on the Northwest Coast,* 172.

40 "Man and His Works," *Daily Republican,* July 28, 1893, 3.

41 R. Wetherill, letter to Marcia Billings, September 21, 1890, in *Richard Wetherill: Anasazi. Pioneer Explorer of Southwestern Ruins,* 346.

42 McNitt, *Richard Wetherill: Anasazi. Pioneer Explorer of Southwestern Ruins,* 54.

43 Mason, "The Story of the Discovery and Early Exploration of the Cliff Houses at the Mesa Verde," in *Richard Wetherill: Anasazi. Pioneer Explorer of Southwestern Ruin,* 325–27.

44 McNitt, *Richard Wetherill: Anasazi. Pioneer Explorer of Southwestern Ruins,* 33.

45 "The Cliff Dwellers! The Wetherill Collection on Exhibition at Denver," *Grand Junction News,* March 21, 1891, 1.

46 A. Phillips, "Archaeological Expeditions into Southeastern Utah and Southwestern Colorado between 1888–1898 and the Dispersal of the Collections," 114.

47 Phillips, "Archaeological Expeditions into Southeastern Utah and Southwestern Colorado between 1888–1898 and the Dispersal of the Collections," 105.

48 F. Hyde, Frederick E. Hyde Journals, 1892–1893, University of Utah Libraries, Special Collections, ACCN 0093.

49 Mason, "The Story of the Discovery and Early Exploration of the Cliff Houses at the Mesa Verde," 326.

50 "Around the World in Ten Days," *Huntsville Weekly Democrat,* October 11, 1893, 2.

51 "A Visit to Niagara Falls and the World's Fair," *Cambridge Transcript,* November 3, 1893, 1.

52 F. Cushing, "Excerpts from the Diary of Frank Hamilton Cushing at the World's Fair."

53 Boas, "Ethnology at the Exposition," 78–83.

54 J. Snead, *Ruins and Rivals: The Making of Southwest Archaeology*, 23.

55 Correspondence with B. K. Wetherill, folder 252, Box 18, Manuscript and Pamphlet File, Department of Anthropology Records, National Anthropological Archives, Smithsonian Institution.

56 Correspondence with B. K. Wetherill, folder 252, Box 18, Manuscript and Pamphlet File, Department of Anthropology Records, National Anthropological Archives, Smithsonian Institution.

57 Gillmor and Wetherill, *Traders to the Navajos*, 35.

58 R. Wetherill, letter to Prof. F. W. Putnam, April 7, 1890, in *Richard Wetherill: Anasazi. Pioneer Explorer of Southwestern Ruins*, 330.

59 Hinsley, "Anthropology as Education and Entertainment: Frederic Ward Putnam at the World's Fair," 10.

60 E. Wicker, *Banking Panics of the Gilded Age*, 58–59.

61 "The San Juan Gold Fields, Reports from the Scene of Excitement in Southeastern Utah," *Idaho Springs News*, January 6, 1893, 2.

62 McNitt, *Richard Wetherill: Anasazi. Pioneer Explorer of Southwestern Ruins*, 47.

63 "Taken Up!" *Mancos Times*, June 23, 1893, 4.

64 *Mancos Times*, May 5, 1893, 4.

65 D. Browman, "The Origin of the 'Chicago Method' Excavation Techniques: Contributions of William Nickerson and Frederick Starr."

66 W. Holmes, "The World's Fair Congress of Anthropology," *American Anthropologist*, 423–34.

67 Holmes, "The World's Fair Congress of Anthropology," 423–34.

68 D. Browman, *Cultural Negotiations: The Role of Women in the Founding of Americanist Archaeology*, 60–61.

69 A. James, "Were the Cliff Dwellers White?" *Modern World and Business Woman's Magazine*, 47–49.

70 Cushing, "Excerpts from the Diary of Frank Hamilton Cushing at the World's Fair," 190.

71 J. Watkins, "Through Wary Eyes: Indigenous Perspectives on Archaeology," *Annual Review of Anthropology*, 441.

72 C. Abbott. "Paleolithic Man: A Last Word" *Science*, 344–45.

73 Holmes, "The World's Fair Congress of Anthropology," 423–34.

74 Holmes, "The World's Fair Congress of Anthropology," 423–34.

75 J. Ingham, *Biographical Dictionary of American Business Leaders*, 36.

76 S. Ewen and E. Ewen, *Channels of Desire: Mass Images and the Shaping of American Consciousness*.

77 "Benjamin T. Babbitt," *New York Times*, October 21, 1889.

78 F. Hyde, Frederick E. Hyde Journals, 1892–1893, University of Utah Libraries, Special Collections, ACCN 0093.

Chapter 4

1   McNitt, *Richard Wetherill: Anasazi. Pioneer Explorer of Southwestern Ruins*, 66.

2   "The Cliff Dwellers Discussed in a Series of Papers at the Woman's Club," *Brooklyn Daily Eagle*, February 12, 1895, 5.

3   McNitt, *Richard Wetherill: Anasazi. Pioneer Explorer of Southwestern Ruins*, 45.

4   Hyde, Frederick E. Hyde Journals, 1892–1893, University of Utah Libraries, Special Collections, ACCN 0093.

5   R. Wetherill, letter to Mr. Hyde, 1893, American Museum of Natural History, Division of Anthropology Archives, 1897–45.

6   Phillips, "Archaeological Expeditions into Southeastern Utah and Southwestern Colorado between 1888–1898 and the Dispersal of the Collections," 108.

7   M. Wheeler, *Archaeology from the Earth*, 1.

8   C. Renfrew and P. Bahn, *Archaeology Theories, Methods, and Practice*, 22.

9   M. Carver, "Burial as Poetry: The Context of Treasure in Anglo-Saxon Graves," 27.

10 B. Fagan, *A Little History of Archaeology*, 3.

11 H. Vyse, *Operations carried on at the pyramids of Gizeh in 1837: with an account of a voyage into Upper Egypt, and an appendix*, 286–306.

12 C. Moorehead, *Lost and Found: The 9,000 Treasures of Troy. Heinrich Schliemann and the Gold That Got Away*, 120.

13 Browman, "The Origin of the 'Chicago Method' Excavation Techniques: Contributions of William Nickerson and Frederick Starr."

14 "Archaeology and Ethnology," *American Naturalist*, 590.

15 R. Wetherill, letter to Mr. Hyde, 1893, American Museum of Natural History, Division of Anthropology Archives, 1897–45.

16 Epigrams, Discussion of the human condition, date unknown, Canyons of the Ancients, 2004.84.D.53.O.

17 F. Blackburn and R. Williamson, *Cowboys and Cave Dwellers: Basketmaker Archaeology in Utah's Grand Gulch*, 35.

18 D. Keller et al., *Final Report for Surface Cleanup of Cultural Sites in Grand Gulch*, 13–14.

19 F. Blackburn and V. Atkins, "Anasazi Basketmaker Papers from the 1990 Wetherill–Grand Gulch Symposium," 45.

20 A. Hayes, "The Chicago Connection: 100 Years in the Life of the C. H. Green Collection," 121–28.

21 J. Knipmeyer, "Some Historic Signatures of the Four Corners Region," 37.

22 McNitt, *Richard Wetherill: Anasazi. Pioneer Explorer of Southwestern Ruins*, 63; Blackburn, *The Wetherills: Friends of Mesa Verde*, 49.

23 L. Wade, "Human Footprints Near Ice Age Lake Suggest Surprisingly Early Arrival in the Americas," *Science*.

24 L. Tate and the San Juan County Historical Society, *Early San Juan County*, 27.
25 Blackburn, *The Wetherills: Friends of Mesa Verde*, 45.
26 W. Hurst and C. Turner II, "Rediscovering the 'Great Discovery': Wetherill's First Cave 7 and Its Record of Basketmaker Violence," 156.
27 H., "Recent Finds in Utah," *Archaeologist* 2 (1894): 154.
28 H., "Recent Finds in Utah," 154.
29 B. Wetherill, *The Wetherills of the Mesa Verde: Autobiography of Benjamin Alfred Wetherill*, 178.
30 Hurst and Turner, "Rediscovering the 'Great Discovery': Wetherill's First Cave 7 and Its Record of Basketmaker Violence," 158.
31 Hurst and Turner, "Rediscovering the 'Great Discovery': Wetherill's First Cave 7 and Its Record of Basketmaker Violence," 156.
32 H., "Recent Finds in Utah," 154.
33 C. Wetherill, "The Cliff Dwellers. An Interesting Review of Ancient Customs," *Mancos Times*, April 28, 1893, 1.
34 Wetherill, *The Wetherills of the Mesa Verde: Autobiography of Benjamin Alfred Wetherill*, 116.
35 L. Balenquah, *The Memory of Water: Elements and Ancestry in Bears Ears—Part 1.*
36 "Archaeology and Ethnology," *American Naturalist*, 589–94.
37 H., "Recent Finds in Utah," 154–55.
38 R. Wetherill, letter to B. Talbot B. Hyde, December 17, 1893, American Museum of Natural History, Division of Anthropology Archives, 1897–45.
39 H., "Recent Finds in Utah," 154–55.
40 R. Wetherill, letter to B. Talbot B. Hyde, December 17, 1893, American Museum of Natural History, Division of Anthropology Archives, 1897–45.
41 Wetherill, *The Wetherills of the Mesa Verde: Autobiography of Benjamin Alfred Wetherill*, 114.
42 H., "Recent Finds in Utah," 154–55.
43 R. Wetherill, letter to B. Talbot B. Hyde, December 17, 1893, American Museum of Natural History, Division of Anthropology Archives, 1897–45.
44 McNitt, *Richard Wetherill: Anasazi. Pioneer Explorer of Southwestern Ruins*, 67.
45 Knipmeyer, "Some Historic Signatures of the Four Corners Region," 37.
46 R. Wetherill, letter to B. Talbot Hyde, February 4, 1894, American Museum of Natural History, Division of Anthropology Archives, 1897–45.
47 Snead, *Ruins and Rivals: The Making of Southwest Archaeology*, 32–33.
48 R. Wetherill, letter to B. Talbot B. Hyde, March 28, 1894, American Museum of Natural History, Division of Anthropology Archives, 1897–45.
49 Hurst and Turner, "Rediscovering the 'Great Discovery': Wetherill's First Cave 7 and Its Record of Basketmaker Violence," 147.

50 R. Wetherill, letter to B. Talbot Hyde, February 4, 1894, American Museum of Natural History, Division of Anthropology Archives, 1897–45.

51 R. Wetherill, letter to B. Talbot Hyde, February 4, 1894, American Museum of Natural History, Division of Anthropology Archives, 1897–45.

52 R. Wetherill, letter to B. Talbot B Hyde, March 28, 1894, American Museum of Natural History, Division of Anthropology Archives, 1897–45.

53 McNitt, *Richard Wetherill: Anasazi. Pioneer Explorer of Southwestern Ruins,* 258.

54 R. Wetherill, letter to B. Talbot B. Hyde, March 28, 1894, American Museum of Natural History, Division of Anthropology Archives, 1897–45.

55 R. Wetherill, letter to B. Talbot B. Hyde, September 4, 1895, American Museum of Natural History, Division of Anthropology Archives, 1897–45.

56 G. Nordenskiöld, letter to Richard Wetherill, 1893, Canyons of the Ancients, 2001.2.D.1.O, 1893.

57 Phillips, "Archaeological Expeditions into Southeastern Utah and Southwestern Colorado between 1888–1898 and the Dispersal of the Collections,"113.

58 "Basket People," *Rocky Mountain Sun,* November 24, 1894, 1.

Chapter 5

1 J. Powell, "On Limitations to the Use of Some Anthropologic Data," 73–75.

2 G. Sayre, "The Mound Builders and the Imagination of American Antiquity in Jefferson, Bartram, and Chateaubriand," 227.

3 Sayre, "The Mound Builders and the Imagination of American Antiquity in Jefferson, Bartram, and Chateaubriand," 227, 241.

4 Ohio Historical Society, *Ohio History,* 225.

5 Fagan, *A Little History of Archaeology,* 77, 79.

6 S. Sawyer, *Myths and Mysteries of Tennessee: True Stories of the Unsolved and Unexplained,* 100–105.

7 J. Blitz, *Moundville,* 8.

8 G. Willey and J. Sabloff, *A History of American Archaeology,* 47.

9 Wetherill, "The Cliff Dwellers. An Interesting Review of Ancient Customs," 1.

10 Wetherill, *The Wetherills of the Mesa Verde: Autobiography of Benjamin Alfred Wetherill,* 166.

11 H. Gillman, "December Meeting. The 'Cardiff Giant' Controversy," 159–64.

12 F. Kelsey, "Archaeological Forgeries from Michigan," 48–59.

13 Kelsey, "Archaeological Forgeries from Michigan," 48–59.

14 Kelsey, "Archaeological Forgeries from Michigan," 58–59.

15 S. Tribble, "Mounds, Myths, and Grave Mistakes: Wills De Hass and the Growing Pains of Nineteenth-Century Archaeology," 30–31.

16   Tribble, "Mounds, Myths, and Grave Mistakes: Wills De Hass and the Growing Pains of Nineteenth-Century Archaeology," 31.

17   WJ McGee, "Man and the Glacial Period," *American Anthropologist*, 85.

18   "Indian Mounds," *Salt Lake Herald*, November 22, 1885.

19   C. Thomas, *Report on the Mound Explorations of the Bureau of Ethnology*.

20   Thomas, *Report on the Mound Explorations of the Bureau of Ethnology*.

21   "Indian Mounds," *Salt Lake Herald*, November 22, 1885, 7.

22   T. Jefferson, *Notes on the State of Virginia*.

23   C. Thomas, *Work in Mound Exploration of the Bureau of Ethnology*, 6–8.

24   "Indian Mounds," *Salt Lake Herald*, November 22, 1885, 7.

25   Thomas, *The Problem of the Ohio Mounds*, 10–13.

26   Thomas, *Work in Mound Exploration of the Bureau of Ethnology*, 4.

27   Thomas, *Report on the Mound Explorations of the Bureau of Ethnology*.

28   *New York Herald*, February 8, 1891, 25.

29   V. Deloria Jr., *Custer Died for Your Sins*.

30   F. Putnam, "A Problem in American Anthropology," *Science*, 225.

31   Putnam, "A Problem in American Anthropology," 232.

32   Putnam, "A Problem in American Anthropology," 233.

33   Meltzer, "When Destiny Takes a Turn for the Worse: William Henry Holmes and, Incidentally, Franz Boas in Chicago, 1892–97," 192.

34   Meltzer, "When Destiny Takes a Turn for the Worse: William Henry Holmes and, Incidentally, Franz Boas in Chicago, 1892–97," 195.

35   Hinsley, "Anthropology as Education and Entertainment: Frederic Ward Putnam at the World's Fair," 73.

36   D. Browman, "The Peabody Museum, Frederic W. Putnam, and the Rise of U.S. Anthropology, 1866–1903," *American Anthropologist*, 508–19.

Chapter 6

1   "A Weird Spectacle. Description of the Great Rattlesnake Dance of the Hopis. With Rattlers in Their Mouths. How the Serpents Were Captured and the Part They Played. A Strange Indian Ceremony," *Evening Star*, 16.

2   "A Weird Spectacle. Description of the Great Rattlesnake Dance of the Hopis. With Rattlers in Their Mouths. How the Serpents Were Captured and the Part They Played. A Strange Indian Ceremony," *Evening Star*, 16.

3   "A Weird Spectacle. Description of the Great Rattlesnake Dance of the Hopis. With Rattlers in Their Mouths. How the Serpents Were Captured and the Part They Played. A Strange Indian Ceremony," *Evening Star*, 16.

4   L. Dilworth, "Representing the Hopi Snake Dance," *Imagining Indians in the Southwest: Persistent Visions of a Primitive Past*, 453–56.

5 Dilworth, "Representing the Hopi Snake Dance," 457.

6 Dunbar-Ortiz, *An Indigenous Peoples' History of the United States*, 159–60.

7 Dilworth, "Representing the Hopi Snake Dance," 454.

8 R. Wetherill, letter to B. T. B. Hyde, October 16, 1894, American Museum of Natural History, Division of Anthropology Archives, 1897–45.

9 T. Hyde, Excavation in the Tsegi by the Wetherills 1894 or 1895 expedition, Canyons of the Ancients, 2001.18.D.22.O.

10 R. Wetherill, letter to Baron C. Nordenskiöld, July 6, 1895, Canyons of the Ancients, 2000.19.D.773.O.

11 K. Gabriel, *Marietta Wetherill: Life with the Navajos in Chaco Canyon*, 39.

12 Gabriel, *Marietta Wetherill: Life with the Navajos in Chaco Canyon*, 27.

13 V. Waters, letter to Mabel C. Wright, September 15, 1957, Canyons of the Ancients, 2004.84.D.139.O.

14 Gabriel, *Marietta Wetherill: Life with the Navajos in Chaco Canyon*, 25–37.

15 Gabriel, *Marietta Wetherill: Life with the Navajos in Chaco Canyon*, 39–40.

16 Gabriel, *Marietta Wetherill: Life with the Navajos in Chaco Canyon*, 41.

17 Gabriel, *Marietta Wetherill: Life with the Navajos in Chaco Canyon*, 41.

18 Gabriel, *Marietta Wetherill: Life with the Navajos in Chaco Canyon*, 41.

19 Gabriel, *Marietta Wetherill: Life with the Navajos in Chaco Canyon*, 42.

20 Gabriel, *Marietta Wetherill: Life with the Navajos in Chaco Canyon*, 44.

21 W. Campbell et al., "Naasgo: Moving Forward—Dine Archaeology in the Twenty-First Century," *KIVA*, 3–4.

22 P. Iverson, *Diné: A History of the Navajos*.

23 Iverson, *Diné: A History of the Navajos*, 51–57.

24 K. M'Closkey, *Swept under the Rug. A Hidden History of Navajo Weaving*, 29.

25 G. Pepper, "Pueblo Bonito," *Anthropological Papers of the American Museum of Natural History, Vol. XXVII*, 13.

26 Gabriel, *Marietta Wetherill: Life with the Navajos in Chaco Canyon*, 43.

27 "Latest Local News," *San Juan Times*, October 18, 1895, 5.

28 Gabriel, *Marietta Wetherill: Life with the Navajos in Chaco Canyon*, 45.

29 Gabriel, *Marietta Wetherill: Life with the Navajos in Chaco Canyon*, 46.

30 R. Vivian and B. Hilpert, *The Chaco Handbook: An Encyclopedic Guide*, 127.

31 Gabriel, *Marietta Wetherill: Life with the Navajos in Chaco Canyon*, 46–47.

32 McNitt, *Richard Wetherill: Anasazi. Pioneer Explorer of Southwestern Ruins*, 113.

33 Gabriel, *Marietta Wetherill: Life with the Navajos in Chaco Canyon*, 49–50.

34 Vivian and Hilpert, *The Chaco Handbook: An Encyclopedic Guide*.

35 Gabriel, *Marietta Wetherill: Life with the Navajos in Chaco Canyon*, 53.

36 Blackburn, *The Wetherills: Friends of Mesa Verde*, 153.

37 McNitt, *Richard Wetherill: Anasazi. Pioneer Explorer of Southwestern Ruins*, 113.

38 AMNH, *Annual Report of the President, Act of Incorporation, Contract with the*

Department of Public Parks, Constitution, By-Laws and List of Members for the Year 1895, 10.

39   AMNH, *Annual Report of the President, Act of Incorporation, Contract with the Department of Public Parks, Constitution, By-Laws and List of Members for the Year 1895*, 18.

40   R. Wetherill, letter to B. T. B. Hyde, October 1, 1895, American Museum of Natural History, Division of Anthropology Archives, 1897–45.

Chapter 7

1   G. Pepper, letter to Mr. George G. Heye, Director, December 4, 1923, The Latin American Library, Tulane University.

2   Snead, *Ruins and Rivals: The Making of Southwest Archaeology*, 38.

3   A. Hayes et al., *Archaeological Surveys of Chaco Canyon New Mexico. Publications in Archaeology 18A Chaco Canyon Studies*, 38.

4   D. Brugge, *A History of the Chaco Navajos*, 155.

5   Gabriel, *Marietta Wetherill: Life with the Navajos in Chaco Canyon*.

6   D. Two Bears, "Navajo Archaeologist Is Not an Oxymoron: A Tribal Archaeologist's Experience," 383.

7   K. Dring et al., "Authoring and Authority in Eastern Pequot Community Heritage and Archaeology," 364.

8   Brugge, *A History of the Chaco Navajos*, 155.

9   Brugge, *A History of the Chaco Navajos*, 159.

10   G. Pepper, George Pepper Diary, GHP Reel 1 1886 2_000, August 16–19, 1896, The Latin American Library, Tulane University.

11   Pepper, George Pepper Diary, GHP Reel 1 1886 2_000, August 20, 1896, The Latin American Library, Tulane University.

12   Pepper, George Pepper Diary, GHP Reel 1 1886 2_000, August 20–1, 1896, The Latin American Library, Tulane University.

13   Pepper, George Pepper Diary, GHP Reel 1 1886 2_000, August 21, 1896, The Latin American Library, Tulane University.

14   H. Holt, "A Cultural Resource Management Dilemma: Anasazi Ruins and the Navajos," 596.

15   P. Crown, "Room 28 in Pueblo Bonito: Background, Research Questions, and Methods."

16   Pepper, "Pueblo Bonito," 129.

17   Pepper, "Pueblo Bonito," 129–34.

18   Pepper, "Pueblo Bonito."

19   Pepper, "Pueblo Bonito," 137.

20   Pepper, "Pueblo Bonito," 143.

21 G. Pepper, "The Exploration of a Burial Room in Pueblo Bonito, New Mexico," 196–252.

22 Pepper, "The Exploration of a Burial Room in Pueblo Bonito, New Mexico," 196–252.

23 G. Pepper, "Mosaic Objects from Pueblo Bonito, Chaco Cañon, N.M. Presented before the Mid-winter meeting of Section H., Anthropology, at New Haven, December 27–28–29, 1898, The Latin American Library, Tulane University.

24 H. Mattson and J. Kocer, "Ornaments, Mineral Specimens, and Shell Specimens from Room 28," 80–100.

25 Pepper, "The Exploration of a Burial Room in Pueblo Bonito, New Mexico," 247.

26 F. Mathien, "Identifying Sources of Prehistoric Turquoise in North America: Problems and Implications for Interpreting Social Organization," 17–37.

27 Pepper, "Pueblo Bonito," 195.

28 G. Pepper, Untitled lecture, undated, The Latin American Library, Tulane University, 7–8.

29 R. Wetherill, letter to B. T. B. Hyde, October 23, 1896, American Museum of Natural History, Division of Anthropology Archives, 1897–45.

30 R. Wetherill, letter to B. T. B. Hyde, October 23, 1896, American Museum of Natural History, Division of Anthropology Archives, 1897–45.

31 Gillmor and Wetherill, *Traders to the Navajos*, 47.

32 Gabriel, *Marietta Wetherill: Life with the Navajos in Chaco Canyon*, 61–63.

Chapter 8

1 R. Wetherill, letter to B. T. B Hyde, October 23, 1896, American Museum of Natural History, Division of Anthropology Archives, 1897–45.

2 R. Wetherill, letter to B. T. B. Hyde, October 1, 1896, American Museum of Natural History, Division of Anthropology Archives, 1897–45.

3 R. Wetherill, letter to B. T. B Hyde, February 15, 1897, American Museum of Natural History, Division of Anthropology Archives, 1897–45.

4 Blackburn and Williamson, *Cowboys and Cave Dwellers: Basketmaker Archaeology in Utah's Grand Gulch*, 61.

5 Copy, the Expedition of 1896 and 1897 Grand Gulch, American Museum of Natural History, Division of Anthropology Archives, 1897–45.

6 Blackburn and Williamson, *Cowboys and Cave Dwellers*, 61.

7 Gabriel, *Marietta Wetherill: Life with the Navajos in Chaco Canyon*, 65.

8 Copy, the Expedition of 1896 and 1897 Grand Gulch, American Museum of Natural History, Division of Anthropology Archives, 1897–45.

9 Gabriel, *Marietta Wetherill: Life with the Navajos in Chaco Canyon*, 65.

10 Gabriel, *Marietta Wetherill: Life with the Navajos in Chaco Canyon*, 66.

11   Copy, the Expedition of 1896 and 1897 Grand Gulch, American Museum of Natural History, Division of Anthropology Archives, 1897–45.

12   Gabriel, *Marietta Wetherill: Life with the Navajos in Chaco Canyon*, 66.

13   Copy, the Expedition of 1896 and 1897 Grand Gulch, American Museum of Natural History, Division of Anthropology Archives, 1897–45.

14   Gabriel, *Marietta Wetherill: Life with the Navajos in Chaco Canyon*, 66.

15   B. Lipe, "Introduction to the 1979 Notes on 'Archaeological Research at the Turkey Pen Site.'"

16   Gabriel, *Marietta Wetherill: Life with the Navajos in Chaco Canyon*, 66.

17   Lipe, "Introduction to the 1979 Notes on 'Archaeological Research at the Turkey Pen Site.'"

18   Gabriel, *Marietta Wetherill: Life with the Navajos in Chaco Canyon*, 67.

19   Gabriel, *Marietta Wetherill: Life with the Navajos in Chaco Canyon*, 68.

20   Gabriel, *Marietta Wetherill: Life with the Navajos in Chaco Canyon*, 68.

21   Gabriel, *Marietta Wetherill: Life with the Navajos in Chaco Canyon*, 69.

22   "Archaeology and Ethnology," *American Naturalist*, 589–94.

23   Gabriel, *Marietta Wetherill: Life with the Navajos in Chaco Canyon*, 69.

24   Gabriel, *Marietta Wetherill: Life with the Navajos in Chaco Canyon*, 69.

25   W. Echo-Hawk, "Tribal Efforts to Protect Against Mistreatment of Indian Dead: The Quest for Equal Protection of the Laws," 2.

26   R. Wetherill, letter to B. T. B Hyde, February 15, 1897, American Museum of Natural History, Division of Anthropology Archives, 1897–45.

27   R. Wetherill, letter to B. T. B Hyde, February 15, 1897, American Museum of Natural History, Division of Anthropology Archives, 1897–45.

28   Gabriel, *Marietta Wetherill: Life with the Navajos in Chaco Canyon*, 77–84.

29   McNitt, *Richard Wetherill: Anasazi. Pioneer Explorer of Southwestern Ruins*, 162.

30   Copy, the Expedition of 1896 and 1897 Grand Gulch, American Museum of Natural History, Division of Anthropology Archives, 1897–45.

31   Gabriel, *Marietta Wetherill: Life with the Navajos in Chaco Canyon*, 83–84.

32   Knipmeyer, "Some Historic Signatures of the Four Corners Region," 37.

33   Copy, the Expedition of 1896 and 1897 Grand Gulch, American Museum of Natural History, Division of Anthropology Archives, 1897–45.

34   Gabriel, *Marietta Wetherill: Life with the Navajos in Chaco Canyon*, 85.

35   Unknown, letter to Friend Hyde, October 24, 1897, American Museum of Natural History, Division of Anthropology Archives, 1897–45.

36   Gabriel, *Marietta Wetherill: Life with the Navajos in Chaco Canyon*, 86.

37   Snead, *Ruins and Rivals: The Making of Southwest Archaeology*, 49.

38   Pepper, "Pueblo Bonito," 205.

39   G. Pepper, Pepper Papers, Box 2, 1897 Field Notes, The Latin American Library, Tulane University.

40 Pepper, "Pueblo Bonito," 210–13.
41 Pepper, Pepper Papers, Box 2, 1897 Field Notes, The Latin American Library, Tulane University.
42 Pepper, "Pueblo Bonito," 216.
43 Pepper, Pepper Papers, Box 2, 1897 Field Notes, The Latin American Library, Tulane University.
44 Pepper, "Pueblo Bonito," 269.
45 R. Wetherill, letter to Friend Hyde, October 24, 1897, American Museum of Natural History, Division of Anthropology Archives, 1897–45.
46 R. Wetherill, letter to Friend Hyde, October 24, 1897, American Museum of Natural History, Division of Anthropology Archives, 1897–45.
47 Gabriel, *Marietta Wetherill: Life with the Navajos in Chaco Canyon*, 85.
48 R. Wetherill, letter to Friend Hyde, October 24, 1897, American Museum of Natural History, Division of Anthropology Archives, 1897–45.
49 R. Wetherill, letter to Friend Hyde, October 24, 1897, American Museum of Natural History, Division of Anthropology Archives, 1897–45.
50 Gabriel, *Marietta Wetherill: Life with the Navajos in Chaco Canyon*, 89.
51 Gabriel, *Marietta Wetherill: Life with the Navajos in Chaco Canyon*, 96.
52 R. Wetherill, letter to Friend Hyde, October 26, 1897, American Museum of Natural History, Division of Anthropology Archives, 1897–45.
53 Brugge, *A History of the Chaco Navajos*, 159.
54 Gabriel, *Marietta Wetherill: Life with the Navajos in Chaco Canyon*, 87.
55 Gabriel, *Marietta Wetherill: Life with the Navajos in Chaco Canyon*, 87.
56 Gabriel, *Marietta Wetherill: Life with the Navajos in Chaco Canyon*, 95.
57 Deloria, *Custer Died for Your Sins*.
58 G. Chapin, "A Navajo Myth from the Chaco Canyon," 63–67.

Chapter 9

1 Wetherill, *The Wetherills of the Mesa Verde: Autobiography of Benjamin Alfred Wetherill*, 128.
2 Wetherill, *The Wetherills of the Mesa Verde: Autobiography of Benjamin Alfred Wetherill*, 269.
3 R. Wetherill, letter to Friend Hyde, December 23, 1894, American Museum of Natural History, Division of Anthropology Archives, 1897–45.
4 Snead, *Ruins and Rivals: The Making of Southwest Archaeology*, 40; McNitt, *Richard Wetherill: Anasazi. Pioneer Explorer of Southwestern Ruins*, 163.
5 McNitt, *Richard Wetherill: Anasazi. Pioneer Explorer of Southwestern Ruins*, 173.
6 P. Steeves, "Academia, Archaeology, CRM, and Tribal Historic Preservation."

7   Wetherill, *The Wetherills of the Mesa Verde: Autobiography of Benjamin Alfred Wetherill*, 189–94.

8   M'Closkey, *Swept under the Rug: A Hidden History of Navajo Weaving*, 49–52.

9   Brugge, *A History of the Chaco Navajos*, 161.

10 Gabriel, *Marietta Wetherill: Life with the Navajos in Chaco Canyon*, 115.

11 J. Schmedding, *Cowboy and Indian Trader*, 112.

12 M'Closkey, *Swept under the Rug: A Hidden History of Navajo Weaving*, 18–19, 214.

13 G. Pepper, "The Making of a Navajo Blanket," *Everybody's Magazine* (1902), Canyons of the Ancients, 2000.19.D.1484.O, 34.

14 Pepper, "The Making of a Navajo Blanket," 34.

15 Pepper, "The Making of a Navajo Blanket," 42.

16 R. McPherson, *Traders, Agents, and Weavers: Developing the Northern Navajo Region*, 205.

17 Pepper, "The Making of a Navajo Blanket," 36–37.

18 Pepper, "The Making of a Navajo Blanket," 42.

19 M'Closkey, *Swept under the Rug: A Hidden History of Navajo Weaving*, 85.

20 M'Closkey, *Swept under the Rug: A Hidden History of Navajo Weaving*, 55, 122.

21 Pepper, "The Making of a Navajo Blanket," 42.

22 R. Wetherill, letter to Friend Hyde, July 3, 1898, American Museum of Natural History, Division of Anthropology Archives, 1897–45.

23 R. Wetherill, letter to Friend Hyde, December 23, 1894, American Museum of Natural History, Division of Anthropology Archives, 1897–45.

24 R. Wetherill, letter to Friend Hyde, July 3, 1898, American Museum of Natural History, Division of Anthropology Archives, 1897–45.

25 R. Wetherill, letter to Friend Hyde, July 3, 1898, American Museum of Natural History, Division of Anthropology Archives, 1897–45.

Chapter 10

1   *Mancos Times*, March 18, 1898, 4.

2   Gillmor and Wetherill, *Traders to the Navajos*, 47.

3   Brugge, *A History of the Chaco Navajos*, 161.

4   R. Wetherill, letter to Friend Hyde, March 28, 1898, American Museum of Natural History, Division of Anthropology Archives, 1897–45.

5   Pepper, "Pueblo Bonito," 298.

6   Pepper, "Pueblo Bonito," 316.

7   Pepper, "Pueblo Bonito," 320.

8   Pepper, "Pueblo Bonito," 324.

9   M. Jesup, "Report of the President," 14.

10   G. Pepper, letter to Mr. B. T. B. Hyde, July 30, 1898, American Museum of Natural History, Division of Anthropology Archives, 1897–45.

11   S. Freed et al., "Capitalist Philanthropy and Russian Revolutionaries: The Jesup North Pacific Expedition (1897–1902)," 7–24.

12   Reyman, "The History of Archaeology and the Archaeological History of Chaco Canyon, New Mexico," 42.

13   Jesup, "Report of the President," 14–15.

14   Jesup, "Report of the President," 14–15.

15   Pepper, "Pueblo Bonito," 23.

16   Pepper, "Pueblo Bonito," 23.

17   Schmedding, *Cowboy and Indian Trader*, 181.

18   Gabriel, *Marietta Wetherill: Life with the Navajos in Chaco Canyon*, 109.

19   A. Schultz, *Biographical Memoir of Aleš Hrdlička 1869–1943. National Academy Biographical Memoirs XXIII*, 305–6.

20   A. Hrdlička, "The Medico-Legal Aspect of the Case of Maria Barbella," 213–300.

21   Schultz, *Biographical Memoir of Aleš Hrdlička 1869–1943*, 310–14.

22   Pepper, "Pueblo Bonito," 376.

23   V. Lyman, letter to *New Mexico* magazine for Marietta Wetherill and Mabel C. Wright, August 26, 1954, Canyons of the Ancients, 2004.84.D.190.O.

24   Brugge, *A History of the Chaco Navajos*, 161.

25   W. Campbell. "Na'nilkad bee na'niltin—Learning from Herding: An Ethnoar-chaeological Study of Historic Pastoralism on the Navajo Nation," 295–315.

26   A. Hrdlička, letter to Professor Fred. W. Putnam, October 16, 1900, Peabody Museum of Archaeology and Ethnology at Harvard University, 999–24 Frederic Ward Putnam papers, Box 2, Folder 12.

27   F. Putnam, Notes Pueblo Bonito, September 1899, Peabody Museum of Archae-ology and Ethnology at Harvard University, 99–22–00/1.1.1.

28   R. Wetherill, letter to Friend Hyde, October 24, 1897, American Museum of Natural History, Division of Anthropology Archives, 1897–45.

29   G. Pepper, letter to Mr. B. T. B. Hyde, American Museum of Natural History, Division of Anthropology Archives, 1897–45.

Chapter 11

1   Wetherill, *The Wetherills of the Mesa Verde: Autobiography of Benjamin Alfred Wetherill*, 181.

2   "Cliff Dwellers of Colorado," *Philadelphia Times*, July 4, 1898, 2.

3   "Cliff Dwellers of Colorado," *Philadelphia Times*, July 4, 1898, 2.

4   "Mrs. McClurg's Last Lecture," *Daily Morning Journal and Courier*, October 31, 1895, 2.

5 "Cliff Dwellers of Colorado," *Philadelphia Times*, July 4, 1898, 2.

6 R. Keller and M. Turek, *American Indians and National Parks*, 33.

7 Browman, *The Role of Women in the Founding of Americanist Archaeology*, 37–39.

8 A. Fletcher, "On the Preservation of Archaeologic Monuments," 317.

9 Fletcher, "On the Preservation of Archaeologic Monuments," 317.

10 R. Lee, "The Antiquities Act of 1906," 223–24.

11 A. Fletcher and T. E. Stevenson, "Report on the Committee on the Preservation of Archaeologic Remains on the Public Lands," 35–37.

12 Lee, "The Antiquities Act of 1906," 224.

13 Lee, "The Antiquities Act of 1906," 224.

14 Lee, "The Antiquities Act of 1906," 225–26.

15 Lee, "The Antiquities Act of 1906," 227–29.

16 Lee, "The Antiquities Act of 1906," 278–81.

17 "Territorial Happenings," *Santa Fe New Mexican*, May 1, 1900, 1.

18 Brugge, *A History of the Chaco Navajos*, 169.

19 "Items from Denver," *New Castle Nonpareil*, June 28, 1900, 1.

20 "Enthusiastic Annual Meeting of the Colorado Cliff Dwellers Association," *Weekly Gazette*, August 21, 1901, 5.

21 "A New National Park on the Site of a Pre-Historic City," *San Francisco Examiner*, January 5, 1901, 21.

22 "Prehistoric Ruins," *Record*, June 28, 1900, 4.

23 Keller and Turek, *American Indians and National Parks*, 33–34.

24 "A New National Park on the Site of a Pre-Historic City," *San Francisco Examiner*, January 5, 1901, 21.

25 Lee, "The Antiquities Act of 1906," 218.

Chapter 12

1 "Loot," in *The Oxford English Dictionary, Second Edition, Volume IX*, ed. J. A. Simpson and E. S. C. Weiner (Oxford: Clarendon Press, 1989), 21.

2 Wetherill, *The Wetherills of the Mesa Verde: Autobiography of Benjamin Alfred Wetherill*, 119.

3 AMNH, *Annual Report of the President, Treasurer's Report, List of Accessions, Act of Incorporation, Constitution, By-Laws and List of Members for the Year 1901*, 20–21.

4 AMNH, *Annual Report of the President, Treasurer's Report, List of Accessions, Act of Incorporation, Constitution, By-Laws and List of Members for the Year 1901*, 25.

5 Gabriel, *Marietta Wetherill: Life with the Navajos in Chaco Canyon*, 98.

6 Gabriel, *Marietta Wetherill: Life with the Navajos in Chaco Canyon*, 118.

7 Gillmor and Wetherill, *Traders to the Navajos*, 49.

8 Wetherill, *The Wetherills of the Mesa Verde: Autobiography of Benjamin Alfred Wetherill*, 250.

9 *Western Liberal*, October 25, 1901, 1.

10 *Western Liberal*, October 25, 1901, 1.

11 "Special Land Agent," *Record Union*, July 13, 1897, 5.

12 McNitt, *Richard Wetherill: Anasazi. Pioneer Explorer of Southwestern Ruins*, 190.

13 McNitt, *Richard Wetherill: Anasazi. Pioneer Explorer of Southwestern Ruins*, 201.

14 F. Levine, "Homestead in Ruins: Richard Wetherill's Homestead in Chaco Canyon," 49.

15 A. Hayes et al., *Archaeological Surveys of Chaco Canyon, New Mexico*, 10, 34.

16 R. Van Dyke et al., *Chaco Landscapes: Data, Theory and Management*, 22.

17 Brugge, *A History of the Chaco Navajos*, 171.

18 McNitt, *Richard Wetherill: Anasazi. Pioneer Explorer of Southwestern Ruins*, 205.

19 "New Mexico's Pre-Historic Ruins," *Albuquerque Citizen*, April 10, 1902, 7.

20 "Enthusiastic Annual Meeting of the Colorado Cliff Dwellers Association," *Weekly Gazette*, August 21, 1901, 5.

21 Browman, *The Role of Women in the Founding of Americanist Archaeology*.

22 Robertson, *The Magnificent Mountain Women: Adventures in the Colorado Rockies*, 68.

23 "A New National Park on the Site of a Pre-Historic City," *San Francisco Examiner*, January 5, 1901, 21.

24 "Enthusiastic Annual Meeting of the Colorado Cliff Dwellers Association," *Weekly Gazette*, August 21, 1901, 5.

25 J. Wetherill, "Notes on the Discovery of Keet Seel," *Plateau Magazine* 27.3 (1995): 18–20. Canyons of the Ancients, 2004.84.D.13.O.

26 "Enthusiastic Annual Meeting of the Colorado Cliff Dwellers Association," *Weekly Gazette*, August 21, 1901, 5.

27 Lee, "The Antiquities Act of 1906," 230.

28 A. Chamberlain, "In Memoriam: John Wesley Powell, 1834–1902," *Journal of American Folklore*, 202.

29 Wetherill, *The Wetherills of the Mesa Verde: Autobiography of Benjamin Alfred Wetherill*, 283.

30 Wetherill, *The Wetherills of the Mesa Verde: Autobiography of Benjamin Alfred Wetherill*, 269.

31 Wetherill, *The Wetherills of the Mesa Verde: Autobiography of Benjamin Alfred Wetherill*, 271, 283.

32 AMNH, *Annual Report of the President, Treasurer's Report, List of Accessions, Act of Incorporation, Constitution, By-Laws and List of Members for the Year 1901*, 20–21.

33 R. Wetherill, letter to B. T. B. Hyde, April 17, 1901, American Museum of Natural History, Division of Anthropology Archives, 1897–45.

34 "The Looker-on," *Brooklyn Life*, March 8, 1902, 9.

35 R. Wetherill, letter to Fred Hyde, March 21, 1902, American Museum of Natural History, Division of Anthropology Archives, 1897–45.

36 "Improvements. Hyde Exploration Company Is Developing the Navajo Land. New Buildings," *Albuquerque Citizen*, April 3, 1902, 1.

37 "Santa Fe," *Albuquerque Citizen*, April 16, 1902, 6.

38 "Hyde Exploring Expedition," *Albuquerque Citizen*, July 21, 1902.

39 Wetherill and Horabin, proprietors of Navajo Indian Trading Post, letter to "Mine Own Peoples" [Mary and Martha Wetherill], ca. 1903, Canyons of the Ancients, 2000.19.D.365.O.

40 McNitt, *Richard Wetherill: Anasazi. Pioneer Explorer of Southwestern Ruins*, 252.

41 G. Pepper, letter to Professor F. W. Putnam, July 26, 1902, Peabody Museum of Archaeology and Ethnology at Harvard University, 999–24 Frederic Ward Putnam papers, Box 2, Folder 13.

42 "Agreement Between the Hyde Exploring Expedition and Doctor A. Hrdlicka" (March 21, 1903) Museum of the American Indian/Heye Foundation Records, NMAI.AC.001_188_12, National Museum of the American Indian Archives Center, Smithsonian Institution.

43 A. Schultz, *Biographical Memoir of Aleš Hrdlička 1869–1943. National Academny Biographical Memoirs XXIII*, 307–8.

44 H. Haynes, "Progress of American Archaeology during the Past Ten Years," 17–39.

45 Wetherill and Horabin, proprietors of Navajo Indian Trading Post, letter to "Mine Own Peoples" [Mary and Martha Wetherill], ca. 1903, Canyons of the Ancients, 2000.19.D.365.O.

46 McPherson, *Traders, Agents, and Weavers: Developing the Northern Navajo Region*, 78.

47 McPherson, *Traders, Agents, and Weavers: Developing the Northern Navajo Region*, 60.

48 Brugge, *A History of the Chaco Navajos*, 179.

Chapter 13

1 Gabriel, *Marietta Wetherill: Life with the Navajos in Chaco Canyon*, 183.

2 Wetherill, *The Wetherills of the Mesa Verde: Autobiography of Benjamin Alfred Wetherill*, 280.

3 Gabriel, *Marietta Wetherill: Life with the Navajos in Chaco Canyon*, 184.

4 Gabriel, *Marietta Wetherill: Life with the Navajos in Chaco Canyon*, 186.

5 Gabriel, *Marietta Wetherill: Life with the Navajos in Chaco Canyon*, 183.

6 R. Wetherill II, oral history interview conducted by Richard N. Sandlin, December 1–4, 1977.

7 McNitt, *Richard Wetherill: Anasazi. Pioneer Explorer of Southwestern Ruins*, 216–17.

8 Gabriel, *Marietta Wetherill: Life with the Navajos in Chaco Canyon*, 95.

9 B. T. B. Hyde, letter to George H. Pepper, October 20, 1904, George Pepper: Correspondence; Museum of the American Indian/Heye Foundation Records.

10 Phillips, "Archaeological Expeditions into Southeastern Utah and Southwestern Colorado between 1888–1898 and the Dispersal of the Collections," 116.

11 S. K. Lothrop, "George Gustav Heye. 1874–1956," 66.

12 G. Pepper, "The Museum of the American Indian, Heye Foundation," 403, 406.

13 R. Woodbury and N. F. S. Woodbury, "The Rise and Fall of the Bureau of American Ethnology," 289.

14 Woodbury and Woodbury, "The Rise and Fall of the Bureau of American Ethnology," 289.

15 N. Parezo and D. Fowler, *Anthropology Goes to the Fair: The 1904 Louisiana Purchase Exposition*, 36–46.

16 Boas, "The Bureau of American Ethnology," 830.

17 Parezo and Fowler, *Anthropology Goes to the Fair: The 1904 Louisiana Purchase Exposition*, 45–46.

18 Holmes, "Appendix II. Report on the Bureau of American Ethnology," 47.

19 Holmes, "Appendix II. Report on the Bureau of American Ethnology," 47–49.

20 R. Halley, *Tennessee Archaeology at the Louisiana Purchase Exposition*, 3.

21 Parezo and Fowler, *Anthropology Goes to the Fair: The 1904 Louisiana Purchase Exposition*, 100.

22 Gabriel, *Marietta Wetherill: Life with the Navajos in Chaco Canyon*, 187.

23 F. Boas, "The History of Anthropology," 521.

24 Lee, "The Antiquities Act of 1906," 232–33.

25 Lee, "The Antiquities Act of 1906," 234.

26 T. Seymour, "Twenty-Fifth Annual Report of the Council of the Archaeological Institute of America," 1–10.

27 Lee, "The Antiquities Act of 1906," 237.

28 S. Livick, "A Feud That Sparked the Move of Manitou," *Dolores Star*.

29 Wetherill, *The Wetherills of the Mesa Verde: Autobiography of Benjamin Alfred Wetherill*, 280.

30 S. Redman, *Bone Rooms: From Scientific Racism to Human Prehistory in Museums*, 65.

31 Schmedding, *Cowboy and Indian Trader*, 65.

32 Schmedding, *Cowboy and Indian Trader*, 96–97.

33 Schmedding, *Cowboy and Indian Trader*, 206–7. In typical fashion, Mamie remembered the day differently. She was the first to meet Finn and there were more guns and more drama.

34 McPherson, *Traders, Agents, and Weavers: Developing the Northern Navajo Region*, 104.

35 Gabriel, *Marietta Wetherill: Life with the Navajos in Chaco Canyon*, 109.

36 R. Wetherill II, oral history interview conducted by Richard N. Sandlin, December 1–4, 1977.

Chapter 14

1 Lee, "The Antiquities Act of 1906," 237.

2 Lee, "The Antiquities Act of 1906," 238.

3 Thompson, "Edgar Lee Hewett and the Political Process," 309.

4 R. Tsosie, "Indigenous Rights and Archaeology," 68.

5 Watkins, "Beyond the Margin: American Indians, First Nations, and Archaeology in North America," 275.

6 C. Bowditch, "Report of the Committee on American Archaeology," 41.

7 C. Bowditch and E. Hewett, "Report of the Committee on American Archaeology," 50–60.

8 Keller and Turek, *American Indians and National Parks.*

9 Jones, *Being and Becoming Ute: The Story of an American Indian People*, 223.

10 Robertson, *The Magnificent Mountain Women: Adventures in the Colorado Rockies*, 72.

11 "Enthusiastic Annual Meeting of the Colorado Cliff Dwellers Association," *Weekly Gazette*, August 21, 1901, 5.

12 Bowditch and Hewett, "Report of the Committee on American Archaeology," 59.

13 McNitt, *Richard Wetherill: Anasazi. Pioneer Explorer of Southwestern Ruins*, 212–13.

14 Gabriel, *Marietta Wetherill: Life with the Navajos in Chaco Canyon*, 103.

15 J. Moen and E. Tallman, "The Panic of 1907."

16 Schmedding, *Cowboy and Indian Trader*, 112.

17 McPherson, *Traders, Agents, and Weavers Developing the Northern Navajo Region*, 87, 111.

18 Iverson, *Diné: A History of the Navajos*, 210.

19 Lee, "The Antiquities Act of 1906," 246.

Chapter 15

1 Schmedding, *Cowboy and Indian Trader*, 191–205.

2 R. Wetherill II, oral history interview conducted by Richard N. Sandlin, December 1–4, 1977.

3 Schmedding, *Cowboy and Indian Trader*, 205.

4 McNitt, *Richard Wetherill: Anasazi. Pioneer Explorer of Southwestern Ruins*, 248–53.

5 Brugge, *A History of the Chaco Navajos*, 201.

6 Schmedding, *Cowboy and Indian Trader*, 218–19.

7 Brugge, *A History of the Chaco Navajos*, 214–15.

8 Schmedding, *Cowboy and Indian Trader*, 307.

9 Schmedding, *Cowboy and Indian Trader*, 98–100.

10 Brugge, *A History of the Chaco Navajos*, 201.

11 R. Wetherill II, oral history interview conducted by Richard N. Sandlin, December 1–4, 1977.

12 R. Wetherill II, oral history interview conducted by Richard N. Sandlin, December 1–4, 1977.

13 Gabriel, *Marietta Wetherill: Life with the Navajos in Chaco Canyon*, 203.

14 Gabriel, *Marietta Wetherill: Life with the Navajos in Chaco Canyon*, 204.

15 Gillmor and Wetherill, *Traders to the Navajos*, 81.

16 Gillmor and Wetherill, *Traders to the Navajos*, 97.

17 Gillmor and Wetherill, *Traders to the Navajos*, 182.

18 Gillmor and Wetherill, *Traders to the Navajos*, 161.

19 H. Hassell, *Rainbow Bridge*, 38.

20 H. Rothman, "Ruins, Reputations, and Regulation: Byron Cummings, William B. Douglass, John Wetherill, and the Summer of 1909," 326.

21 Gillmor and Wetherill, *Traders to the Navajos*, 62.

22 Hassell, *Rainbow Bridge*, 43.

23 Hassell, *Rainbow Bridge*, 38.

24 Rothman, "Ruins, Reputations, and Regulation: Byron Cummings, William B. Douglass, John Wetherill, and the Summer of 1909," 334.

25 Gillmor and Wetherill, *Traders to the Navajos*, 166.

26 Gillmor and Wetherill, *Traders to the Navajos*, 166.

27 Hassell, *Rainbow Bridge*, 47.

28 Hassell, *Rainbow Bridge*, 48.

29 Hassell, *Rainbow Bridge*, 49.

30 Hassell, *Rainbow Bridge*, 49.

31 Hassell, *Rainbow Bridge*, 50.

32 Gillmor and Wetherill, *Traders to the Navajos*, 171.

33 Hassell, *Rainbow Bridge*, 57.

34 Hassell, *Rainbow Bridge*, 54.

35 Gillmor and Wetherill, *Traders to the Navajos*, 205.

36 McPherson, "Of Papers and Perception: Utes and Navajos in Journalistic Media, 1900–1930," 207–8.

37 M'Closkey, *Swept under the Rug: A Hidden History of Navajo Weaving*, 43.

38   Gillmor and Wetherill, *Traders to the Navajos*, 66.

39   Gillmor and Wetherill, *Traders to the Navajos*, 188.

Chapter 16

1   R. Wetherill II, oral history interview conducted by Richard N. Sandlin, December 1–4, 1977.

2   R. Wetherill II, oral history interview conducted by Richard N. Sandlin, December 1–4, 1977.

3   Brugge, *A History of the Chaco Navajos*, 252–55.

4   Brugge, *A History of the Chaco Navajos*, 252–55.

5   Brugge, *A History of the Chaco Navajos*, 253.

6   Brugge, *A History of the Chaco Navajos*, 253.

7   Brugge, *A History of the Chaco Navajos*, 253–54.

8   Brugge, *A History of the Chaco Navajos*, 253–54.

9   Brugge, *A History of the Chaco Navajos*, 254.

10   Gabriel, *Marietta Wetherill: Life with the Navajos in Chaco Canyon*, 209–10.

11   "Women Left at Mercy of the Murderers of Wetherill," *Albuquerque Morning Journal*, June 30, 1910, 6.

12   Gabriel, *Marietta Wetherill: Life with the Navajos in Chaco Canyon*, 210.

13   Gabriel, *Marietta Wetherill: Life with the Navajos in Chaco Canyon*, 210.

14   Gabriel, *Marietta Wetherill: Life with the Navajos in Chaco Canyon*, 210.

15   Gabriel, *Marietta Wetherill: Life with the Navajos in Chaco Canyon*, 211.

16   Gabriel, *Marietta Wetherill: Life with the Navajos in Chaco Canyon*, 212.

17   Gabriel, *Marietta Wetherill: Life with the Navajos in Chaco Canyon*, 212–13.

18   "Women Left at Mercy of the Murderers of Wetherill," *Albuquerque Morning Journal*, June 30, 1910, 6.

19   Gabriel, *Marietta Wetheril:l Life with the Navajos in Chaco Canyon*, 213.

20   R. Wetherill II, oral history interview conducted by Richard N. Sandlin, December 1–4, 1977.

21   R. Wetherill II, oral history interview conducted by Richard N. Sandlin, December 1–4, 1977.

22   Gabriel, *Marietta Wetherill: Life with the Navajos in Chaco Canyon*, 213–4.

23   Prudden, *Life and Death of Richard Wetherill*, 20.

24   Gabriel, *Marietta Wetherill: Life with the Navajos in Chaco Canyon*, 217–8.

25   Gabriel, *Marietta Wetherill: Life with the Navajos in Chaco Canyon*, 216.

26   Wetherill, *The Wetherills of the Mesa Verde: Autobiography of Benjamin Alfred Wetherill*, 282.

27   "How Wetherill Met Death at Navajos' Hands," *Deseret News*, June 24, 1910, 1.

28   "Indian Trader in New Mexico Killed," *El Paso Herald*, June 23, 1910, 7.

29 "Richard Wetherill, Pioneer Indian Trader, Shot Dead by Navajo," *Albuquerque Morning Journal*, June 24, 1910, 1.

30 "Husband Killed in Indian Outbreak," *Tiller and Toiler*, July 15, 1910, 2.

31 S. T. Shelton, letter to Mr. Paul A. F. Walter, January 28, 1910.

32 S. F. Stacher, letter to Mr. Alfred Hardy, March 7, 1910.

33 S. F. Stacher, letter to the Commissioner of Indian Affairs, April 4, 1910.

34 S. F. Stacher, letter to Supt. Peter Paquett, May 7, 1910.

35 B. P. Six, letter to the Commissioner of Indian Affairs, May 28, 1910.

36 E. Quick, Affidavit of Eleanor L. Quick at Gallup, September 5, 1910.

37 Quick, Affidavit of Eleanor L. Quick at Gallup, September 5, 1910.

38 Gabriel, *Marietta Wetherill: Life with the Navajos in Chaco Canyon*, 204.

39 Quick, Affidavit of Eleanor L. Quick at Gallup, September 5, 1910.

40 S. F. Stacher, letter to the Commissioner of Indian Affairs, June 27, 1910.

41 Gabriel, *Marietta Wetherill: Life with the Navajos in Chaco Canyon*, 218–19.

42 W. T. Shelton, letter to Supt. Peter Paquette, July 25, 1910.

43 T. M. Prudden, letter to Robert G. Valentine, Commissioner of Indian Affairs, July 19, 1910, Bureau of Land Management, Canyons of the Ancients, 2004.84.D.12.O.

44 T. M. Prudden, letter to Robert G. Valentine, Commissioner of Indian Affairs, July 19, 1910, Bureau of Land Management, Canyons of the Ancients, 2004.84.D.12.O.

45 Prudden, *Life and Death of Richard Wetherill*, 10–11.

46 Prudden, *Life and Death of Richard Wetherill*, 18.

47 Prudden, *Life and Death of Richard Wetherill*, 14.

48 Gabriel, *Marietta Wetherill: Life with the Navajos in Chaco Canyon*, 23.

49 R. Wetherill II, oral history interview conducted by Richard N. Sandlin, December 1–4, 1977.

50 Gabriel, *Marietta Wetherill: Life with the Navajos in Chaco Canyon*, 232–36.

51 Gabriel, *Marietta Wetherill: Life with the Navajos in Chaco Canyon*, 219.

52 Gabriel, *Marietta Wetherill: Life with the Navajos in Chaco Canyon*, 207.

53 US Census Bureau, "Fourteenth Census of the United States: 1920–Population, Navajo County, Arizona."

Chapter 17

1 A. Kidder, "Samuel James Guernsey," 135–37.

2 R. Greengo, "Alfred Vincent Kidder," 320–25.

3 Kidder and Guernsey, *Archaeological Explorations in Northeastern Arizona. Smithsonian Institution Bureau of American Ethnology Bulletin*, 13.

4 Kidder and Guernsey, *Archaeological Explorations in Northeastern Arizona*, 13.

5   Kidder and Guernsey, *Archaeological Explorations in Northeastern Arizona*, 14.

6   Kidder and Guernsey, *Archaeological Explorations in Northeastern Arizona*, 15.

7   Kidder and Guernsey, *Archaeological Explorations in Northeastern Arizona*, 17–19.

8   Kidder and Guernsey, *Archaeological Explorations in Northeastern Arizona*, 19.

9   Kidder and Guernsey, *Archaeological Explorations in Northeastern Arizona*, 19.

10   Kidder and Guernsey, *Archaeological Explorations in Northeastern Arizona*, 24–26.

11   Kidder and Guernsey, *Archaeological Explorations in Northeastern Arizona*, 27.

12   Kidder and Guernsey, *Archaeological Explorations in Northeastern Arizona*, 29–30.

13   Kidder and Guernsey, *Archaeological Explorations in Northeastern Arizona*, 31.

14   S. Guernsey and A. Kidder, *Basket-maker Caves of Northeastern Arizona. Report on the Explorations, 1916–17*, iii.

15   Kidder and Guernsey, *Archaeological Explorations in Northeastern Arizona*, 91–92.

16   Kidder and Guernsey, *Archaeological Explorations in Northeastern Arizona*, 91–92.

17   Kidder and Guernsey, *Archaeological Explorations in Northeastern Arizona*, 212.

18   Kidder and Guernsey, *Archaeological Explorations in Northeastern Arizona*, 204.

19   D. Browman and D. Givens, "Stratigraphic Excavation: The First 'New Archaeology,'" 81.

20   Browman and Givens, "Stratigraphic Excavation: The First 'New Archaeology,'" 82.

21   S. Nash, "Time for Collaboration: A. E. Douglass, Archaeologists, and the Establishment of Tree-Ring Dating in the American Southwest," 268–69.

22   Willey and Sabloff, *A History of American Archaeology*, 98–103.

23   D. Browman, "Spying by American Archaeologists in World War I (with a minor linkage to the development of the Society for American Archaeology)," 10–17.

24   Browman, "Spying by American Archaeologists in World War I (with a minor linkage to the development of the Society for American Archaeology)," 10–17.

25   J. Wetherill, letter to Talbot Hyde, December 15, 1918, American Museum of Natural History, Division of Anthropology Archives, 1897–45.

26   Kroeber "Frederic Ward Putnam," 718.

Chapter 18

1   Wetherill, *The Wetherills of the Mesa Verde: Autobiography of Benjamin Alfred Wetherill*, 30.

2   Pepper, "Pueblo Bonito."

3   "George Hubbard Pepper," *American Anthropologist*, 567.

4 Phillips, "Archaeological Expeditions into Southeastern Utah and Southwestern Colorado between 1888–1898 and the Dispersal of the Collections," 116.

5 Phillips, "Archaeological Expeditions into Southeastern Utah and Southwestern Colorado between 1888–1898 and the Dispersal of the Collections," 116–17.

6 G. Pepper, Letter to Mr. George G. Heye, Director, December 4, 1923, The Latin American Library, Tulane University.

7 Lothrop, "George Gustav Heye. 1874–1956," 66.

8 G. Pepper, "The Museum of the American Indian, Heye Foundation," 416–18.

9 Phillips, "Archaeological Expeditions into Southeastern Utah and Southwestern Colorado between 1888–1898 and the Dispersal of the Collections," 117.

10 Pepper, "The Museum of the American Indian, Heye Foundation," 403.

11 Lothrop, "George Gustav Heye. 1874–1956," 66–67.

12 K. Carlson, "Nels C. Nelson: Danish-American Archaeologist," 47–63.

13 Lipe, "Introduction to the 1979 notes on 'Archaeological Research at the Turkey Pen Site.'"

14 Dring et al. "Authoring and Authority in Eastern Pequot Community Heritage and Archaeology," 367.

15 F. McManamon, "Developments in American Archaeology: Fifty Years of the National Historic Preservation Act," 567.

16 M. Bawaya, "Archaeology: Curation in Crisis," 1025–26.

Chapter 19

1 B. Fagan, *Chaco Canyon: Archaeologists Explore the Lives of an Ancient Society*, 33.

2 Hayes et al., *Archaeological Surveys of Chaco Canyon, New Mexico. Publications in Archaeology 18A Chaco Canyon Studies*, 10.

3 Willey and Sabloff, *A History of American Archaeology*, 106–7.

4 Fagan, *Chaco Canyon: Archaeologists Explore the Lives of an Ancient Society*, 37–38.

5 Fagan, *Chaco Canyon: Archaeologists Explore the Lives of an Ancient Society*, 58.

6 Willey and Sabloff, *A History of American Archaeology*, 58.

7 B. Glasrud, "Under the Radar Blacks in New Mexico History," 1–20.

8 N. Judd, "The Present Status of Archaeology in the United States," 401.

9 Judd, "The Present Status of Archaeology in the United States," 403.

10 Judd, "The Present Status of Archaeology in the United States," 403–8.

11 J. Sprinkle Jr., *Crafting Preservation Criteria: The National Register of Historic Places and American Historic Preservation*, 7–8.

12 United States Code: Historic Sites, Buildings, Objects, and Antiquities, 16 U.S.C. §§ 461–467 (Suppl. 1 1934).

13 Sprinkle, *Crafting Preservation Criteria: The National Register of Historic Places and American Historic Preservation*, 12.

14 S. Anfinson, *Practical Heritage Management: Preserving a Tangible Past*, 222.

15 J. Paige, *The Civilian Conservation Corps and the National Park Service, 1933–1942: An Administrative History*, 110–14.

16 R. Richert and R. Vivian, *Ruins Stabilization in the Southwestern United States*, 8–9.

17 Richert and Vivian, *Ruins Stabilization in the Southwestern United States*, 3.

18 K. Harry et al., *Cultural Resources Archaeology: An Introduction*, 8–10.

19 B. Means, "Introduction: 'Alphabet Soup' and American Archaeology," 9.

20 T. Thiessen, *Emergency Archeology in the Missouri River Basin: The Role of the Missouri River Basin Project and the Midwest Archeological Center in the Interagency Archeological Salvation Program, 1946–1975.*

21 B. Means, "Labouring in the Fields of the Past: Geographic Variation in New Deal Archaeology across the Lower 48 United States," 4–7.

Chapter 20

1 A. Rains and L. Henderson, *With Heritage So Rich*, 11–12.

2 Rains and Henderson, *With Heritage So Rich*, 18.

3 L. Sebastian, *Preserving America's Past*, 2.

4 National Historic Preservation Act, as amended (54 USC 3000 et seq: Historic Preservation)

5 "Directory," National Conference of State Historic Preservation Officers.

6 A. Klesert, "A View from Navajoland on the Reconciliation of Anthropologists and Native Americans," 18.

7 "Federally Recognized Indian Tribes and Resources for Native Americans," USA.Gov.

8 "THPO Directory," National Association of Tribal Historic Preservation Officers.

9 Reyman, "The History of Archaeology and the Archaeological History of Chaco Canyon, New Mexico," 45.

10 R. Van Dyke et al., *Chaco Landscapes: Data, Theory and Management*, 24.

11 Van Dyke et al., *Chaco Landscapes: Data, Theory and Management*, 25.

12 Van Dyke et al., *Chaco Landscapes: Data, Theory and Management*, 25.

13 Van Dyke et al., *Chaco Landscapes: Data, Theory and Management*, 25.

14 T. Ferguson et al., "Co-Creation of Knowledge by the Hopi Tribe and Archaeologists," 255.

15 Louis Berger and Associates, *Abbott Farm: National Historic Landmark.*

16 C. Tolmie and P. Branstner, *Section 106 Archaeological Properties Identification Report, Obama Presidential Center (OPC) Mobility Improvements to Support the South Lakefront Framework Plan (SLFP), Cook County, Illinois.*

17 "More Concerns About the Obama Center as Archaeology Report on Jackson Park Faces New Scrutiny," *Cultural Landscape Foundation*.

18 Memorandum of Agreement among Federal Highway Administration, Illinois State Historic Preservation Officer, Advisory Council on Historic Preservation Regarding Projects in Jackson Park in Chicago, Cook County, Illinois.

Chapter 21

1   D. Guinand, "BLM Is Restoring Historic 'Turkey Pen' Ruin," *Times-Independent*, July 31, 1980, 9.

2   M. Powers, *The Salvage of Archaeological Data from Turkey Pen Ruin, Grand Gulch Primitive Area, San Juan County, Utah*, 1.

3   American Antiquities Act of 1906, 16 USC 431–433.

4   United States v. Diaz, 499 F.2d 113 (9th Cir. 1974), rev'g 368 F. Supp. 856 (D. Ariz. 1973).

5   R. Collins and M. Michel, "Preserving the Past: Origins of the Archaeological Resources Protection Act of 1979," 85.

6   Collins and Michel, "Preserving the Past: Origins of the Archaeological Resources Protection Act of 1979," 85.

7   United States v. Smyer, 596 F.2d 939 (10th Cir. 1979), cert. denied, 444 U.S. 843 (1979).

8   United States of America, Plaintiff-Appellant v. Kyle R. Jones, Thayde L. Jones and Robert E. Gevara, Defendants-Appellees. 607 F.2d 269 (1979).

9   Collins and Michel, "Preserving the Past: Origins of the Archaeological Resources Protection Act of 1979," 87.

10 United States General Accounting Office, *Cultural Resources Problems Protecting and Preserving Federal Archeological Resources*, Report to Congressional Requesters.

11 S. Koyiyumptewa, "A Hopi Perspective on Archaeological Resource Crime: Safeguarding Ancestral Footprints," 27.

12 B. Chapoose, "Remnants of a Lifeway, Sources of Strength," 35–36.

13 Collins and Michel, "Preserving the Past: Origins of the Archaeological Resources Protection Act of 1979," 84.

14 Watkins, "Beyond the Margin: American Indians, First Nations, and Archaeology in North America," 276.

15 D. Green and H. Hanks, "Prosecuting without Regulations: ARPA Successes and Failures," 103.

16 "Letters to the Editor," *San Juan Record*, August 14, 1980, 16.

17 "Letters to the Editor," *San Juan Record*, September 4, 1980, 2, 17.

18 United States General Accounting Office, *Cultural Resources Problems Protect-*

ing and Preserving Federal Archeological Resources, Report to Congressional Requesters.

19 J. Fryar, "Historical Perspective on Enforcing the Archaeological Resources Protection Act and the Native American Graves Protection and Repatriation Act," 11–13.

20 United States Government Accountability Office, *Native American Cultural Resources Improved Information Could Enhance Agencies' Efforts to Analyze and Respond to Risks of Theft and Damage*, Report to the Committee on Indian Affairs, US Senate.

Chapter 22

1 J. Battillo et al., "Tale of a Test Pit: The Research History of a Midden Column from the Turkey Pen Site, Utah."

2 D. Aasen, "Pollen, Macrofossil, and Charcoal Analyses of Basketmaker Coprolites from Turkey Pen Ruin, Cedar Mesa, Utah."

3 C. Cooper et al., "Short-Term Variability of Human Diet at Basketmaker II Turkey Pen Ruins, Utah: Insights into Domesticate Use and Supplementation from Bulk and Single Amino Acid Isotope Analysis of Hair," 10–18.

4 R. Matson, "Turkey Pen Excavation."

5 N. Akins, *A Biocultural Approach to Human Burials from Chaco Canyon*.

6 Hurst and Turner II "Rediscovering the 'Great Discovery': Wetherill's First Cave 7 and Its Record of Basketmaker Violence," 143–91.

7 P. Geib and W. Hurst, "Should Dates Trump Context? Evaluation of the Cave 7 Skeletal Assemblage Radiocarbon Dates," 2760.

8 D. Kennett et al., "Archaeogenomic Evidence Reveals Prehistoric Matrilineal Dynasty."

9 Wetherill, *The Wetherills of the Mesa Verde: Autobiography of Benjamin Alfred Wetherill*, 111.

10 K. Claw et al., "Chaco Canyon Dig Unearths Ethical Concerns," 177.

11 J. Reardon and K. TallBear, "'Your DNA Is Our History': Genomics, Anthropology, and the Construction of Whiteness as Property," S233–45.

12 Kennett et al., "Archaeogenomic Evidence Reveals Prehistoric Matrilineal Dynasty."

13 Claw et al., "Chaco Canyon Dig Unearths Ethical Concerns," 177.

14 G. A. Clark, "NAGPRA, the Conflict between Science and Religion, and the Political Consequences."

15 L. Wade, "An Archaeology Society Hosted a Talk against Returning Indigenous Remains. Some Want a New Society."

16 Public Law 101–601—Nov. 16, 1990.

17   United States Senate, "Providing for the Protection of Native American Graves and the Repatriation of Native American Remains and Cultural Patrimony."

18   T. Ferguson, "Native Americans and the Practice of Archaeology," 70.

19   T. Ferguson et al., "Co-Creation of Knowledge by the Hopi Tribe and Archaeologists," 249–62.

20   L. Kuwanwisiwma, "The Collaborative Road: A Personal History of the Hopi Cultural Preservation Office," 9–10.

21   S. Atalay, *Community-Based Archaeology: Research with, by, and for Indigenous and Local Communities.*

22   D. Williams and G. Shipley, "Scientific Consequentialism: Potential Problems with an Outcome-Driven Form of Indigenous Archaeology," 64.

23   C. Colwell-Chanthaphonh et al., "The Premise and Promise of Indigenous Archaeology," 228–38.

24   P. Crown, "Room 28 in Pueblo Bonito Background, Research Questions, and Methods," 2.

25   Claw et al., "Chaco Canyon Dig Unearths Ethical Concerns," 179.

26   S. Wolverton et al., "Archaeology, Heritage, and Moral Terrains: Two Cases from the Mesa Verde Region," 29.

Chapter 23

1   A. Klesert, "A View from Navajoland on the Reconciliation of Anthropologists and Native Americans," 17.

2   N. Laluk, "Changing How Archaeology Is Done in Native American Contexts: An Ndee (Apache) Case Study," 53–73.

3   V. Deloria Jr., *God Is Red: A Native View of Religion*, 10.

4   S. Dowlin, "Maria Pearson: A Warrior and Peacemaker in Two Worlds," 72–79.

5   C. Colwell-Chanthaphonh et al. "The Premise and Promise of Indigenous Archaeology," 229.

6   E. Greer, "Na Wai E Ho ʻōla I Nā Iwi? Who Will Save the Bones: Native Hawaiians and the Native American Graves Protection and Repatriation Act," 39–40.

7   J. Keenan, "Seminole Indian Remains Reburied at Historic Sioux Indian Site," *Associated Press*, August 11, 1989.

8   A. Arieff, "A Different Sort of (P)Reservation: Some Thoughts on the National Museum of the American Indian," 79.

9   Public Law 101–185 — Nov. 28, 1989.

10   R. Preucel, "An Archaeology of NAGPRA: Conversations with Suzan Shown Harjo," 2–3.

11   I. Jacknis, "A New Thing? The NMAI in Historical and Institutional Perspective," 511–42.

12 R. Seidemann, "NAGPRA at 20: What Have the States Done to Expand Human Remains Protections?" 200–203.

13 Friends Committee on National Legislation. Letter from Representatives of Various Religious and Other Organizations to Members of the Senate Select Committee on Indian Affairs and House Committee on Interior and Insular Affairs.

14 M. Schillaci and W. Bustard, "Controversy and Conflict: NAGPRA and the Role of Biological Anthropology in Determining Cultural Affiliation," 357.

15 43 CFR § 10.14.

16 J. Vela, "Returning Geronimo to His Homeland: The Application of NAGPRA and Broken Treaties to the Case of Geronimo's Repatriation," S184–86.

17 Schillaci and Bustard, "Controversy and Conflict: NAGPRA and the Role of Biological Anthropology in Determining Cultural Affiliation," 358–59.

18 Schillaci and Bustard, "Controversy and Conflict: NAGPRA and the Role of Biological Anthropology in Determining Cultural Affiliation," 359–60.

19 Schillaci and Bustard, "Controversy and Conflict: NAGPRA and the Role of Biological Anthropology in Determining Cultural Affiliation," 363–65.

20 "Tribes Celebrate Mesa Verde Repatriation," *Indian Country Today*, September 17, 2020.

21 L. Kuwanwisiwma, "The Collaborative Road: A Personal History of the Hopi Cultural Preservation Office," 10–11.

22 M. F. Brown and M. Bruchac, "NAGPRA from the Middle Distance: Legal Puzzles and Unintended Consequences," 198.

23 Crown, "Room 28 in Pueblo Bonito: Background, Research Questions, and Methods," 2.

24 S. Nash and C. Colwell, "NAGPRA at 30: The Effects of Repatriation," 225–39.

25 Department of the Interior, "Native American Graves Protection and Repatriation Act Systematic Process of Disposition and Repatriation of Native American Human Remains, Funerary Objects, Sacred Objects, and Objects of Cultural Patrimony," 63202–60.

Chapter 24

1 W. Davis and J. Till, "The Lime Ridge Clovis Site: Old and New Data."

2 R. Burrillo, "The Archaeology of Bears Ears," 9–18.

3 R. Fitzsimmons, "Honoring 114 Years of the Antiquities Act, Critical to the Protection of Bears Ears."

4 R. Robinson, *Voices from Bears Ears: Seeking Common Ground on Sacred Land*, 119–20.

5 R. Johannsen, "Public Land Withdrawal Policy and the Antiquities Act," 439–65.

6   Public Law 96–487, Alaska National Interest Lands Conservation Act, December 2, 1980.

7   National Trust for Historic Preservation, "Broad Coalition Sues to Stop Trump Administration's Unlawful Dismemberment of the Bears Ears National Monument," *National Trust for Historic Preservation.*

8   National Park Service, "Arizona May Put People with Minimal Training in Charge of Identifying Archaeological Sites," *NPS Archaeology E-Gram.*

9   J. Fowler, Re: Regulation Identifier Number 1024-AE49. Letter to the Keeper of the National Register of Historic Places, National Park Service from the Advisory Council on Historic Preservation.

10   National Trust for Historic Preservation, Statement of the National Trust for Historic Preservation, Tom Cassidy, Vice President for Government Relations and Policy Subcommittee for Indigenous Peoples of the United States, Natural Resources Committee, United States House of Representatives.

11   J. Swarner, "Oak Flat Historic Designation a Win for Mine Opponents, but Fight Continues."

12   United States Department of Agriculture, Final Environmental Impact Statement, Resolution Copper Project and Land Exchange.

13   National Trust for Historic Preservation, Statement of the National Trust for Historic Preservation, Tom Cassidy, Vice President for Government Relations and Policy Subcommittee for Indigenous Peoples of the United States, Natural Resources Committee, United States House of Representatives.

14   Swarner, "Oak Flat Historic Designation a Win for Mine Opponents, but Fight Continues."

15   V. Grussing, "Re: National Park Service (NPS) Regulation Identifier Number 1024-AE49."

16   L. Llewellyn and C. Perser, *NEPA and the Environmental Movement: A Brief History.*

17   L. Friedman, "Trump Weakens Major Conservation Law to Speed Construction Permits."

18   T. Roosevelt, "Address at Dickinson, Dakota Territory."

Epilogue

1   Wetherill, *The Wetherills of the Mesa Verde: Autobiography of Benjamin Alfred Wetherill,* 283–84.

2   Wetherill, *The Wetherills of the Mesa Verde: Autobiography of Benjamin Alfred Wetherill,* 276.

3   Al and Mary Wetherill Address Book, Bureau of Land Management, Canyons of the Ancients, 2000.19.D.1332.O.

4 Wetherill, *The Wetherills of the Mesa Verde: Autobiography of Benjamin Alfred Wetherill*, 289.

5 "George Hubbard Pepper," 566–72.

6 A Noyes, "B. Talbot Hyde."

7 "Benjamin Talbot Babbitt Hyde," 628.

8 Wetherill, *The Wetherills of the Mesa Verde: Autobiography of Benjamin Alfred Wetherill*, 230.

9 Wetherill, *The Wetherills of the Mesa Verde: Autobiography of Benjamin Alfred Wetherill*, 237.

10 M. Wright, letter to Harry F. Evans, July 5, 1957, Bureau of Land Management, Canyons of the Ancients, 2004.84.D.140.O.

11 Watkins, "Beyond the Margin: American Indians, First Nations, and Archaeology in North America," 277.

12 D. Two Bears. "'Ihoosh'aah, Learning by Doing: The Navajo Nation Archeology Department Student Training Program," 190.

13 Steeves, "Academia, Archaeology, CRM, and Tribal Historic Preservation," 131.

14 J. Altscul and T. Klein, "Forecast for the US CRM Industry and Job Market, 2022–2031," 1–16.

Bibliography

Aasen, Diane K. "Pollen, Macrofossil, and Charcoal Analyses of Basketmaker Coprolites from Turkey Pen Ruin, Cedar Mesa, Utah." MA thesis, Washington State University.

Abbott, Charles Conrad. "Paleolithic Man: A Last Word." *Science* (1892): 344–45.

"Agreement Between the Hyde Exploring Expedition and Doctor A. Hrdlcika," March 21, 1903. Museum of the American Indian/Heye Foundation Records, NMAI.AC.001_188_12, National Museum of the American Indian Archives Center, Smithsonian Institution.

Akins, Nancy J. *A Biocultural Approach to Human Burials from Chaco Canyon, New Mexico*. Santa Fe: Branch of Cultural Research, US Department of the Interior, National Park Service, 1986.

Al and Mary Wetherill Address Book. Bureau of Land Management, Canyons of the Ancients, 2000.19.D.1332.O.

Altscul, Jeffrey H., and Terry H. Klein. "Forecast for the US CRM Industry and Job Market, 2022–2031." *Advances in Archaeological Practice* (2022): 1–16.

American Museum of Natural History. *Annual Report of the President, Act of Incorporation, Contract with the Department of Public Parks, Constitution, By-Laws and List of Members for the Year 1895*. New York: American Museum of Natural History, 1895.

American Museum of Natural History. *Annual Report of the President, Treasurer's Report, List of Accessions, Act of Incorporation, Constitution, By-Laws and List of Members for the Year 1901*. New York, 1902.

Anfinson, Scott F. *Practical Heritage Management: Preserving a Tangible Past*. Lanham: Rowman and Littlefield, 2019.

"An Antiquarian in Trouble." *Muscatine News-Tribune*, September 20, 1891.

"Archaeology and Ethnology." *American Naturalist* 24.282 (1890): 589–94.

Arieff, Allison. "A Different Sort of (P)Reservation: Some Thoughts on the

National Museum of the American Indian." *Museum Anthropology* 19.2 (1995): 78–90.

"Around the World in Ten Days." *Huntsville Weekly Democrat*, October 11, 1893.

Atalay, Sonya. *Community-Based Archaeology: Research with, by, and for Indigenous and Local Communities*. Berkeley: University of California Press, 2012.

Balenquah, Lyle. *The Memory of Water: Elements and Ancestry in Bears Ears—Part 1*. Courtesy of the Crow Canyon Archaeological Center.

Bandelier, Adolph. "Report on the Ruins of the Pueblo of Pecos." In *Papers of the Archaeological Institute of America. American Series*. Boston: Cupples, Upham, and Co., 1883.

"Basket People." *Rocky Mountain Sun*, November 24, 1894.

Battillo, Jenna, R. G. Matson, and William D. Lipe. "Tale of a Test Pit: The Research History of a Midden Column from the Turkey Pen Site, Utah." Presented at the 84th Annual SAA Meeting, Albuquerque, New Mexico, 2019.

Bawaya, Michael. "Archaeology: Curation in Crisis." *Science* 317.5841 (2007): 1025–26.

Bear, Casey. "'The Spirits Are Still There': A Personal Reflection on Bears Ears National Monument." *National Trust for Historic Preservation*, May 24, 2017. https://savingplaces.org/stories/mark-maryboy-personal-reflection-bears-ears-national-monument#.X2DA5GhKjIU.

Beck, David. *Unfair Labor? American Indians and the 1893 World's Columbian Exposition in Chicago*. Lincoln: University of Nebraska Press, 2019.

"Benjamin Talbot Babbitt Hyde." *The Historical Encyclopedia of New Mexico*. Albuquerque, 1945.

"Benjamin T. Babbitt." *New York Times*, October 21, 1889.

Blackburn, Fred M. *The Wetherills: Friends of Mesa Verde*. Korea: Durango Herald Small Press, 2009.

Blackburn, Fred M., and Victoria M. Atkins. "Anasazi Basketmaker Papers from the 1990 Wetherill–Grand Gulch Symposium." In *Anasazi Basketmaker Papers from the 1990 Wetherill–Grand Gulch Symposium*, edited by Victoria M. Atkins, 41–102. Salt Lake City: United States Department of the Interior, Bureau of Land Management, 1993.

Blackburn, Fred M., and Ray A. Williamson. *Cowboys and Cave Dwellers: Basketmaker Archaeology in Utah's Grand Gulch*. Santa Fe: School of American Research Press, 1997.

Blitz, John H. *Moundville*. Tuscaloosa: University of Alabama Press, 2005.

Boas, Franz. "The Bureau of American Ethnology." *Science* 16.412 (1902): 828–31.

Boas, Franz. "Ethnology at the Exposition." In *Coming of Age in Chicago: The 1893 World's Fair and the Coalescence of American Anthropology*, edited by

Curtis M. Hinsley and David R. Wilcox, 78–83. Lincoln: University of Nebraska Press, 2016.

Boas, Franz. "The History of Anthropology." *Science* 20.512 (1904): 513–24.

Bowditch, Charles P. "Report of the Committee on American Archaeology." *American Journal of Archaeology* 10 (1906): 40–2.

Bowditch, Charles P., and Edgar L. Hewett. "Report of the Committee on American Archaeology." *American Journal of Archaeology* 11 (1907): 50–60.

Browman, David L. "The Origin of the 'Chicago Method' Excavation Techniques: Contributions of William Nickerson and Frederick Starr." *Bulletin of the History of Archaeology* 23.2 (2013). http://doi.org/10.5334/bha.2324.

Browman, David L. "The Peabody Museum, Frederic W. Putnam, and the Rise of U.S. Anthropology, 1866–1903." *American Anthropologist* 104.2 (2002): 508–19.

Browman, David L. *Cultural Negotiations: The Role of Women in the Founding of Americanist Archaeology*. Lincoln: University of Nebraska Press, 2013.

Browman, David L. "Spying by American Archaeologists in World War I (with a minor linkage to the development of the Society for American Archaeology)." *Bulletin of the History of Archaeology* 21.2 (2011): 10–17.

Browman, David L., and Douglas R. Givens. "Stratigraphic Excavation: The First 'New Archaeology.'" *American Anthropologist* 98.1 (1996): 80–95.

Browman, David L., and Stephen Williams. *Anthropology at Harvard. A Biographical History, 1790–1940*. Cambridge: Peabody Museum Press, 2013.

Brown, M. F., and M. Bruchac. "NAGPRA from the Middle Distance: Legal Puzzles and Unintended Consequences." In *Imperialism, Art, and Restitution*, edited by H. Merryman, 193–217. Cambridge: University of Cambridge Press, 2006.

Brugge, David M. *A History of the Chaco Navajos*. Albuquerque: US Department of the Interior, 1980.

"The Bureau of Ethnology." *Science* 16.408 (1902): 676–77.

Burrillo, R. E. "The Archaeology of Bears Ears." *SAA Archaeological Record* (2017): 9–18.

Campbell, Wade. "Na'nilkad bee na'niltin—Learning from Herding: An Ethnoarchaeological Study of Historic Pastoralism on the Navajo Nation." *Kiva* 87.3 (2021): 295–315.

Campbell, Wade, Kerry F. Thompson, and Richard Begay. "Naasgo: Moving Forward—Dine Archaeology in the Twenty-First Century." *KIVA* (2021): 1–15.

Carlson, Kathleen Nielsen. "Nels C. Nelson: Danish-American Archaeologist." *The Bridge* 18.1: 47–63.

Carver, Martin. "Burial as Poetry: The Context of Treasure in Anglo-Saxon Graves." In *Treasure in the Medieval West*, edited by Elizabeth M. Tyler, 25–48. Suffolk: York Medieval Press, 2000.

Chamberlain, Alex F. "In Memoriam: Frank Hamilton Cushing." *Journal of American Folklore* 13.49 (1900): 129–34.

Chamberlain, Alexander F. "In Memoriam: John Wesley Powell, 1834–1902." *Journal of American Folklore* 15.58 (1902): 199–204.

Chapin, Frederick Hastings. *The Land of the Cliff-dwellers*. Boston: Appalachian Mountain Club, 1892.

Chapin, Gretchen. "A Navajo Myth from the Chaco Canyon." *New Mexico Anthropologist* 4.4 (1940): 63–67.

Chapoose, Betsy. "Remnants of a Lifeway, Sources of Strength." *Archaeology Southwest Magazine* 34.2&3 (2020): 35–36.

Chester, Hilary Lynn. "Frances Eliza Babbitt and the Growth of Professionalism of Women in Archaeology." In *New Perspectives on the Origins of Americanist Archaeology*, edited by David L. Browman and Stephen Williams, 164–84. Tuscaloosa: University of Alabama Press, 2002.

Clark, G. A. "NAGPRA, the Conflict between Science and Religion, and the Political Consequences." *Society for American Archaeology Bulletin* 16.5 (1998).

Claw, Katrina G., Dorothy Lippert, Jessica Bardill, Anna Cardova, Keolu Fox, Joseph M. Yracheta, Alyssa C. Bader, Deborah A. Bolnick, Ripan S. Malhi, Kimberly TallBear, and Nanibaa' A. Garrison. "Chaco Canyon Dig Unearths Ethical Concerns." *Human Biology* 89.3 (2017): 177–80.

"The Cliff Dwellers Discussed in a Series of Papers at the Woman's Club." *Brooklyn Daily Eagle*, February 12, 1895.

"Cliff Dwellers' Homes." *Lenora News*, November 14, 1901.

"Cliff Dwellers of Colorado." *Philadelphia Times*, July 4, 1898.

"The Cliff Dwellers! The Wetherill Collection on Exhibition at Denver." *Grand Junction News*, March 21, 1891.

Cole, Fay-Cooper. "In Memoriam Franz Boas." *American Journal of Sociology* 48.5 (1943): 603.

Collins, Robert B., and Mark P. Michel. "Preserving the Past: Origins of the Archaeological Resources Protection Act of 1979." In *A History of the Archaeological Resources Protection Act: Law and Regulations*, edited by Janet L. Friedman, 84–89. *American Archaeology* 5.2, 1985.

Colwell-Chanthaphonh, Chip. *Inheriting the Past: The Making of Arthur C. Parker and Indigenous Archaeology*. Tucson: University of Arizona Press, 2016.

Colwell-Chanthaphonh, Chip, T. J. Ferguson, Dorothy Lippert, Randall H. McGuire, George P. Nicholas, Joe E. Watkins, and Larry J. Zimmerman. "The

Premise and Promise of Indigenous Archaeology." *American Antiquity* 75.2 (2010): 228–38.

Cooper, Catherine, Karen Lupo, R. G. Matson, William D. Lipe, Colin Smith, and Michael P. Richards. "Short-Term Variability of Human Diet at Basket-maker II Turkey Pen Ruins, Utah: Insights into Domesticate Use and Supplementation from Bulk and Single Amino Acid Isotope Analysis of Hair." *Journal of Archaeological Science: Reports*, 5 (2016): 10–18.

Copy, the Expedition of 1896 and 1897 Grand Gulch. American Museum of Natural History, Division of Anthropology Archives, 1897–45.

Correspondence with B. K. Wetherill, folder 252, Box 18, Manuscript and Pamphlet File, Department of Anthropology Records, National Anthropological Archives, Smithsonian Institution.

Crown, Patricia L. "Room 28 in Pueblo Bonito: Background, Research Questions, and Methods." In *The House of the Cylinder Jars: Room 28 in Pueblo Bonito, Chaco Canyon*, edited by Patricia L. Crown, 1–13. Albuquerque: University of New Mexico Press, 2020.

Cushing, Frank Hamilton. "Excerpts from the Diary of Frank Hamilton Cushing at the World's Fair." In *Coming of Age in Chicago. The 1893 World's Fair and the Coalescence of American Anthropology*, edited by Curtis M. Hinsley and David R. Wilcox, 153–211. Lincoln: University of Nebraska Press, 2016.

Cushing, Frank Hamilton. "Monthly Report of Mr. Frank Hamilton Cushing." In *Coming of Age in Chicago. The 1893 World's Fair and the Coalescence of American Anthropology*, edited by Curtis M. Hinsley and David R. Wilcox, 212–31. Lincoln: University of Nebraska Press, 2016.

Davis, William E., and Jonathan D. Till. "The Lime Ridge Clovis Site: Old and New Data." *Archaeology Southwest Magazine* 28.3&4 (2014).

Deloria Jr., Vine. *Custer Died for Your Sins*. Scribner, 2018.

Deloria Jr., Vine. *God Is Red: A Native View of Religion*. Fulcrum, 2003.

Department of the Interior. "Native American Graves Protection and Repatriation Act, Systematic Process of Disposition and Repatriation of Native American Human Remains, Funerary Objects, Sacred Objects, and Objects of Cultural Patrimony." *Federal Register* 87.200 (2022): 63202–60.

Dilworth, Leah. "Representing the Hopi Snake Dance." In *Imagining Indians in the Southwest: Persistent Visions of a Primitive Past*, 453–96. Washington: Smithsonian Institution Press, 1996.

"Directory." National Conference of State Historic Preservation Officers. https://ncshpo.org/directory/.

Dowlin, Sheryl L. "Maria Pearson: A Warrior and Peacemaker in Two Worlds." In *Women Who Speak for Peace*, edited by Colleen E. Kelley and Anna L. Eblen, 71–86. Lanham: Rowman and Littlefield, 2002.

Dring, Katherine Sebastian, et al. "Authoring and Authority in Eastern Pequot Community Heritage and Archaeology." *Archaeologies: Journal of the World Archaeological Congress* 15.3 (2019): 355–58.

Dunbar-Ortiz, Roxanne. *An Indigenous Peoples' History of the United States.* Boston: Beacon Press, 2014.

Echo-Hawk, Walter R. "Tribal Efforts to Protect against Mistreatment of Indian Dead: The Quest for Equal Protection of the Laws." *Native American Rights Fund Legal Review* 14.1 (1989): 1–5.

"Enthusiastic Annual Meeting of the Colorado Cliff Dwellers Association." *Weekly Gazette*, August 21, 1901.

Epigrams, Discussion of the human condition, date unknown. Bureau of Land Management, Canyons of the Ancients, 2004.84.D.53.O.

Ewen, Stuart, and Elizabeth Ewen. *Channels of Desire: Mass Images and the Shaping of American Consciousness.* Minneapolis: University of Minnesota Press, 1992.

Ewing, Heather. *The Lost World of James Smithson: Science, Revolution and the Birth of the Smithsonian.* New York: Bloomsbury, 2010.

Executive Order 11593, *Protection and Enhancement of the Cultural Environment,* 3 CFR 1971 Comp. p. 154.

Fagan, Brian. *Chaco Canyon: Archaeologists Explore the Lives of an Ancient Society.* Oxford: Oxford University Press, 2005.

Fagan, Brian. *A Little History of Archaeology.* London: Yale University Press, 2018.

"Federally Recognized Indian Tribes and Resources for Native Americans." USA. Gov. https://www.usa.gov/tribes#:~:text=for%20Native%20Americans -,Federally%20Recognized%20Indian%20Tribes,contracts%2C%20grants %2C%20or%20compacts.

Ferguson, T. J. "Native Americans and the Practice of Archaeology." *Annual Review of Anthropology* 25 (1996): 63–79.

Ferguson, T. J., Stewart B. Koyiyumptewa, and Maren P. Hopkins. "Co-Creation of Knowledge by the Hopi Tribe and Archaeologists." *Advances in Archaeological Practice* 3.3 (2015): 249–62.

Fewkes, Jesse Walter. *Antiquities of the Mesa Verde National Park, Cliff Palace.* Washington, DC: Government Printing Office, 1911.

Fitzsimmons, Regina. "Honoring 114 Years of the Antiquities Act, Critical to the Protection of Bears Ears." *Friends of Cedar Mesa,* June 10, 2020. https://www .friendsofcedarmesa.org/honoring-114-years-of-the-antiquities-act-critical -to-the-protection-of-bears-ears/.

Fletcher, Alice C. "On the Preservation of Archaeologic Monuments." *Proceedings of the American Association for the Advancement of Science* 36 (1888): 317.

Fletcher, Alice C., and T. E. Stevenson. "Report on the Committee on the Preservation of Archaeologic Remains on the Public Lands." *Proceedings of the American Association for the Advancement of Science* 37 (1889): 35–7.

Fowler, John M., Re: Regulation Identifier Number 1024-AE49. Letter to the Keeper of the National Register of Historic Places, National Park Service from the Advisory Council on Historic Preservation, April 26, 2019.

Freed, Stanley A., Ruth S. Freed, and Laila Williamson. "Capitalist Philanthropy and Russian Revolutionaries: The Jesup North Pacific Expedition (1897–1902)." *American Anthropologist* 90.1 (1988): 7–24.

Friedman, Lisa. "Trump Weakens Major Conservation Law to Speed Construction Permits." *New York Times*, August 4, 2020. https://www.nytimes.com/2020/07/15/climate/trump-environment-nepa.html.

Friends Committee on National Legislation. Letter from Representatives of Various Religious and Other Organizations to Members of the Senate Select Committee on Indian Affairs and House Committee on Interior and Insular Affairs, 1990.

Fryar, John. "Historical Perspective on Enforcing the Archaeological Resources Protection Act and the Native American Graves Protection and Repatriation Act." *Archaeology Southwest* 34.2&3 (2020): 11–13.

Gabriel, Kathryn. *Marietta Wetherill: Life with the Navajos in Chaco Canyon.* Albuquerque: University of New Mexico Press, 1992.

Geib, Phil R., and Winston B. Hurst. "Should Dates Trump Context? Evaluation of the Cave 7 Skeletal Assemblage Radiocarbon Dates." *Journal of Archaeological Science* 40 (2013): 2754–70.

"George Hubbard Pepper." *American Anthropologist* 26 (1924): 566–72.

Gillman, Henry. "December Meeting. The 'Cardiff Giant' Controversy." *Proceedings of the Massachusetts Historical Society, 1869–1870.* Vol. 11 (1869–1870): 159–64.

Gillmor, Frances, and Louisa Wade Wetherill. *Traders to the Navajos.* Boston: Houghton Mifflin, 1934.

Glasrund, Bruce A. "Under the Radar: Blacks in New Mexico History." In *African American History in New Mexico: Portraits from Five Hundred Years*, edited by Bruce A. Glasrund, 1–20. Albuquerque: University of New Mexico Press, 2013.

"Grand Valley!" *Grand Junction News*, December 2, 1882.

Green, Dee F., and Herrick Hanks. "Prosecuting without Regulations: ARPA Successes and Failures," "A History of the Archaeological Resources Protection Act: Law and Regulations." In *A History of the Archaeological Resources Protection Act: Law and Regulations*, edited by Janet L. Friedman, 103–105. *American Archaeology* 5.2 (1985).

Greengo, Robert E. "Alfred Vincent Kidder." *American Anthropologist* 70.2 (1968): 320–25.

Greer, E. Sunny. "Na Wai E Ho ʻōla I Nā Iwi? Who Will Save the Bones: Native Hawaiians and the Native American Graves Protection and Repatriation Act." *Asian-Pacific Law and Policy Journal* 14.1 (2012): 33–52.

Grussing, Valerie J. "Re: National Park Service (NPS) Regulation Identifier Number 1024-AE49." Letter from the NATHPO to the Keeper of the National Register of Historic Places, July 3, 2019. http://www.nathpo.org/wp-content/uploads/2019/07/NRHP-Proposed-Rule_NATHPO-Comment-Letter-on-Tribal-Consultation.pdf.

Guernsey, Samuel James, and Alfred Vincent Kidder. *Basket-maker Caves of Northeastern Arizona. Report on the Explorations, 1916–17.* Cambridge: Peabody Museum, 1921.

Guinand, Debbie. "BLM Is Restoring Historic 'Turkey Pen' Ruin." *Times-Independent,* July 31, 1980.

Gulliford, Andrew. *Preserving Western History.* Albuquerque: University of New Mexico Press, 2005.

H. "Recent Finds in Utah." *Archaeologist* 2 (1894): 154–55.

Halley, R. A. *Tennessee Archaeology at the Louisiana Purchase Exposition.* Nashville: Cumberland Press, 1904.

Harris, Ann G. Esther Tuttle, and Sherwood D. Tuttle. *Geology of National Parks, Sixth Edition.* Dubuque: Kendall/Hunt Publishing Company, 2004.

Harry, Karen G., Thomas W. Newmann, and Robert M. Sanford. *Cultural Resources Archaeology: An Introduction.* Lanham: AltaMira Press, a Division of Rowman and Littlefield, 2010.

Hassell, Hank. *Rainbow Bridge.* Logan: Utah State University Press 1999.

Hayes, Alden C., David M. Brugge, and W. James Judge. *Archaeological Surveys of Chaco Canyon, New Mexico. Publications in Archaeology 18A, Chaco Canyon Studies.* Washington, DC: US Department of the Interior, 1981.

Hayes, Ann. "The Chicago Connection: 100 Years in the Life of the C. H. Green Collection." In *Anasazi Basketmaker Papers from the 1990 Wetherill–Grand Gulch Symposium,* edited by Victoria M. Atkins, 121–28. Salt Lake City: United States Department of the Interior, Bureau of Land Management, 1993.

Haynes, Henry W. "Progress of American Archaeology during the Past Ten Years." *American Journal of Archaeology* 4.1 (1900): 17–39.

Headline Story of the Wetherill Family. *Mancos Times-Tribune,* Mancos, Colorado, June 19, 1980. 2004.84.D.81.0, Bureau of Land Management, Canyons of the Ancients National Monument, US Department of the Interior, Dolores, Colorado.

Hinsley, Curtis M. "Anthropology as Education and Entertainment. Frederic

Ward Putnam at the World's Fair." In *Coming of Age in Chicago: The 1893 World's Fair and the Coalescence of American Anthropology*, edited by Curtis M. Hinsley and David R. Wilcox, 1–77. Lincoln: University of Nebraska Press, 2016.

Hinsley, Curtis M., Jr., and Alfred M. Tozzer. "The Problem with Mr. Hewett: Academics and Popularizers in American Archaeology, c. 1910." *History of Anthropology Newsletter* 7.5 (1980): 7–10.

Hinsley, Curtis M., and David R. Wilcox, "Introduction: The Chicago Fair and American Anthropology in 1893." In *Coming of Age in Chicago: The 1893 World's Fair and the Coalescence of American Anthropology*, edited by Curtis M. Hinsley and David R. Wilcox, xv-xli. Lincoln: University of Nebraska Press, 2016.

Holmes, William Henry. "Appendix II. Report on the Bureau of American Ethnology." *Annual Report of the Board of Regents of the Smithsonian Institution* (1904): 46–54.

Holmes, William Henry. "A Quarry Workshop of the Flaked-Stone Implement Makers in the District of Columbia." *American Anthropologist* 3.1 (1890): 1–26.

Holmes, William Henry. "The World's Fair Congress of Anthropology." *American Anthropologist* 6.4 (1893): 423–34.

Holt, H. Barry. "A Cultural Resource Management Dilemma: Anasazi Ruins and the Navajos." *American Antiquity* 48.3 (1983): 594–99.

Hough, Walter. "William Henry Holmes." *American Anthropologist* 35.4 (1933): 752–64.

"How Wetherill Met Death at Navajos' Hands." *Deseret News*, June 24, 1910.

Hrdlička, Alex, letter to Professor Fred. W. Putnam, October 16, 1900. Peabody Museum of Archaeology & Ethnology at Harvard University, 2–12.

Hrdlička, Alois F. "The Medico-Legal Aspect of the Case of Maria Barbella." *State Hospital Bulletin Vol. III, No. 2.* Utica: State Hospitals Press, 1897.

Hurst, Winston, and Christy G. Turner II. "Rediscovering the 'Great Discovery': Wetherill's First Cave 7 and Its Record of Basketmaker Violence." In *Anasazi Basketmaker Papers from the 1990 Wetherill–Grand Gulch Symposium*, edited by Victoria M. Atkins, 143–92. Salt Lake City: United States Department of the Interior, Bureau of Land Management, 1993.

"Husband Killed in Indian Outbreak." *Tiller and Toiler*, July 15, 1910.

"Hyde Exploring Expedition." *Albuquerque Citizen*, July 21, 1902.

Hyde, B. Talbot B., letter to George H. Pepper, October 20, 1904. George Pepper: Correspondence. Museum of the American Indian/Heye Foundation Records.

Hyde, Frederick E. (1892–1893). Frederick E. Hyde Journals, 1892–1893. University of Utah Libraries, Special Collections, ACCN 0093.

Hyde, Talbot. Excavation in the Tsegi by the Wetherills 1894 or 1895 Expedition. Bureau of Land Management, Canyons of the Ancients, 2001.18.D.22.O.

"Improvements. Hyde Exploration Company Is Developing the Navajo Land. New Buildings." *Albuquerque Citizen*, April 3, 1902.

"Indian Mounds." *Salt Lake Herald*, November 22, 1885.

"Indian Trader in New Mexico Killed." *El Paso Herald*, June 23, 1910.

Ingham, John N. *Biographical Dictionary of American Business Leaders*. Westport: Greenwood Press, 1983.

"Items from Denver." *New Castle Nonpareil*, June 28, 1900, 1.

"It Is Now History." *Daily Independent*, November 6, 1893.

Iverson, Peter. *Diné: A History of the Navajos*. Albuquerque: University of New Mexico Press, 2002.

Jacknis, Ira. "A New Thing? The NMAI in Historical and Institutional Perspective." *American Indian Quarterly* 30.3/4 (2006): 511–42.

James, Anthony. "Were the Cliff Dwellers White?" *Modern World and Business Woman's Magazine* (1908): 47–49.

Jefferson, Thomas. *Notes on the State of Virginia*. London: John Stockdale, 1787.

Jesup, Morris K. "Report of the President." *American Museum of Natural History Annual Report of the President*. New York: American Museum of Natural History, 1898.

Johannsen, Richard M. "Public Land Withdrawal Policy and the Antiquities Act." *Washington Law Review* 56 (1981): 439–65.

Jones, Sondra G. *Being and Becoming Ute: The Story of an American Indian People*. Salt Lake City: University of Utah Press, 2019.

Judd, Neil M. "The Present Status of Archaeology in the United States." *American Anthropologist* 31.3 (1929): 401–18.

Keenan, Joseph. "Seminole Indian Remains Reburied at Historic Sioux Indian Site." Associated Press, August 11, 1989. https://apnews.com /df3456299ad80580872863599de40ed0.

Keller, Donald R., Richard V. Ahlstrom, and Dana Hartman. *Final Report for Surface Cleanup of Cultural Sites in Grand Gulch*. Submitted to the Bureau of Land Management by the Museum of Northern Arizona Department of Anthropology, 1974.

Keller, Robert H., and Michael F. Turek. *American Indians and National Parks*. Tucson: University of Arizona Press, 1999.

Kelsey, Francis W. "Archaeological Forgeries from Michigan." *American Anthropologist* 10.1 (1908): 48–59.

Kennett, Douglass J., Stephen Plog, Richard J. George, Brendan J. Culleton, Adam S. Watson, Pontus Skoglund, Nadin Rohland, Swapan Mallick, Kristin Stewardson, Logan Kistler, Steven A. LeBlanc, Peter M. Whiteley, David

Reich, and George H. Perry. "Archaeogenomic Evidence Reveals Prehistoric Matrilineal Dynasty." *Nature Community* 8.14115 (2017). doi.org/10.1038 %2Fncomms14115.

Kidder, A. V. "Samuel James Guernsey." *American Anthropologist* 39.1 (1937): 135–37.

Kidder, Alfred Vincent, and Samuel James Guernsey. *Archaeological Explorations in Northeastern Arizona. Smithsonian Institution Bureau of American Ethnology Bulletin* 65. Washington, DC: Government Printing Office, 1919.

Klesert, Anthony L. "A View from Navajoland on the Reconciliation of Anthropologists and Native Americans." *Human Organization* 51.1 (1992): 17–22.

Knipmeyer, James H. "Some Historic Signatures of the Four Corners Region." In *Anasazi Basketmaker Papers from the 1990 Wetherill–Grand Gulch Symposium*, edited by Victoria M. Atkins, 33–40. Salt Lake City: United States Department of the Interior, Bureau of Land Management, 1993.

Koenig, Seymour H., and Harriet Koenig. *Acculturation in the Navajo Eden: New Mexico, 1550–1750.* New York: YBK Publishers, 2005.

Koyiyumptewa, Stewart B. "A Hopi Perspective on Archaeological Resource Crime: Safeguarding Ancestral Footprints." *Archaeology Southwest Magazine* 34.2&3 (2020): 26–27.

Kroeber, Alfred Louis. "Frederic Ward Putnam." *American Anthropologist* 17.4 (1915): 712–18.

Kuwanwisiwma, Leigh J. "The Collaborative Road: A Personal History of the Hopi Cultural Preservation Office." In *Footprints of Hopi History: Hopihiniwtiput Kukveni'at*, edited by Leigh J. Kuwanwisiwma, T. J. Ferguson, and Chip Colwell. Tucson: University of Arizona Press, 2018.

Laluk, Nicholas C. "Changing How Archaeology Is Done in Native American Contexts: An Ndee (Apache) Case Study." *Journal of Social Archaeology* 21.1 (2021): 53–73.

"The Latest." *Parker Pilot*, September 18, 1891.

"Latest Local News." *San Juan Times*, October 18, 1895.

Lee, Ronald Freeman. "The Antiquities Act of 1906." *Journal of the Southwest. A Special Issue: The Antiquities Act of 1906* 42.2 (2000): 197–269.

"Letters to the Editor." *San Juan Record*, August 14, 1980.

"Letters to the Editor." *San Juan Record*, September 4, 1980.

Levine, Frances. "Homestead in Ruins: Richard Wetherill's Homestead in Chaco Canyon." In *From Chaco to Chaco: Papers in Honor of Robert H. Lister and Florence C. Lister*, edited by Meliha S. Duran and David T. Kirkpatrick, 45–59. Archaeological Society of New Mexico Papers.

Lipe, Bill. "Introduction to the 1979 Notes on 'Archaeological Research at the Turkey Pen Site'" (2015).

Livick, Shannon. "A Feud That Sparked the Move of Manitou." *Dolores Star*, February 7, 2013.

Llewellyn, Lynn G., and Clare Perser. *NEPA and the Environmental Movement: A Brief History*. Prepared for Environmental Studies Division, Office of Research and Monitoring, Environmental Protection Agency, 1973.

"The Looker-on." *Brooklyn Life*, March 8, 1902.

"Loot." In *The Oxford English Dictionary, Second Edition, Volume IX*, edited by J. A. Simpson and E. S. C. Weiner. Oxford: Clarendon Press, 1989.

Lothrop, S. K. "George Gustav Heye. 1874–1956." *American Antiquity* 23.1 (1957): 66–67.

Louis Berger and Associates. *Abbott Farm: National Historic Landmark* (1996). doi:10.7282/T3G44TBR.

Lyman, Vanallen, letter to *New Mexico* magazine for Marietta Wetherill and Mabel C. Wright. August 26, 1954. Bureau of Land Management, Canyons of the Ancients, 2004.84.D.190.O.

"Man and His Works." *Daily Republican*, July 28, 1893.

Mancos Times. May 5, 1893.

Mason, Charlie. "The Story of the Discovery and Early Exploration of the Cliff Houses at the Mesa Verde." In *Richard Wetherill: Anasazi. Pioneer Explorer of Southwestern Ruins*, by Frank McNitt. Albuquerque: University of New Mexico Press, 1966.

Mathien, Frances Joan. "Identifying Sources of Prehistoric Turquoise in North America: Problems and Implications for Interpreting Social Organization." *BEADS: Journal of the Society of Bead Researchers* 12 (2000): 17–37.

Matson, R. G. "Turkey Pen Excavation." Cedar Mesa Research Materials, 2018. http://hdl.handle.net/2376/5302.

Mattson, Hannah V., and Jacqueline M. Kocer. "Ornaments, Mineral Specimens, and Shell Specimens from Room 28." In *The House of the Cylinder Jars: Room 28 in Pueblo Bonito, Chaco Canyon*, edited by Patricia L. Crown, 80–100. Albuquerque: University of New Mexico Press, 2020.

M'Closkey, Kathy. *Swept under the Rug: A Hidden History of Navajo Weaving*. Albuquerque: University of New Mexico Press, 2002.

McClurg, Virginia Donaghe. "Colorado." In *Evenings with Colorado Poets: A Compilation of Selections from Colorado Poets and Verse-writers*, edited by Francis S. Kinder and F. Clarence Spencer, 12. Denver: Chain & Hardy, 1894.

McGee, WJ. "Man and the Glacial Period." *American Anthropologist* 6.1 (1893): 85–95.

McManamon, Francis P. "Developments in American Archaeology: Fifty Years of the National Historic Preservation Act." *Annual Review of Anthropology* 47(2018): 553–74.

McNitt, Frank. *Richard Wetherill: Anasazi. Pioneer Explorer of Southwestern Ruins*. Albuquerque: University of New Mexico Press, 1966.

McPherson, Robert S. "Of Papers and Perception: Utes and Navajos in Journalistic Media, 1900–1930." *Utah Historical Quarterly* LXVII.3 (1999): 196–219.

McPherson, Robert. *Traders, Agents, and Weavers Developing the Northern Navajo Region*. Norman: University of Oklahoma Press, 2017.

Means, Bernard K. "Introduction: 'Alphabet Soup' and American Archaeology." In *Shovel Ready Archaeology and Roosevelt's New Deal for America*, edited by Bernard K. Means, 1–20. Tuscaloosa: University of Alabama Press, 2013.

Means, Bernard K. "Labouring in the Fields of the Past: Geographic Variation in New Deal Archaeology across the Lower 48 United States." *Bulletin of the History of Archaeology* 25.2 (2015): 1–11.

Meltzer, David J. "In the Heat of Controversy. C.C. Abbott, the American Paleolithic, and the University Museum, 1889–1893." In *Philadelphia and the Development of Americanist Archaeology*, edited by Don D. Fowler and David R. Wilcox, 48–87. Tuscaloosa: University Press, 2003.

Meltzer, David J. "When Destiny Takes a Turn for the Worse: William Henry Holmes and, Incidentally, Franz Boas in Chicago, 1892–97." *Histories of Anthropology Annual* 6 (2010): 171–224.

Memorandum of Agreement among Federal Highway Administration, Illinois State Historic Preservation Officer, Advisory Council on Historic Preservation Regarding Projects in Jackson Park in Chicago, Cook County, Illinois. https://www.chicago.gov/content/dam/city/depts/dcd/supp_info/jackson/final_moa_for_signature_111020.pdf.

Miller, Darlis. *Matilda Coxe Stevenson: Pioneering Anthropologist*. Norman: University of Oklahoma, 2007.

Miscellaneous Documents of the House of Representatives for the Second Session of the Fifty-Second Congress, 1892–1893. Washington, DC: Government Printing Office, 1893.

Moen, Jon R., and Ellis W. Tallman. "The Panic of 1907." *Federal Reserve History* (2015). https://www.federalreservehistory.org/essays/panic-of-1907.

Moorehead, Caroline. *Lost and Found: The 9,000 Treasures of Troy. Heinrich Schliemann and the Gold That Got Away*. New York: Penguin, 1997.

Moorehead, Warren King. "The Ancient Man: The Anthropological Exhibit at the World's Fair. It Will Open Next Month. The Work Which Has Been Done by Professor Putnam." In *Coming of Age in Chicago: The 1893 World's Fair and the Coalescence of American Anthropology*, edited by Curtis M. Hinsley and David R. Wilcox, 369–74. Lincoln: University of Nebraska Press, 2016.

"More Concerns about the Obama Center as Archaeology Report on Jackson Park Faces New Scrutiny." *Cultural Landscape Foundation*. https://www.tclf

.org/more-concerns-about-obama-center-archaeology-report-jackson-park
-faces-new-scrutiny.

"Mrs. McClurg's Last Lecture." *Daily Morning Journal and Courier*, October 31,
1895.

Nash, Stephen E. "Time for Collaboration: A. E. Douglass, Archaeologists, and
the Establishment of Tree-Ring Dating in the American Southwest." *Journal
of the Southwest* 40.3 (1998): 261–305.

Nash, Stephen E., and Chip Colwell. "NAGPRA at 30: The Effects of Repatriation." *Annual Review of Anthropology* 49: 225–39.

National Park Service. "Arizona May Put People with Minimal Training in
Charge of Identifying Archaeological Sites." *NPS Archaeology E-Gram*, April
2018. https://www.nps.gov/archeology/pubs/egrams/1804.pdf.

National Trust for Historic Preservation. "Broad Coalition Sues to Stop Trump
Administration's Unlawful Dismemberment of the Bears Ears National Monument." *National Trust for Historic Preservation*, December 6, 2017: https://
savingplaces.org/press-center/media-resources/broad-coalition-sues-to
-stop-trump-administrations-unlawful-dismemberment-of-the-bears-ears
-national-monument#.X2DOwWhKjIU.

National Trust for Historic Preservation. Statement of the National Trust for
Historic Preservation, Tom Cassidy, Vice President for Government Rela-
tions and Policy, Subcommittee for Indigenous Peoples of the United States,
Natural Resources Committee, United States House of Representatives,
March 12, 2020. https://docs.house.gov/meetings/AP/AP06/20190226
/108950/HHRG-116-AP06-Wstate-CassidyT-20190226.pdf.

"New Mexico's Pre-Historic Ruins." *Albuquerque Citizen*, April 10, 1902.

"A New National Park on the Site of a Pre-Historic City." *San Francisco Examiner*,
January 5, 1901.

New York Herald, February 8, 1891. www.loc.gov/item/sn83030313/1891–02–08
/ed-1/.

Nordenskiöld, Gustaf. *The Cliff Dwellers of the Mesa Verde*. Colorado: Mesa Verde
Museum Association, 1893.

Nordenskiöld, Gustaf, letter to Richard Wetherill. 1893. Bureau of Land Management, Canyons of the Ancients, 2001.2.D.1.O, 1893.

Nordenskiöld, Gustaf. *Letters of Gustaf Nordenskiöld*. Edited by Irving L. Dia-
mond and Daniel M. Olson. Colorado: Mesa Verde Museum Association,
1991.

"A Noted Baron Arrested." *Colorado Daily Chieftain*, September 19, 1891.

Noyes, Alexander Dana. "B. Talbot Hyde." Century Association Biographical
Archive. Earliest Members of the Century Association (1934). https://
centuryarchives.org/caba/bio.php?PersonID=1487.

Ohio Historical Society. *Ohio History, Volume 10*. Columbus: Fred J. Heer, 1901.

"The Ohio Mounds." *Cambridge City Tribune*, December 13, 1888.

Paige, John C. *The Civilian Conservation Corps and the National Park Service, 1933–1942: An Administrative History*. Washington, DC: National Park Service, 1985.

Parezo, Nancy J., and Don D. Fowler. *Anthropology Goes to the Fair: The 1904 Louisiana Purchase Exposition*. Lincoln: University of Nebraska Press, 2007.

Peabody, Charles. "Frederic Ward Putnam." *Journal of American Folklore* 28.109 (1915): 302–6.

Pepper, George H. "The Exploration of a Burial Room in Pueblo Bonito, New Mexico." In *Putnam Anniversary Volume, Anthropological Essays Presented to Frederic Ward Putnam in Honor of His Seventieth Birthday*, edited by Franz Boas, Roland B. Dixon, F. W. Hodge, Alfred L. Kroeber, and Harlan I. Smith, 196–252. New York: G. E. Stechert, 1909.

Pepper, George. George Pepper Diary. GHP Reel 1 1886 2_000. The Latin American Library, Tulane University.

Pepper, George H., letter to Mr. B.T.B. Hyde. American Museum of Natural History, Division of Anthropology Archives, 1897–45.

Pepper, George H., letter to Mr. B.T.B. Hyde. July 30, 1898. American Museum of Natural History, Division of Anthropology Archives, 1897–45.

Pepper, George, letter to Mr. George G. Heye, Director. December 4, 1923. The Latin American Library, Tulane University.

Pepper, George H., letter to Professor F. W. Putnam. July 26, 1902. Peabody Museum of Archaeology & Ethnology at Harvard University, 2–13.

Pepper, George. "The Making of a Navajo Blanket." *Everybody's Magazine* (1902). Canyons of the Ancients, 2000.19.D.1484.O.

Pepper, George. "Mosaic Objects from Pueblo Bonito, Chaco Cañon, N.M." Presented before the Mid-winter meeting of Section H., Anthropology, at New Haven, December 27–29, 1898. The Latin American Library, Tulane University.

Pepper, George H. "The Museum of the American Indian, Heye Foundation." *Geographical Review* 2.6 (1916): 401–18.

Pepper, George. Pepper Papers, Box 2, 1897 Field Notes. The Latin American Library, Tulane University.

Pepper, George. "Pueblo Bonito." *Anthropological Papers of the American Museum of Natural History, Vol. XXVII*. New York: Order of the Trustees, 1920.

Phillips, Ann. "Archaeological Expeditions into Southeastern Utah and Southwestern Colorado between 1888–1898 and the Dispersal of the Collections." In *Anasazi Basketmaker Papers from the 1990 Wetherill–Grand Gulch Sym-*

posium, edited by Victoria M. Atkins, 103–20. Salt Lake City: United States Department of the Interior, Bureau of Land Management, 1993.

Powell, John Wesley. "On Limitations to the Use of Some Anthropologic Data." In *First Annual Report of the Bureau of Ethnology to the Secretary of the Smithsonian Institution, 1879–'80*, edited by John Wesley Powell, 73–75. Washington, DC: Government Printing Office, 1881.

Powers, Margaret A. *The Salvage of Archaeological Data from Turkey Pen Ruin, Grand Gulch Primitive Area, San Juan County, Utah*. Contributions to Anthropology Series, No. 808. San Juan County Archaeological Research Center and Library, 1984.

Pratt, Charles Eadward. *The Quaker Doctrine of the Inward Light Vindicated with Some Criticism of Thomas Kimber's Review of an Essay by Augustine Jones, upon the Principles, Methods, and History of the Society of Friends*. Boston: Geo. C. Herbert, 1874.

"Prehistoric Ruins." *Record*, June 28, 1900.

Preucel, Robert W. "An Archaeology of NAGPRA: Conversations with Suzan Shown Harjo." *Journal of Social Archaeology* (2011): 1–13.

Prudden, letter to R. P. Holcombe, September 6, 1910.

Prudden, Mitchell T. *Life and Death of Richard Wetherill* (1910–1912). Bureau of Land Management, Canyons of the Ancients, 2000.19.D.782.O.

Prudden, T. M., letter to Robert G. Valentine, Commissioner of Indian Affairs. July 19, 1910. Bureau of Land Management, Canyons of the Ancients, 2004.84.D.12.O.

Putnam, Charles E. *A Vindication of the Authenticity of the Elephant Pipes and Inscribed Tablets in the Museum of the Davenport Academy of Natural Sciences from the Accusations of the Bureau of Ethnology of the Smithsonian Institution*. Davenport: Glass and Hoover, 1885.

Putnam, Frederic Ward. Letter to George Davis. In *Coming of Age in Chicago: The 1893 World's Fair and the Coalescence of American Anthropology*, edited by Curtis M. Hinsley and David R. Wilcox, PP. Lincoln: University of Nebraska Press, 2016.

Putnam, Dr. Frederic W. Notes Pueblo Bonito, September 1899. Peabody Museum of Archaeology & Ethnology at Harvard University, 400010001.

Putnam, Frederic Ward. "A Problem in American Anthropology." *Science* 10.243 (1899): 225–36.

Putnam, Frederic Ward. *The Serpent Mound of Adams County, Ohio, and Its Preservation by the Peabody Museum of American Archaeology and Ethnology*. Salem Press, 1888.

Putnam, Frederic Ward. "The Serpent Mound of Ohio." *Century Illustrated Monthly Magazine* 39 (1889).

Quick, Eleanor L. Affidavit of Eleanor L. Quick at Gallup. September 5, 1910. http://wetherillfamily.com/.

Rains, Albert, and Laurance G. Henderson. *With Heritage So Rich*. New York: Random House, 1999.

Reardon, Jenny, and Kim TallBear. "'Your DNA Is Our History': Genomics, Anthropology, and the Construction of Whiteness as Property." *Current Anthropology* 53.5 (2012): S233–45.

Redman, Samuel J. *Bone Rooms: From Scientific Racism to Human Prehistory in Museums*. Cambridge: Harvard University Press, 2016.

Renfrew, Colin, and Paul Bahn. *Archaeology Theories, Methods, and Practice*, 6th ed. London: Thames and Hudson, 2012.

Reyman, Jonathan E. "The History of Archaeology and the Archaeological History of Chaco Canyon, New Mexico." In *Tracing Archaeology's Past: The Historiography of Archaeology*, edited by Andrew L. Christenson. Carbondale: Southern Illinois University Press, 1989.

"Richard Wetherill, Pioneer Indian Trader, Shot Dead by Navajo." *Albuquerque Morning Journal*, June 24, 1910.

Richert, Roland Von S., and R. Gordon Vivian. *Ruins Stabilization in the Southwestern United States*. Washington, DC: US Department of the Interior, 1974.

Riding In, James. "Six Pawnee Crania Historical and Contemporary Issues Associated with the Massacre and Decapitation of Pawnee Indians in 1869." In *Native Historians Write Back: Decolonizing American Indian History*, edited by Susan A. Miller and James Riding In, 101–19. Lubbock: Texas Tech University Press, 2011.

Riley, Ramon, and John R. Welch. "An Apache Perspective on Archaeological Resource Crime: Everything Is a Sacred, Living Entity." *Archaeology Southwest Magazine* 34.2&3 (2021): 23–25.

Robertson, Janet. *The Magnificent Mountain Women: Adventures in the Colorado Rockies*. Lincoln: University of Nebraska Press, 2003.

Robinson, Rebecca M. *Voices from Bears Ears: Seeking Common Ground on Sacred Land*. Tucson: University of Arizona Press, 2018.

Rohner, Ronald P. "Franz Boas: Ethnographer on the Northwest Coast." In *Pioneers of American Anthropology: The Uses of Biography*, edited by June Helm, 149–212. Seattle: University of Washington Press, 1966.

Roosevelt, Theodore. "Address at Dickinson, Dakota Territory, July 4, 1886." In *In the Words of Theodore Roosevelt: Quotations from the Man in the Arena*, edited by Patricia O'Toole. Ithaca: Cornell University Press, 2012.

Rothman, Hal K. "Ruins, Reputations, and Regulation: Byron Cummings, William B. Douglass, John Wetherill, and the Summer of 1909." *Journal of the Southwest* 35.3 (1993): 318–40.

"The San Juan Gold Fields, Reports from the Scene of Excitement in Southeastern Utah." *Idaho Springs News*, January 6, 1893.

"Santa Fe." *Albuquerque Citizen*, April 16, 1902.

Sawyer, Susan. *Myths and Mysteries of Tennessee: True Stories of the Unsolved and Unexplained.* Connecticut: Morris, 2013.

Sayre, Gordon M. "The Mound Builders and the Imagination of American Antiquity in Jefferson, Bartram, and Chateaubriand." *Early American Literature* 33.3 (1998): 225–49.

Schillaci, Michael A., and Wendy J. Bustard. "Controversy and Conflict: NAGPRA and the Role of Biological Anthropology in Determining Cultural Affiliation." *Political and Legal Anthropology Review* 33.2 (2010): 352–73.

Schmedding, Joseph. *Cowboy and Indian Trader*. Albuquerque: University of New Mexico Press, 1951.

Schultz, Adolph H. *Biographical Memoir of Aleš Hrdlička 1869–1943*. National Academy Biographical Memoirs XXIII. 1944.

Sebastian, Lynne. *Preserving America's Past*. Prepared for the Society for American Archaeology M.A.T.R.I.X Project on Undergraduate Curricula Archaeology, 2002.

Seidemann, Ryan M. "NAGPRA at 20: What Have the States Done to Expand Human Remains Protections?" *Museum Anthropology* 33.2 (2010): 199–209.

Seymour, Thomas Day. "Twenty-Fifth Annual Report of the Council of the Archaeological Institute of America." *American Journal of Archaeology* 8 (1904): 1–10.

Shelton, S. T., letter to Mr. Paul A. F. Walter. January 28, 1910. http://wetherillfamily.com/.

Shelton, W. T., letter to Supt. Peter Paquette. July 25, 1910. http://wetherillfamily.com/.

Six, B. P., letter to the Commissioner of Indian Affairs. May 28, 1910. http://wetherillfamily.com/.

Snead, James E. *Ruins and Rivals: The Making of Southwest Archaeology*. Tucson: University of Arizona Press, 2001.

"Special Land Agent." *Record Union*, July 13, 1897.

Sprinkle, Jr., John H. *Crafting Preservation Criteria: The National Register of Historic Places and American Historic Preservation*. New York: Routledge, 2014.

Stacher, S. F., letter to the Commissioner of Indian Affairs. April 4, 1910. http://wetherillfamily.com/.

Stacher, S. F., letter to the Commissioner of Indian Affairs. June 27, 1910. http://wetherillfamily.com/.

Stacher, S. F., letter to Mr. Alfred Hardy. March 7, 1910. http://wetherillfamily.com/.

Stacher, S. F., letter to Supt. Peter Paquett. May 7, 1910. http://wetherillfamily
.com/.

Steeves, Paulette. 2015. "Academia, Archaeology, CRM, and Tribal Historic Preservation." *Archaeologies: Journal of the World Archaeological Congress*. DOI:
10.1007/s11759–015–9266-y.

Swarner, Jessica. "Oak Flat Historic Designation a Win for Mine Opponents, but
Fight Continues." *Tucson Sentinel*, March 14, 2016. http://www.tucsonsentinel
.com/local/report/031416_oak_flat/oak-flat-historic-designation-win
-mine-opponents-but-fight-continues/.

"Taken Up!" *Mancos Times*, June 23, 1893.

Tate, LaVerne, and San Juan County Historical Society. *Early San Juan County*.
Charleston: Arcadia, 2008.

"Territorial Happenings." *Santa Fe New Mexican*, May 1, 1900.

Thiessen, Thomas D. *Emergency Archeology in the Missouri River Basin: The Role
of the Missouri River Basin Project and the Midwest Archeological Center in the
Interagency Archeological Salvation Program, 1946–1975*. Midwest Archeological Center Special Report No. 2.2 (1999).

Thomas, Cyrus. *The Problem of the Ohio Mounds*. Washington, DC: Government
Printing Office, 1889.

Thomas, Cyrus. *Report on the Mound Explorations of the Bureau of Ethnology*.
Washington, DC: Smithsonian Institution, 1894.

Thomas, Cyrus. *Work in Mound Exploration of the Bureau of Ethnology*. Washington, DC: Government Printing Office, 1887.

Thompson, Raymond Harris. "Edgar Lee Hewett and the Political Process."
Journal of the Southwest 42.2 (2000): 271–318.

"THPO Directory." National Association of Tribal Historic Preservation Officers. https://members.nathpo.org/thpodirectory/FindStartsWith?term
=%23%21.

Tolmie, Clare, and Paula Porubcan Branstner. *Section 106 Archaeological Properties Identification Report, Obama Presidential Center (OPC) Mobility Improvements to Support the South Lakefront Framework Plan (SLFP), Cook
County, Illinois*. Board of Trustees of the University of Illinois, Illinois State
Archaeological Survey, 2018. https://www.chicago.gov/content/dam/city
/depts/dcd/supp_info/jackson/2018–03–19-Arch-Report.pdf.

Tribble, Scott. "Mounds, Myths, and Grave Mistakes: Wills De Hass and the
Growing Pains of Nineteenth-Century Archaeology." *West Virginia History*
7.1 (2013): 23–37.

"Tribes Celebrate Mesa Verde Repatriation." *Indian Country Today*, September 17, 2020. https://indiancountrytoday.com/the-press-pool/tribes
-celebrate-mesa-verde-repatriation.

Tsosie, Rebecca. "Indigenous Rights and Archaeology." *Native Americans and Archaeologists: Stepping Stones to Common Ground*. Walnut Creek: AltaMira Press, 1997, 64–76.

Two Bears, Davina. "'Ihoosh'aah, Learning by Doing: The Navajo Nation Archeology Department Student Training Program." In *Collaborating at the Trowel's Edge: Teaching and Learning in Indigenous Archaeology*, edited by Stephen W. Silliman, 188–210. Tucson: University of Arizona Press, 2008.

Two Bears, Davina R. "Navajo Archaeologist Is Not an Oxymoron: A Tribal Archaeologist's Experience." *American Indian Quarterly* 30.3/4 (2006): 381–87.

Unknown, letter to Friend Hyde. October 24, 1897. American Museum of Natural History, Division of Anthropology Archives, 1897–45.

US Census Bureau. "Fourteenth Census of the United States: 1920-Population, Navajo County, Arizona." 1920. Accessed at www.ancestry.com.

United States Code. 43 CFR § 10.14.

United States Code. Public Law 96–487, Alaska National Interest Lands Conservation Act, December 2, 1980.

United States Code. American Antiquities Act of 1906, 16 USC 431–33.

United States Code. Historic Sites, Buildings, Objects, and Antiquities, 16 U.S.C. §§ 461–67 (Suppl. 1 1934).

United States Code. National Historic Preservation Act, as amended (54 USC 3000 et seq: Historic Preservation).

United States Code. Public Law 101–85—Nov. 28, 1989.

United States Department of Agriculture. *Final Environmental Impact Statement: Resolution Copper Project and Land Exchange*, 2021. https://www .resolutionmineeis.us/documents/final-eis.

United States General Accounting Office. *Cultural Resources Problems Protecting and Preserving Federal Archeological Resources*. Report to Congressional Requesters, December 1987.

United States Government Accountability Office. *Native American Cultural Resources: Improved Information Could Enhance Agencies' Efforts to Analyze and Respond to Risks of Theft and Damage*. Report to the Committee on Indian Affairs, US Senate, March 2021.

United States of America, Plaintiff-Appellant v. Kyle R. Jones, Thayde L. Jones and Robert E. Gevara, Defendants-Appellees. 607 F.2d 269 (1979).

United States v. Diaz, 499 F.2d 113 (9th Cir. 1974), rev'g 368 F. Supp. 856 (D. Ariz. 1973).

United States v. Smyer, 596 F.2d 939 (10th Cir. 1979), cert. denied, 444 U.S. 843 (1979).

Van Dyke, Ruth, Stephen Lekson, Carrie Heitman, and Julian Thomas. *Chaco*

Landscapes: Data, Theory and Management. Prepared by the University of Colorado for Chaco Culture National Historical Park, 2016.

Vela, Jaime Geronimo. "Returning Geronimo to His Homeland: The Application of NAGPRA and Broken Treaties to the Case of Geronimo's Repatriation." *American Journal of Indigenous Studies* (2017): S178–93.

"A Visit to Niagara Falls and the World's Fair." *Cambridge Transcript*, November 3, 1893.

Vivian, R. Gwinn, and Bruce Hilpert. *The Chaco Handbook: An Encyclopedic Guide.* Salt Lake City: University of Utah Press, 2012.

Vyse, Colonel Howard. *Operations carried on at the pyramids of Gizeh in 1837: with an account of a voyage into Upper Egypt, and an appendix.* London: J. Fraser, 1840.

Wade, Lizzie. "An Archaeology Society Hosted a Talk against Returning Indigenous Remains. Some Want a New Society." *Science*, April 19, 2021. doi: 10.1126/science.abjo843.

Wade, Lizzie. "Human Footprints Near Ice Age Lake Suggest Surprisingly Early Arrival in the Americas." *Science*, September 23, 2021. doi: 10.1126/science.acx9187.

Waters, Victor L., letter to Mabel C. Wright. September 15, 1957. Bureau of Land Management, Canyons of the Ancients, 2004.84.D.139.O.

Watkins, Joe E. "Beyond the Margin: American Indians, First Nations, and Archaeology in North America." *American Antiquity* 68.2 (2003): 273–85.

Watkins, Joe. "Through Wary Eyes: Indigenous Perspectives on Archaeology." *Annual Review of Anthropology* 34 (2005): 429–49.

"A Weird Spectacle. Description of the Great Rattlesnake Dance of the Hopis. With Rattlers in Their Mouths. How the Serpents Were Captured and the Part They Played. A Strange Indian Ceremony." *Evening Star*, October 26, 1895.

Wells, Ida B., Frederick Douglass, Irvine Garland Penn, and Ferdinand Lee Barnett. *The Reason Why the Colored American Is Not in the World's Columbian Exposition.* Chicago, 1893.

Western Liberal. October 25, 1901.

Wetherill, Al. Al Wetherill's Journal Tan and Wine Ledger Book, AWD #1. Bureau of Land Management, Canyons of the Ancients National Monument, Department of the Interior, 2000.19.D.253.O.

Wetherill, Benjamin Alfred. *The Wetherills of the Mesa Verde: Autobiography of Benjamin Alfred Wetherill.* Edited by Maurine S. Fletcher. Lincoln: University of Nebraska Press, 1977.

Wetherill, C. "The Cliff Dwellers. An Interesting Review of Ancient Customs." *Mancos Times*, April 28, 1893.

Wetherill, John, letter to Talbot Hyde, December 15, 1918. American Museum of Natural History, Division of Anthropology Archives, 1897–45.

Wetherill, John. "Notes on the Discovery of Keet Seel." *Plateau Magazine* 27.3 (1995): 18–20. Bureau of Land Management, Canyons of the Ancients, 2004.84.D.13.O.

Wetherill, Richard, letter to B. Talbot Hyde. February 4, 1894. American Museum of Natural History, Division of Anthropology Archives, 1897–45.

Wetherill, Richard, letter to B. Talbot B. Hyde. December 17, 1893. American Museum of Natural History, Division of Anthropology Archives, 1897–45.

Wetherill, Richard, letter to B. Talbot B. Hyde. March 28, 1894. American Museum of Natural History, Division of Anthropology Archives, 1897–45.

Wetherill, Richard, letter to B. T. B. Hyde. October 16, 1894. American Museum of Natural History, Division of Anthropology Archives, 1897–45.

Wetherill, Richard, letter to B. Talbot B. Hyde. September 4, 1895. American Museum of Natural History, Division of Anthropology Archives, 1897–45.

Wetherill, Richard, letter to B. T. B. Hyde. October 1, 1895. American Museum of Natural History, Division of Anthropology Archives, 1897–45.

Wetherill, Richard, letter to B. T. B. Hyde. October 1, 1896. American Museum of Natural History, Division of Anthropology Archives, 1897–45.

Wetherill, Richard, letter to B. T. B. Hyde. October 23, 1896. American Museum of Natural History, Division of Anthropology Archives, 1897–45.

Wetherill, Richard, letter to B. T. B. Hyde. February 15, 1897. American Museum of Natural History, Division of Anthropology Archives, 1897–45.

Wetherill, Richard, letter to B. T. B. Hyde. April 17, 1901. American Museum of Natural History, Division of Anthropology Archives, 1897–45.

Wetherill, Richard, letter to Baron C. Nordenskiöld. July 6, 1895. Bureau of Land Management, Canyons of the Ancients, 2000.19.D.773.O.

Wetherill, Richard, letter to Fred Hyde. March 21, 1902. American Museum of Natural History, Division of Anthropology Archives, 1897–45.

Wetherill, Richard, letter to Friend Hyde. October 24, 1897. American Museum of Natural History, Division of Anthropology Archives, 1897–45.

Wetherill, Richard, letter to Friend Hyde. December 23, 1894. American Museum of Natural History, Division of Anthropology Archives, 1897–45.

Wetherill, Richard, letter to Friend Hyde. March 28, 1898. American Museum of Natural History, Division of Anthropology Archives, 1897–45.

Wetherill, Richard, letter to Friend Hyde. July 3, 1898. American Museum of Natural History, Division of Anthropology Archives, 1897–45.

Wetherill, Richard, letter to Friend Hyde. October 26, 1897. American Museum of Natural History, Division of Anthropology Archives, 1897-45.

Wetherill, Richard, letter to Marcia Billings. September 21, 1890. In *Richard Wetherill: Anasazi. Pioneer Explorer of Southwestern Ruins*, by Frank McNitt, 345–46. Albuquerque: University of New Mexico Press, 1966.

Wetherill, Richard, letter to Marcia Billings. Undated. In *Richard Wetherill: Anasazi. Pioneer Explorer of Southwestern Ruins*, by Frank McNitt, 348. Albuquerque: University of New Mexico Press, 1966.

Wetherill, Richard, letter to Mr. Hyde. 1893. American Museum of Natural History, Division of Anthropology Archives, 1897–45.

Wetherill, Richard, letter to Prof. F. W. Putnam. April 7, 1890. In *Richard Wetherill: Anasazi. Pioneer Explorer of Southwestern Ruins*, by Frank McNitt, PP. Albuquerque: University of New Mexico Press, 1966.

Wetherill II, Richard, oral history interview conducted by Richard N. Sandlin, December 1–4, 1977.

Wetherill and Horabin, proprietors of Navajo Indian Trading Post, letter to "Mine Own Peoples" [Mary and Martha Wetherill], ca. 1903. Bureau of Land Management, Canyons of the Ancients, 2000.19.D.365.O.

Wheeler, Sir Mortimer. *Archaeology from the Earth*. Oxford: Clarendon Press, 1954.

Wicker, Elmus. *Banking Panics of the Gilded Age*. Cambridge: Cambridge University Press, 2000.

Willey, Gordon R., and Jeremy A. Sabloff. *A History of American Archaeology*. San Francisco: W. H. Freeman, 1974.

Williams, Deborah H., and Gerhard P. Shipley. "Scientific Consequentialism: Potential Problems with an Outcome-Driven Form of Indigenous Archaeology." *Archaeological Discovery* 8 (2020): 63–83.

Wilson, Thomas. "Archaeology and Anthropology." *American Naturalist* 22.255 (1888): 271–75.

Wolverton, Steve, Robert Melchior Figueroa, and Porter Swentzell. "Archaeology, Heritage, and Moral Terrains: Two Cases from the Mesa Verde Region." *Ethnobiology Letters* 7.2 (2016): 23–31.

"Women Left at Mercy of the Murderers of Wetherill." *Albuquerque Morning Journal*, June 30, 1910.

Woodbury, Richard B., and Nathalie F. S. Woodbury. "The Rise and Fall of the Bureau of American Ethnology." *Journal of the Southwest* 41.3 (1999): 283–96.

Wright, Mabel C., letter to Harry F. Evans. July 5, 1957. Bureau of Land Management, Canyons of the Ancients, 2004.84.D.140.O.

Index

Page numbers in italics refer to figures.

Pathological Institute, New York State
  Hospital, 106
Patrick, L. C., 7
Peabody, Charles, 176
Peabody, Lucy, 116, 123, 139–40, 144
Peabody Museum of Archaeology &
  Ethnology (Cambridge, MA), 25,
  29, 72, 111, 170, 176
Pearson, Maria (Running Moccasin),
  214–15
Penn, William, 3
Pepper, George Hubbard, 72–82, 87–
  93, 96–105, 105, 108–9, 119, 128–31,
  131, 134–35, 177–81, 184, 212, 218;
  death of, 236
phrenology, 107
Pidgeon, William, 52
Pompeii, 111
pothunters and pothunting, 41, 95,
  118, 144, 186–88, 202–3
Powell, John Wesley, 23–24, 27, 51–54,
  104; death of, 125, 135
Pracht, Max, 114–15
preservation: and archaeology, 111–12,
  139, 216; and conservation, 144;
  legislation, 112–14, 117, 138–40, 143,
  148; and protection, 3, 187, 228, 230;
  of public lands, 120–21; as unresolved issue, 117
Prudden, Mitchell, 60–62, 96, 156,
  162, 166–67
public lands: archaeological sites on,
  24; and legislation, 112–13; and
  natural wonders, 112; preservation
  of, 120–21; and timber, 121
Pueblo Bonito (Chaco Canyon,
  NM), 64–68, 83, 98, 101–5, 114–21,
  129–32, 134–35, 141, 152, 158–60,
  162–64, 168, 171, 175, 178, 184–85,
  211–12; architecture of, 76, 108;

artifacts in, 91; auricular landscape
  of, 103; bodies and burials found in,
  78–79, 108–9, 206–7, 222; cylinder
  jars from, 98; diet in, evidence of,
  103; excavations in, vii–viii, 70, 73–
  80, 74, 89–93, 96–98, 103–9, 114,
  116, 119, 129–30, 178, 181, 192, 206–7,
  212, 222; as home, 97, 102, 119, 160,
  168, 238; looting, misuse, plunder
  of, 110, 121; macaws entombed in,
  79; NRHP status, 193; trading post
  in, viii, 96, 131, 152. See also Chaco
  Canyon (New Mexico)
Pueblo del Arroyo (New Mexico),
  121, 164, 184
Pueblo Indians, 49–50, 64–65, 109,
  129, 212
Puerto Rico, 135, 137, 191
Putnam, Frederic Ward, 25–43, 57–58,
  70–72, 103–5, 108–12, 121, 127–30,
  134–39, 170, 179, 195; death of, 177

Quakers, 3, 10–11, 13–15, 62, 70, 92,
  158, 164, 168
Quarrell, Charles and Mike, 199–200
Quetzalcoatl, 34
Quick, Eleanor, 160–62, 164–65

racism, 52, 182, 218
Rainbow Bridge (Utah), 149–56, 184
Rainbow Bridge National Monument
  (Utah), 156
Records of the Past (journal), 124
Records of the Past Exploration
  Society, 124
regulations. See federal regulations
Reisner, George A., 170
religion, and science, 209, 212
remains. See human remains
repatriation, 203–4, 209–24